W omen:
THEORY AND PRACTICE

by Bernard Chapin

Women: Theory and Practice
Published in Chicago by Conservadom Books.
Printed in the United States of America
Copyright © 2007 by Bernard Chapin
ISBN 978-1-60461-271-4

Notices

Bringing to bear a wealth of research, Chapin's own experience as a psychologist and his sharp critical intelligence, *Women: Theory and Practice* takes on the vast catalogue of lies and deceptions perpetrated on behalf of radical feminism by academia, the media and popular culture.

—Harry Stein, Author and Journalist.

The American male, once proud and mighty has been reduced to having to lift up his own toilet seat. In his superb book Bernard Chapin analyzes the calamity to its necessary extent and once you are finished you will find that the smell of gun powder remains with you.

—Roman Genn, Artist and Cartoonist.

Our identity is tied up in our ideas of the relationships between the sexes. When these ideas are distorted, as they have been through political correctness, we, very literally, lose our sense of who we are. When that happens, the most important, but also the most difficult thing we can do is to regain a sense of our selves through honest appraisal of our experience. That is the project in which Bernard Chapin is engaged. His courageous and perceptive book helps to explore ground that we all need to cover.

—Howard S. Schwartz, Professor and author of *The Revolt of the Primitive: An Inquiry into the Roots of Political Correctness.*

Bernard Chapin's writing crackles with energy, but it is not all flair and no substance. Chapin provides solid analysis even as his words fairly seize you by the lapel and shake you awake.

—Shawn Macomber, Phillips Foundation Journalism Fellow.

Women: Theory and Practice, seeks a new center of gravity in the balance of power between the sexes, and suggests a simple solution: authority and responsibility should be universal concepts applied in equal proportion to both men and women. Arguing with wit and brutal clarity, Chapin breaks the rules of establishment discourse by explicitly deconstructing the sad victories of Political Correctness, and by identifying the pernicious impact of "group think" in a free society.

—Mike Lasalle, Editor of *Mensnewsdaily.com*

Bernard Chapin is a confrontational writer. He doesn't wheedle, cajole, or softsell. The reader has to make a choice when he reads Chapin. That's the mark of outstanding polemic performer.

—Hunter Baker, Contributing Editor at *Redstate.com*.

Would that liberals could be so endowed with Chapin's talent.

—G. Lewis, Amazon reviewer.

Bernard Chapin is one of those rare writers who can pack humour and insight into a single sentence, a combination master storyteller and top notch reporter.

—Steve Martinovich, Editor, Enterstageright.com.

This book is dedicated solely to God without Whose assistance I would have never awoken this morning or any other. Thank you for giving me the power to complete this work. Before I sought Your support I never finished anything. Lord, I Thank You.

Worldly Acknowledgements

I thank all of my friends and family for assisting me over the years. I'd like to single out for special mention the names of Karen Chapin, Beth Lindsay, John Kubinski, Dan Synwolt, Vic Forcette, Robert Gatsch, Robert Lynch, William Lynch, Dana Norwick, Thomas Shupe along with his daughter Katie and wife Christine, Paul Granger, Jeffrey "Bubba" Collins, Lisa Granger, Eli Granger, Sophie Granger, Steve Wills, MT, EC, DP, Olivia Penick, Viola Marion Barr, William Barr, and my Uncle Lionel Arnold who died earlier this year. May he Rest in Peace.

Professionally, Mike LaSalle at *Mensnewdaily* and Steve Martinovich at *Enterstageright* continue to be of enormous support and are a couple of Top Dogs. Mike's gotten into the audiofile business and has done a great job with the articles I've written. Steve, unfortunately, continues to be afflicted with a devotion to the Toronto Maple Leafs. James M. Antle "the III" is another guy who has done me a world of good and I appreciate it immensely—the same can be said for other fellows like Jaime Glasov, Shawn Macomber, Kevin Hurley, and Ari "A.J." Kaufman. The Alexander family, Andrew and Rachel, over at *Intellectual Conservative* have been of enormous assistance as has Bill Mayer at *Pipelinenews* along with Bryan Wolfe at *Gopnation* and the Magnificent L.B. "Neal" Neal from *American Daily*. Tony DeSylva at *Conservative-crusader* has been running some of my pieces as of late and I thank him for it. This is also true of Ken Anderson over at *Magic-City-News* and Jim Sesi at *Michnews*. I also must single out the exquisite Hunter Baker and his band of Quakers. Thanks to S.T. Karnick as well who has put up with many of my grammatical questions. In terms of distant motivation, I would like to thank a few conservative greats for the way their genius has inspired me over the years such as Sir Roger Kimball [author's knighting], John Derbyshire, Harry Stein, and the incomparable David Horowitz.

Another professional mention must go to two non-political figures best described as "poker gurus." David Sklansky's and Ed Miller's *No Limit Hold 'em: Theory and Practice* gave me the inspiration for part of my work's title. In June of 2006, I began laughing after realizing that its subtitle would fit my work in the manner of a sheepskin condom. I wish to thank them for that book in particular along with everything else they have written. I'd also like to express gratitude to Mr. Sklansky a second time for a chapter he wrote in *The Theory of Poker* concerning the fundamental theorem of poker. The phrase resulted in my adapting it for a chapter title here. Thank you for your excellence, sirs.

Table of Contents

Preface

I come from a long line of irascibles.

My great-grandfather moved from Ireland to Canada in 1910, and brought my grandfather, Andrew McNamara, with him. Somehow my ancestors managed to survive the potato famine, despite my great-grandfather having a reputation for being "the worst farmer in Ireland"—which, considering his competition, was quite an achievement. His wife, my great-grandmother, marched in Orange Day parades on two continents for at least 80 of her 93 years. As for my grandfather, farm work necessitated his dropping out of school in the second grade, but, unfortunately, the NcNamara's production was not much better on this side of the Atlantic. In his teens, granddad discarded his till, and got a job with the Ford Motor Company in Hamilton, Ontario. It was the last job he would ever work. Eventually, he was transferred to Detroit and a few years later became an American citizen. Before he died in 1984, he sired eight children and was one of the most loved and respected men I have ever known. A few year's later, my grandmother passed away and left me a coffee cup that Ford had bestowed upon him.

Before he became a God-fearing respectable man, my grandfather made extra money "wrasling," which differed radically from what we call wrestling today. One of my uncles described the forbidden brawling as being quite similar to what Clint Eastwood engaged in during the movie Every Which Way but Loose. This side-job ended when he fell in with a group of hyper-Christian fundamentalists. From that point on, there was no more smoking, drinking, dancing, movie watching or even voting in elections. Religion was his purpose, and he instilled it within his children (or tried to at least). My mother was the family's last born, and she read from the Bible at the dinner table everyday during her youth. Hers was an austere life with neither parent having any patience for frivolity or worldly trappings. My Uncle Don attempted to go his own way, and, unbeknownst to my grandfather, became a boxer. He eventually won the Detroit Golden Gloves which resulted in his name being mentioned in the paper and led to my grandfather giving him the beating of a lifetime. Don never boxed again so, yes, my family history is a politically incorrect one, and one that would never be approved by local Department of Child and Family Services agencies of our day. But a politically incorrect family past is something commonly found among Americans. Most of our ancestors would be nothing but pariahs if they were suddenly shuttled forth into the modern age.

By the time I arrived, the Andrew McNamara I met was full of neither fire nor brimstone. To me, he appeared devoid of harshness. All I ever saw him display was humor and kindness. My mother made him promise not to evangelize around her children so he never did—well, intentionally that is. I do recall him once whipping out the Good Book in the midst of an argument with my father, but it was of little use. Dad would sit there puffing on his pipe while ignoring the old man. I recall my grandfather once leaning over to him and saying, "Hey Bob, if God wanted to smoke, don't you think he would have made your mouth into a chimney?" Perhaps I was the only one who laughed, but I am still laughing about it today. I continue to have an appreciation for that man that can never be extinguished.

The patriarch of our clan may not have always been effective, but he sought to influence others whenever he could. I should note though that he was not your stereotypical religious fanatic [who is?]. He lived and worked in an environment saturated with Catholics and seldom agreed with them about anything, but he near universally got along with them and tolerated their diversity. There was not any hate in Andrew McNamara. He had legions of friends, associates, and debating partners during his eight decades of time on this earth. When he died, a contingent of Ulstermen drove down from Ontario to attend his funeral, and I was told that it was presided over by the brother of Reverend Ian Paisley.

I will never forget my grandfather, but it was only after I began writing that I realized there might be something of him in me. While my opinions and ideas are less important and profound—along with my obviously not being a great man in any sense of the term—I have also found it impossible to keep silent about my views and cannot resist an opportunity to broadcast them. Political correctness is the enemy of free speech, and my compulsion to speak freely has made me many enemies. However, in the final analysis, I think that it is better to have stood for something during one's brief existence than to reenter the ground in the form of a never troubled, uncontroversial, and cowardly shadow.

Introduction

Dare to Know.
　　　　　—Immanuel Kant.[1]

Understanding [is] the essential weapon.
Victory is obtained by the intellect.[2]
　　　　　—From the ancient Persian poem "Chatrang namak."

Since the 1960s, apart from Rousseau, much that once was in the western world has been lost.[3] This is the side effect of radicals leaving the streets and becoming ensconced in our universities, public services, non-for-profit foundations and agencies, and even the Senate and Congress of the United States. They see themselves as social engineers, but their intervention has been utterly catastrophic. Cultural Marxism, a synonym for political correctness (PC), has been the main legacy of their decades of rage. It is the vilest of societal overlays and has equated capitalism with selfishness, vilified corporations along with every other non-communal endeavor, lampooned a work ethic which once rightly idolized, shamed the population into inflating the size of our government, and has made large blocks of the citizenry suspicious of all those who fail to meet their exact demographic description.

In terms of its daily impact, it has eroded civility, promoted the use of emotion over reason, and completely undermined the prospects for dispassionate discussion. Rather than make racial hatred a lamentable memory it has attempted to preserve and enshrine it. Political correctness has delegitimized our ability to police our own borders and dubbed as racist the people's simple desire to determine the constitution and census of their own nation. Higher liberal arts education has become a crossword puzzle of interlocking "isms" that exist to tear neighbors apart and isolate us from one another. Our schools encourage a sense of grievance among immigrants and indigenous minorities, while reducing our history to a

3

comic book plot centered on violence and abomination—despite the fact that thousands risk death each year in the hopes of reaching our shores.

Most importantly, in regards to this book, an age of radical critique and contention has fomented a war between the sexes. Only a Manichean view of our social landscape is permitted and its eternal mantra is that "women are good" and "men are bad." Without PC to protect it, the fictions of sexism could never survive because the average social engineer could not refute even basic counter-arguments like "how evil can I be when my closest biological relation, my sister, is unquestionably good?" The only way to maintain the establishment belief system is to silence opposition and tar as misogynists and haters those who question the status quo. The debasing and censure of one sex has resulted in unhappiness for both sexes. Given the way in which critics of human nature have successfully depicted biology as an indicator of moral worth, it seems quite likely that the situation will get far worse before it gets any better. The radicals will continue to preach and talk down to the masses from their privileged perches in our academies, and their tenured status will prevent their termination by more sensible elements.

I decided to write this book as a means to partially correct the argumentative imbalance between the establishment view and the one held by most citizens. *Women: Theory and Practice* was crafted with a quote from George Santayana in mind: "The best men in all ages keep classical traditions alive." And that is precisely what I am trying to do here.

One may already sense that I am not the type of person who will echo Jesse Jackson's chant, "Hey hey, ho ho, Western Civ has got to go."[4] I ardently believe in the western tradition. As an American, I will often mention my country in these pages but this discussion will be appreciated by anyone living in the West, and has considerable application for those residing in the Anglosphere. As for me, my European descent is not something for which I feel any shame. As the Preface suggests, I am proud of my ancestors. I have been an avid appreciator of history since 1974 when I used to sit on my uncle's lap as he read to me from a children's book about the Second World War. I attended four years of college and two-and-a-half years of graduate school, but, for the most part, am an autodidact. The immensity and grandeur of our cultural past became apparent to me long ago, and my appreciation of it grows with each text I consume. The idea that "new" does not always equate with "improved" is something of which I am fully aware.

As a writer, defending the important traditions and achievements of the past is my primary interest. This is particularly true of the relations between men and women. For thousands of years, the sexes have had conflicting interests but functioned in a complementary capacity which allowed them to survive and raise offspring. Just as with my sister, whose ancestors I completely share, there were no firm lines drawn between the moral worth of the sexes. Unfortunately, one cannot say that this remains the case today.

I have written this book as a means to remind society that men and women are both human beings who share many virtues and many faults. Women are no more pure then men are impure. It is regrettable that something so obvious is deemed a provocative statement nowadays but it is. Indeed, enunciating such a perspective can render one beyond the pale in many a professional environment. Larry Summers was released from Harvard University[5] not long after causing an uproar due to his illumination of the irrefutable fact that men and women have different talents and aspirations. Attempts were also been made to remove a sitting judge after he wrote a book containing a chapter entitled "The Cloud Cuckooland of Radical Feminism."[6]

How tempting it would be to hope that works like mine could slow the further decline of our culture—that we might stand athwart history and bellow "Stop!"[7]—but that would be a ridiculously optimistic premise and one that I will not entertain. Our country and community have been under siege for several decades and our opponents are far more vicious and organized than we are. What I hope to do in these pages is to slow down their advance and show others that the thoughts they are afraid to share are held by the rest of us. What was once the counter-culture has become the culture as it is the establishment, yet those of us who question the emotionacs are the ones who are termed radical and extremist. In the chapters that follow, nothing I say would offend anyone born before 1950, but practically all of it is verboten now.

In terms of allegiance, I have always been a member of the "Culture War Has Already Been Lost" school, but perhaps my total pessimism is unwarranted. There is great truth in what David Horowitz said regarding this subject in an interview I once had with him. He observed, "There is nothing irrevocable in human affairs (except death). Yes, the Sixties radicals won the culture war – but like all such victories their gains are limited and the battle is never over."[8] If he is right then there is still a chance to seize victory from their androgynized paws. Books like this one can form the basis for our own Miracle of the Marne. The more twenty-first century samizdat we produce the better. Knowledge does equal power; political correctness is all about keeping people stupid and discouraging them from asking the proper questions. Making sense from the chaos around us is a prerequisite to success.

Fighting political correctness has broad appeal with the overall population. Nobody really understands why they have to display fake sensitivity for their every social interaction. It is only natural for one to resent being told what they can say or cannot say. Most people do not speak up because they do not want to be beaten down. They see what has happened to their less diplomatic peers and silence themselves. Rather than risk their jobs, their friendships, and their prospects over a joke or an opinion they choose to self-censor. Yet if enough of us speak out we can change the course of events. Having the truth on your side does not guarantee influence but it does help. Why should we not be more optimistic about the future? Let us speak truth together to the liars who harass and intimidate us.

Theme.

With so much vile PC in the ether, and so many sacred cows and mascots adopted by our anti-elites, it is necessary to restrict our focus in these pages to an examination of women—a group that embodies half of humanity yet continues to be regarded as minority by the irrational powers that be. Despite their prevalence, they are wrongly thought to be a flamboyant reservoir of sanctity, empathy, and justice within a civilization poisoned by men (who, of course, are woman born). **The main theme of Women: Theory and Practice is that a discrepancy exists between the way women are rumored to function and the way in which they actually do.** The hype surrounding females has grown to bizarre proportions, yet it is totally divergent with their actual ability, achievement, and potential. Our culture has wrongly declared them to be intellectually, morally, and emotionally superior to men. The shine with which women have been burnished is totally synthetic. One cannot help but wonder if their champions believe them to be superheroes in human garb. Indeed, if one only listened to the mainstream media and the speech of our politicians they would come away with the belief that women excel at every task and that there is nothing in this world that they cannot do.

Unfortunately, the rumors of female transcendence are greatly exaggerated. Ironically, the machinations and deceptions of our social engineers only serve to make the glaring normality of the average woman more apparent. There is no correlation between genitalia and nobility.

Inappropriate hoopla merely widens the gap who they are and what they are reputed to be. Women are not demigods. No evidence exists of their being superior to men in most endeavors. Clearly, the sexes do have varying strengths and weaknesses, but the average woman is no more gifted than she is satisfied. Supremacy has been assigned to her, it has not been earned. Women are every bit as fallible as men and, just as with their maligned brothers, are no more likely to be good than evil.

The best phrase in regards to the myth of female grandeur is that "sooner or later you get found out" which is exactly what has happened to countless members of the fairer sex once their inherent mediocrity[9] became known...although, they were the ones most pained by the discovery. Women are no more likely to be an asset to a company, institute, university or place of employment than are men, but it is fashionable to pretend otherwise. We are encouraged to not believe our lying eyes. Faux self-esteem and illusory aptitude cannot increase productivity or efficiency. Rhetoric cannot be substituted for skill, interest, or work ethic in a competitive environment.

Many women, especially those who mistake spin for fact, are quick to experience what I will call a "Tyson Awakening" upon entering the workforce. Any pre-fight swagger and bluster they once had is promptly dispelled after absorbing a few combinations. A couple of uppercuts and jabs cause propaganda to intersect with reality and the results are never pretty. Their dreams become inverted and the knock-out they expected turns out to be their own. No scorecards of judges need be consulted, and the outcome of the theoretical prizefight is disorientation, disillusion, and bitterness. Work proves to be venture fraught with work as opposed one festooned with glorification, heraldry, and the exponential rise of one's ego. They distance between who they are and who they fantasize themselves to be is vaster than they ever anticipated.

Yet society will come to their rescue as PC has a ready-made cure for their every ailment. Their ineptitude (or merely slight trauma) will be transferred from their own bodies onto the back of the apocryphal patriarchy. Once resting there, their artlessness is instantaneously alchemized into oppression. The Sexual Harassment Industry can assist them mightily in this endeavor. PC will allow them to remain employed or be hoisted up the corporate hierarchy due to the leaders of American business being afraid that they will be charged with discrimination or allegations of disproportionate treatment based on sex. If all else fails, and should someone be dumb enough to make a reference or joke around them that is off-color, then they always have the option—which they fortunately do not generally exercise—to claim that the offensive speech made them feel uncomfortable and that they found themselves placed into a "hostile environment;" suggesting that their vocational failure was a foregone conclusion all along. Thus, it would behoove their overseers to simply pay them off.

Most importantly, we are encouraged to remember that any deficiencies women have are not really deficiencies. Their low performance, when it occurs, can be attributed to men selfishly valuing competitiveness over accommodation in their attempts to secure a profit. Their giftedness should have been noticed at outset but was not due to male inferiority. After all, anyone can produce, but how many people can build consensuses and accommodate? Whatever that pap means we are led to believe that these traits are unquestionably good. Furthermore, the task centeredness of their male peers is frequently alienating and gives ground to the accusation that a certain place of employment is not "woman friendly."

Overall, in the context of history, Woman's artificially elevated status is unprecedented. They have been placed upon a pedestal for no coherent reason, and certainly none that has a correlation with their past achievements or future promise. Our nation so favors women that America has become a land of ironclad female privilege. These privileges have been codified into law and have been branded upon our psyches. Our media and government seem to exist solely for the purposes of boosting the morale and self-esteem of women. The belief that government should have an equal regard for the rights of all citizens has now become a sign of misogyny and racism. As of yet we do not live in a matriarchy, but we move further in that direction with each passing day. What can be said is that we now live in a society more matriarchal than it is patriarchal.

Mission.

The last few sentences would qualify me as a chauvinist in the eyes of our cultural magnates, but such a slur would be unfounded. Only in a public square corrupted by Wonderland logic could someone be slandered as chauvinist for stating that women are no better than men. I have been careful not to imply that men are superior to women, and the reasons for my doing so is that I do not believe that they are. While I have no question that biological differences exist between the sexes, I do not hold there to be any disparity in mean cognitive level. This is true in regards to mean Intelligence Quotients (IQs) or in relation to levels of individual general intelligence (G). I have administered nearly a thousand IQ tests since 1994 and my experiences suggest that boys are not born smarter than girls. A plethora of problems face the modern women, but mental capacity is not one of them.

The nuances of my doctrines are not easy to explain in a sound byte, and the taking of a contrarian position in regards to female supremacy has harmed me both romantically and vocationally. The dangers of speaking honestly about the fairer sex are well-known. As Leo Tolstoy famously observed, "When I have one foot in the grave, I will tell the whole truth about women. I shall tell it, jump into my coffin, pull the lid over me and say, 'Do what you like now'."[10] Yes, the price to be paid is severe. Most of us discover that women covet hearing what they want to hear. Thus, Dale Carnegie would not have identified my approach to this conundrum as one in keeping with the correct way to go about making friends and influencing people. Regardless, honest expression is quite pleasurable and rewarding in itself. The same can be said of confronting those who lie in the name of sensitivity. In the future, I will write more expansively about the other areas of PC, but for now we will only examine the hypocrisy of our society in regards to women.

Clearly though, unlike what Tolstoy planned to write, what follows is not a critique of the fairer sex. I am content to describe and analyze the nature of our new dispensation. Like the injunction from Kant, we must dare to know. Were it not for political correctness, however, they would be no dare in the equation. In a society in which cultural Marxism reigns supreme, one becomes a fountain of "hate speech" when they dispute the trendy clichés which currently pass for the gospel. By calling their foes names—haters, racists, homophobes, sexists, and/or misogynists—leftist anti-liberals attempt to win the moral high ground from those who oppose them. Once they have it they are able to dismiss all contrary arguments out-of-hand. The tossing of isms has become a horrific replacement for logic and accuracy. Labels and invective are prefabricated and rarely apply to individual persons. They tell us nothing about reality and are wholly constructed to avoid acknowledging it. Resorting to such methods is but an admission of cowardice and weakness. The PC perception of the world has nothing to do with how it actually is. Conveniently, my foes even question whether there is such a thing as objectivity; a tactic which expedites their massive assaults upon logic.

Why PCniks devote themselves to their novel religion is not always clear. Many do so out of a need to conform, but most adopt the stances they do as a means to feel self-righteous and also to feel as if they have some control over a world they will never understand. Their deconstruction and reconstruction of society psychologically satisfies them as it replaces a life they find detestable. Spinning yarns of conspiracy and accusing others of thought crimes fulfills them. They become morally elevated but demean everyone else in the process. They talk much of diversity yet fail to believe in it. Diversity to them is celebrating those who hold similar opinions.

Nowhere is this truer than with in the women's supremacy movement. Those females who disagree with the cancerous views of activists are dismissed as being afflicted with a false consciousness. When their dogma of these creatures is questioned they become hysterical. Reason is an abhorrent faculty to them. If their beliefs were even partially accurate then contradiction would not so offend them. Aristotle had it right as "it is the mark of an educated mind to be able to entertain a thought without accepting it."[11] One of the most impressive ideas I have ever heard was put forth by Christopher Hitchens in his book *Letters to a Young Contrarian*. He stated that we always profit from debating our opponents as the act of responding to one another propels us farther towards the ultimate truth. I wholly agree with him. Just as doing sets of bench presses causes our pectoral muscles to grow, our minds are strengthened by the process of intellectual repartee.

The Larry Summers incident brought fame to one such person. Professor Nancy Hopkins's response to his speech was as cow-hearted as it could have been. She heard his words and then ran from the room. Had she stayed, she would have "either blacked out or thrown up."[12] The free exchange of thought is anathema to pseudo-scholars like Dr. Hopkins who prefers causing a scene instead.

In light of this eventuality, *Women: Theory and Practice* has little to say to the opposition as they are not the types who are going to read it anyway. This book was written primarily for the benefit of my allies along with the uninitiated, the undecided, and young people in general. Seeing these paragraphs may be the only time in which some college students are ever exposed to ideological heterogeneity. It is for that reason that I encourage conservatives to be as patient as possible with the ignorant. We must present our case and give them a chance to come around; believe it or not, some of them will (I did). We cannot castigate them for mindlessly parroting non-sense if that is all they have ever known. We must remedy their miseducation. Without our alternative missives, developing minds may never realize that there is another way. Were it not for us, they would continue to proselytize themselves before the lecterns of white guiltists, female supremacists, emotionacs, socialists, racists, and those who think Majdanek is a synonym for America.

Perspective.

In an age of tribalism, pseudo-expertise, and overspecialization, there are certain people who would refuse to read this book due to it's not being penned by a woman. That is unfortunate, but my own take on the "fairer sex" (which my biased eyes judge them to be) is invaluable. Indeed, only now, in my middle thirties with my testosterone on the wane am I able to write about them with the proper detachment. It is undeniable, however, that I will always be vested in the women. At some level, my fascination with them will never end.

My perspective on women is colored by a combination of factors; chief among them are personal experience, observation, and interdisciplinary studies. Just as with chess, poker or any other subject that initially confused me, I turned to expert sources as a means to bolster my ability and to help me understand the most beautiful yet perplexing segment of our population.

Foremost among my search has been the field of evolutionary psychology which has impressed me ever since I first stumbled across *Evolutionary Psychiatry* in an Oak Park bookstore back in 1997. This particular branch of psychology, synonymous with sociobiology, is predicated upon the notion that human behavior is a product of evolution. We (generally) act as we do for a reason and our methods have evolved as a time honored way of propagating our species and increasing the likelihood of our individual survival. We are not, and have never been, "blank slates." We emerge from the womb with inclinations forged by millenniums worth of experience. We act as we do for a reason. Our ancestors who behaved in a similar fashion perpetuated their genes and produced more offspring than those who did not. Members of our species who failed to adapt to the rigors of their environment did not propagate and duly died off. Our progenitors have bequeathed to us a legacy that we cannot ignore. In essence, who we are is largely the product of millions of decisions made long before we were born.

A common practice of those opposed to evolutionary psychology is to slander it as being biological determinism but it is not. Just because we are inclined to act in a certain fashion does not mean that we will. *Our genes and our biology merely increase the likelihood of certain behaviors occurring.* They do not independently bring them about. We can and we do resist temptations. In the case of narrator, there have even been a few days in his life when he was hungry but managed to avoid eating. Clearly, humans have free will and are not slaves to their instincts. While one's genetic heritage definitely influences their daily decisions, it does not make the decisions for them. This reality is of crucial importance to women. Our contemporary society persuades women to act in a fashion contrary to their biological interests. Making personal choices to benefit others and not yourself is a one way road to unhappiness and disillusion; which many a modern woman finds herself on sooner rather than later.

The intelligence I have gathered comes from a plethora of sources. Many of these have been rather unusual and some were even painful to read. Devouring *Kiss My Tiara: How to Rule the World as a Smart Mouth Goddess* along *Getting in Touch with Your Inner B*tch* were a serious labor to complete,[13] but I felt it my duty to do so. I have also gone through countless dating manuals, woman's self-help books, feminist treatises, and a brand of publication that most civic authorities wisely prevent children from viewing. I am conscious of the fact that more high-minded authors would disregard such materials, but if I only read what I already agreed with or approved of then I would be no better than my enemies. Some works, such as Nathanson and Young's two magnificent tomes on misandry and Howard S. Schwartz's erudite masterpiece, *The Revolt of the Primitive: An Inquiry into the Roots of Political Correctness*, were euphoric rides indeed.

As with all of my writing *Women: Theory and Practice* is rooted in a myriad of inquiries I first posed long ago. I have been a voluminous reader since the early seventies. Psychology, politics, history, biography, literature, and sports are the bedrock for most of my views. If I had to pick one discipline that has made the largest contribution to my knowledge of psychology it would have to be history. History is the art of inquiry and no other exercise tells us more about the human mind. After all, what is psychology but a series of individual case studies welded together for the purposes of extrapolation? We discern small truths and use them as the basis for a framework of thought. My fascination with the events of yesteryear has given me considerable insight along with a comparative advantage over some of my peers; those psychologists who recite verses of jargon and lingo but rarely communicate much of anything.

My first-hand experiences with women have been extensive, and include successes, failures, and hundreds of interactions that can be best described with the words "no contest." Readers have given me feedback that much of what has happened to me has happened to them as well. Dealing with the fairer sex was never easy for me because, like most of my brothers, I am not rich, poor, ugly or handsome. I am pretty much a regular Joe and that is all I have ever been. I was never popular in school, and never had to worry about juggling a harem. Obviously, alpha males like Matt Damon, Bill Clinton, Tom Brady, and Brad Pitt would have mindsets entirely different from my own.

Regardless of my pedestrian achievements in the realms of love and sex, women continue to be a primary source of inspiration and pleasure for me. Aristotle Onassis was absolutely right when he asserted that without women wealth would have no meaning. Only God could have made such creatures. Their physical appeal is obvious and needs no elaboration. Intellectually, their appeal is also great. Trying to understand them is a splendid challenge. They are generators of eternal amusement, motivation, confusion, exaltation, and frustration. Women provide us with never-ending scenarios and obstacles to negotiate. In alternating intervals, the fairer sex are an avenue to both glory and despair. Without them there is no tomorrow but when we are with them it can seem as if there is no today. Those of us who attempt to elucidate their essence are not unlike the mathematicians who labored to solve Fermat's Last Theorem—except for the fact that the intricacies of women will never fully be known. Certainly, I will not tell you everything there is to know about them here, and I would not be able to do so even if I were given 100,000 pages. Our categorizations and illuminations are merely a series of educated hypotheses which always suffer the flaw of not being divine. What I can do is add to our cumulative knowledge on the subject.

I will stick with what I know in these pages. This is in keeping with the way I live my life as I make an effort to avoid discussing topics of which I know nothing. There will be no soliloquies to be found on theoretical math or Feng shui apartment style. My opinions on those matters are largely indistinguishable from those put forth by chimpanzees or gibbons. I will also leave vicarious subjects, such as childcare and motherhood, to the likes of Dr. Spock. In what follows, I will tackle only the familiar and the defendable.

My profession is that of school psychologist but I will not trouble you with its specifics since I have already outlined them in a book from 2006 called *Escape from Gangsta Island: A School's Progress Decline.* All 12 of the years that I have spent in the vocation have been in an environment saturated with women. There is no question that this has had a major impact upon my perceptions. One could even say that my career has been one long education on the ways of women. The realities that I continually have to deal with leave me astounded by those who pretend that the United States is a Nintendoland vibrating with oppression, and one in which women are trapped below a glass ceiling. To me it looks as if that ceiling is made of cotton candy. Indeed, I have been assigned to some locations in which I was the only male certified staff member; an eventuality that brought about interactions with the rest of the staff which could never be characterized by the words "male privilege" [but I can think of lots of other words to describe it]. The claim that women make for better workers than do men is one I find to be absolutely bizarre.

Despite our political differences, I generally get along rather well with most women. This is principally due to my self-effacing sense of humor and that I have also learned to never make them the butt of my jokes. They sometimes mistake my countenance with that of an insecure person which (platonically) adds to my appeal. What they do not realize is that only a secure and confident person is one who is able make to fun of himself. The act would never be initiated by an unstable or vacillating individual.

In terms of romance, as I gaze back over two decades of dating I can only conclude that my treatment of women has been far above the norm. Physical violence has never been a part of any of my relationships—at least on my end. I have made a habit of never insulting them or putting them down even when they deserve it. I compliment them frequently and say nothing if I do not like something about their appearance. When our relations begin to decline I prefer breaking up with them to initiating a foul drama. Saying goodbye is always preferable to suffering through a recreation of *Madame Butterfly* at a table in a local Thai restaurant. I believe in karma and as a general rule am respectful to others regardless of circumstance. I try to avoid sleeping with women whose personalities I do not like because, regardless of how society may otherwise spin it, women you walk out on after intense, fleeting relationships hate you with an enduring passion. At this point in my life, I favor not making enemies over the etching of notches upon a theoretical bed post.

Just like most people, when it comes to love I have been both lucky and unlucky. I estimate that I have been in love about 10 or 15 times. We all probably remember our defeats more vividly than we do our victories, but, in all honesty, I have probably ladled out as much anguish as I have received. That is to be expected I suppose. I look back on the good times and feel no shortage of pride. My interactions with women never were, and never will be, a waste of time. I have profited from the bonds I formed and believe that my paramours did as well. I am single now and I may die in the same state which is an eventuality to which I have grown accustomed. Admittedly, a life of independence is not for everyone and the more extroverted one is then the more mesmerizing the prospects for marriage are. At one time I very much wanted to get married and have children, yet the importance of this has receded over the years. I will outline the nature of my concerns regarding marriage in the final chapter, but admit that never having children will always bother me to some degree.

Ironically, in another age my liberal inclinations would have made me a high grade feminist as I emphatically believe in equality and fairness. Furthermore, I wish to lord over no one. My devotion to equality has strained many of my romantic relationships, however. Somehow or other, as a child, I never did the memo stating that I was destined to be bossed by the women I fell in love with. Being an inferior based on my sex is not something I can ever tolerate. That is not to say that I am a societal rebel. I always pay for women on dates and do not mind deferring to them about mundane matters, but our affairs often end after I discover that my girlfriend planned on having me cast in the role of peasant for the duration of our relationship.

Preemptions.

a.   The Macho Retort.

After writing a forgettable piece of fiction entitled *Napalm is the Scent of Justice* in 2001 I got a taste of widespread PC criticism for the first time. I enjoyed the irrational responses of my foes so I began blogging and writing short articles about men, women, and feminism. The reaction to my pieces never had anything to do with their substance or argumentation. Defending men and refuting the notion that we are evil oppressors, rapists and louts caused me to become the recipient of extensive politically correct epithets. I was anti-knighted as a sexist, misogynist, [yawn] homophobe, and racist.

According to my opponents, my arguments were but a smoke screen to obscure my own inadequacies. Assaulting the person rather than what they actually said is an enduring characteristic of radicals and I soon discovered that nothing much generative came from my dealings with such people. That I might have had a legitimate viewpoint was never even a consideration. In their opinion, I irrefutably hated women along with everyone else. I also was devoid of self-esteem and had no penis length; due to these factors I then felt a need to pose as a "manly man"[14] in the hopes of compensating for my latent homosexuality. Well, none of these slanders were true and the personal attacks left my positions completely untouched. This meant that I won every argument; although, unlike when I debated in college, there were no judges present to proclaim my victory. I soon realized that I had to answer their invective or else I would be unable to get my point across. I jauntily insulted them right back, but only after demolishing the pseudo-arguments they made.

I will, as preemption, answer some of their calumny here. Wanting to be a "manly man" is a form of psychologizing often showered upon those who question politically correct assumptions. I will not go into more detail about it here as I do so in a later chapter, but I will note that I am not a manly man in the way in which the term is usually defined. I have also have never pretended to be one. Physically, I am quite average and fit the profile more of a librarian than I do that of a hunter or an adventurer. Indeed, I have never gone hunting in my life, and, with the exception of cockroaches, have no interest in killing animals. Drinking heavily is another hallmark of the traditional man but it is not one shared by me. Thousands of writers love to imbibe but I do not. Most of my disinterest stems from the most unmanly of reasons; I get migraine headaches. To me, the pain that liquor creates far outweighs its pleasure. My associations with it are more negative than positive so I only drink when I have too. A man's man would not allow the pangs on the side of his head to come between him and a finished glass of bourbon.[15] For me, it is all too easy to do so. A manly man would also exert some self-control when it came to diet. A tough guy could say the words of which I am incapable: "No thank you. I don't want any more of your free pizza today." Such resolute action is beyond the likes of your Dominos-loving narrator.

b. *Generalizations.*

Most people, the narrator included, devoutly believe that men and women should be treated equally by the government and society at large.

That being said, in order to assess the divergence between reality and fantasy, I will continually discuss the nature of both sexes as opposed to that of women alone. The need to do this is obvious. Elucidating the proclivities of one sex mandates that we continuously juxtapose them with the other as the endemic symbiosis of their relationship cannot be denied. Numerous behaviors and traits that we exhibit are the product of sexual selection. An excellent example of this is the trait of aggression as it has been one coveted by women since the beginning of time.

Science has discovered and verified many enduring differences between the sexes over the course of the last decade, and the depth and power of that research has forced radicals either to ignore it or face extinction. Were they to actually respond to these developments they would quickly find that they had no ground with which to defend. With each passing day and with each new revelation, social constructionists more and more appear to be forgotten figures out of a psychotic Stone Age. All that is left for the enemies of biological difference is to impugn the motives of the researchers themselves. How often have I heard, "Why would you want to study something that?" and "Why would you even want to find that out?" Needless to say, those relics are not moved by any explanation involving the dispassionate pursuit of knowledge or a personal commitment to the discovery of truth.

Only in a highly politicized atmosphere, in the presence of famous politicians or academic luminaries, will these activists take to the ramparts in regards to this subject. Even then they prefer to launch personal attacks or leave the room to faint. Luckily, the days of their organizing demonstrations to protest the work of researchers like Edward O. Wilson are now behind us. In fact, little rancor was showered upon Steven E. Rhoads when he published *Taking Sex Differences Seriously* back in 2004. The book was largely accepted by the mainstream press and its author was even interviewed by *The Today Show* and NPR's *Talk of the Nation*. I emailed Dr. Rhoads and asked him about this. He told me that the social constructionist perspective remains the norm in our universities, but that the influence of the biological perspective on sex differences is growing greatly.[16]

Even in the context of a mountain of contemporary illumination, it must be acknowledged that few conclusions are indisputable or irrefutable. Generalizations are intrinsic to the study of disparity. We can refer to divergent tendencies among a given population and can do so with a high degree of confidence, but we could never do the same thing in regards to individuals. We would expect to find that while women and men differ in a multiple of areas it is never expected that this must be true of a particular person.[17] When analyzing sample populations, the mean, or the average, is what is essential. Conclusions are drawn based on the propensity of their occurring within the average male or female. That outliers exist is a given. In the case of America, a country with about 150 million females, the number of outliers for any particular trait or preference is likely to be quite large. My sister is a case in point. The sciences are largely the domain of men but she is a professor of biology at a university. She has always excelled in math and science. While most women do not fit this profile my sister is unmistakably a female.

The study of history is another area in which our sexual interests diverge. As I alluded to earlier, I have always been an amateur aficionado of the discipline, but have come across few women who share my passion for it. Whenever I meet a woman who openly expresses disdain or disinterest in the subject I make no comment as their opinion is about as unusual as finding out that the tap water I drink comes from Lake Michigan. Should this state of affairs ever be corrected and I meet a woman who cherishes the past as much as I do. I will attribute the finding to statistical variance, but there will be no denying that she is a woman. I could say the same thing about sports, particularly hockey, even though I once ran into a girl who knew more about the game than the majority of my friends.

In the context of race the idea of individual variation is readily apparent. It is well known that most NASCAR fans are white males but no one would ever be taken aback to hear that your narrator has no interest in the sport whatsoever. I remain a Caucasian male despite my lack of affection for the left-hand turn circuit. The same cannot be said of a black male co-worker of mine who loves automobiles and stock car racing in particular.

c.   *Women and Feminists.*

I am perfectly aware that "woman" and "feminist" are not synonymous terms. According to the dictionary definition, feminism is "the doctrine advocating social, political, and all other rights of women equal to those of men."[18] According to that description, I meet the criteria for being a feminist. As stated above, I believe passionately in equality, but that has nothing to do with the modern goals of feminism.

Nowadays, those calling themselves feminists are mostly radical feminists who are about as representative of women on the whole as storm troopers were of Europeans. Radical feminists wish to bestow upon their sisters an infinite number of unearned and undeserved privileges. Christina Hoff Sommers did a marvelous job of teasing out the distinctions between the feminist factions. Those who believe that men and women are entitled to equal pay for equal work and that no legal barriers should exist are dubbed "equity feminists."[19] Sommers holds that most women in America should be included in their ranks. They are the women of the majority, and include the likes of Sommers herself, Carrie Lukas, Wendy McElroy, Daphne Patai, and Danielle Crittenden.

The radical, or gender, feminists are the women of the minority—the Bolsheviks, if you will. Andrea Dworkin, Gloria Steinem, Catharine McKinnon, Shulamith Firestone, and the not so friendly girls at feministing.com are members of this cohort. They are vested in the cause of women's superiority and believe that any law is just if it favors women over men. They display rage over the idea that human nature is intractable, and endlessly hawk conspiracy theories to anyone that will listen. To them, males are always oppressors as the direct sex is a force of evil on this earth. Woman lives in a "state of siege"[20] as the United States is a male dominated "patriarchy." The system exists to "keep women down."[21] In keeping with their irrational perspective, they look to the government to solve their personal problems along with those of a people they do not understand and with whom they never want to interact. They exert a thoroughly horrendous and socialistic influence upon our polity. Even though I admire Dr. Sommers immensely, it has been my experience that most women philosophically fall somewhere in between equity feminism and gender feminism—if only due to the libertarian slant of the average equity feminist [and it is one for which I am enormously grateful] as thirty years of propaganda has had predictable and calamitous effects upon the aggregate outlooks of women.

Speaking of propaganda, unlike Dr. Sommers, the media rarely makes any distinction between radical and equity feminism. More alarmingly, they also intentionally blur the boundaries between women and feminists. Leftist extremist entities like the National Organization of Women (NOW) and the Feminist Majority are described as "women's groups" while their pronouncements are taken to reflect the views of women on the whole. Yet, these radical entities are no more a woman's group than the National Rifle Association is a men's group. If the average woman would make this known to the members of the mainstream media it would markedly improve the political climate for everyone. Thus, due to the inadequacy of our vernacular, in this book, whenever I refer to feminists it will be with the radical variety in mind.

Contrary to the pronouncements of NOW, a recent CBS poll indicated that 68 percent of American women do not consider themselves to be feminists,[22] and that most deem the term repellent. Why wouldn't they? There is nothing attractive about verbally flatulent wildebeests criticizing glamour, grooming, and the need to maintain a healthy body weight. Unfortunately, however, the results of this poll are misleading. Numerous women showcase expectations, attitudes, and behaviors harmonious with the feminist ideal—even if they refuse to take ownership of the feminist label. The feminist ideal continues to titillate as it has elevated Woman to the role of savior. The history of the twentieth century has proven that hailing your constituency as the master race is an excellent way in which to garner public support and power. The refusal of normal women to disavow the outrageous claims and assertions of the feminist minority has made it often difficult to know where the beautiful behind of a woman ends and the gnarled tail of a radical feminist begins.

Thirty years ago, had members of the fairer sex stood up before microphones and told the truth about their lives then we would not be in the predicament we are now in. The world would be a better place had they merely said, "These allegations are false, I don't mind sexual innuendo in the workplace and I've never been raped. I also resent the suggestion that my husband, father, and brother are proto-rapists." Alas, no such undertaking was ever initiated.

Due to their silence concerning the merits of men, women have issued tacit approval to the radical feminist venture. If polls are to be believed their pro-government slant could have something to do with it. They frequently confuse the enrichment of the state with the bettering of the masses. Woman's suffrage is the biggest single factor behind the skyrocketing increase in the size of government and has managed to enlarge the size of the state by a third.[23] Perhaps their love for the nanny state is why so many women wrongly hold feminists to be "fighting the good fight" for them.

George Gilder described their appeal and the effect their positions have had across America: "Though rejecting feminist politics and lesbian posturing, American culture has absorbed the underlying ideology like a sponge. The principal tenets of sexual liberation or sexual liberalism—the obsolescence of masculinity and femininity of sex roles, and of heterosexual monogamy as the moral norm—have diffused through the system and become part of America's conventional wisdom."[24]

Most women are probably cognizant of the disadvantages men face in the status quo, but choose to say nothing because they are afraid of losing the privileges they have acquired. They really cannot be blamed for this as altruism is not the norm among humans. Most of us love getting something for nothing, and a predisposition for "freebies" is found across all civilizations. Feminism remains viable due to our society's lethal mix of inflated female self-esteem and the continuing chivalrous inclinations of the modern male. Women are quite comfortable in demanding what they want and also in saying "Thank you, sir. May I have another?" in response to the favorable treatment they currently receive.

The conundrum in which men find themselves is largely of their own doing. We cannot expect women to do our fighting for us. Most men have refused to stand up to feminists and have acquiesced in the process of the direct sex's diminution and marginalization. The truth was always on our side yet we selected capitulation over self-defense. The outcome has been tragic, unjust, and deplorable, but our own culpability cannot be denied. We have imbued our lives with toxic guilt and allowed hate-mongers to tarnish our history. My book is an attempt to win back some of the logical and moral ground that we have foolishly yielded.

d. Terms.

Lastly, I will avoid using any and all politically correct terminology in this book. They will be no "gender" in these pages. It is a term that radicals have used to erase the unique characteristics of both sexes. Witness the popularity of the phrase "transgendered persons," and the prattle of pseudo-scholars in reference to the existence of a third sex. Just as with boy, I have never bought into the idea that girl is a term of disparagement so I will use it liberally here. To ease the pain of redundancy, I will also call women the fairer sex while calling men the direct sex due to my belief that males generally avoid excessive nuance in our interpersonal relations and are only too pleased to make the exact nature of our needs, desires, and aversions known.

1

The Privileged Sex

If 25 percent of my women friends were really being raped, wouldn't I know it?
—Katie Roiphe[25]

At every age, being a girl rocks. It's your ace in the hole, your backstage pass, your automatic first-class upgrade. Being a girl is what makes you what you are.
—Cameron Tuttle.[26]

If a Martian were to pay an impromptu visit to the United States for the purposes of summing up the interactions between the sexes, I have no doubt that—shortly after ditching his jalopy at a saucer storage facility—he would report his observations in the form of an etched and celestial green drawing. The riveting scene depicted would portray the male in the form of a cat who rested on the lap of his considerably larger female owner. An intimate moment between them would transpire in which she watched television while stroking the back of his head. A bubble next to her face would record the sweet words she said, "Good pussy, good pussy."

Now, one might be tempted to think that a Martian would never use politically incorrect language, but I do not think that this is the case. First, Martians are often better educated than most people realize and this fellow would probably point out to readers that the term pussy, as it used here, is derivative of pusillanimous and has nothing to do with a part of a woman's anatomy. Yes, contrary to what most feministas think, the world, along with the language we use, is not all about women. Second, regardless of the way Martians are commemorated in the timeless verses of Jonathan Richman, their opinions on this subject would be wholly objective and something upon which we could safely rely as only a true radical believer would survey our intersexual landscape and regard our relations as being anything other than preferential to women.

Yet the jaded, politicized and partisan perspective is what passes for truth at the present time. Fanatics see oppression everywhere and our media and politicians encourage us to take them at their word. New York and Los Angeles only look to be zones of anarchic freedom; what they are instead are temples of female oppression and dehumanization which might as well be renamed Kabul and Kandahar. That women, on the whole, are mistreated in America is preposterous, but we are actively lobbied to think otherwise.

The fact of the matter, and it is so important that I will put it into bold print for the benefit of those readers merely skimming these pages, is that **Western women are not oppressed in any way; they are, in fact, the most privileged persons on earth. We know this to be true by the nature of the laws our representatives pass, along with the way those laws are interpreted by our courts and then are enforced by our police. Additionally, the crusade to heighten the status of women at the expense of men showcases the way in which our society is now geared to favor women over all.**

The most damning evidence of their privilege can be found in the way they behave. Do members of the fairer sex, upon encountering men, act in a cowed or intimidated fashion? Absolutely not, simple observation by practically anyone, Martians included, would confirm this to be true. Women today are no more fearful of men than they are a pile of rutabagas or beets. The day in which the average western woman quivers before the average western man is the day in which the French Parliament will invite your humble narrator to fly over and streamline their national bureaucracy.

The modern woman is neither weak nor apprehensive. She is frivolous, well-off, upwardly mobile, and privileged to every extent imaginable. That she may suffer from angst or ennui is granted as victory without effort is an unnatural condition from which only ill-gotten gains can be made. Found status, like found money, is seldom respected. Any disillusion she experiences is likely to be caused by a sea of bewildering lifestyle choices. When thrust into the dragon's treasure room, it is a challenge to decide which objects d'art and doubloons one prefers over the others. No, the decision is not easy and should not be trivialized as it does require effort. A wilderness of options results in a feeling that she no longer has control over her life and no fixed course for the future. Today's woman is not only at liberty to do whatever she wants whenever she wants, but also has been given the wondrous therapeutic tool of being able to blame men should her plans not work out. All but the most deluded realize that the tyranny of men is but a fiction.

The feminist anti-elite reacts with force on the rare occasion in which a member of the sisterhood has the courage to point these facts out. They dub such ladies, "female impersonators,"[27] but they are, instead, ambassadors of truth to a population entirely devoid of it. America has become a place of female transcendence and many of our political discussions are geared towards meeting the wants and needs of our most privileged class.[28] The public square has become a womanspace or a womanchurch.[29] Every time someone somewhere thinks there are not enough women in a particular field, be it among professional opinion journalists[30] or even among largely unpaid bloggers,[31] someone reflexively turns it into a crisis of sexism. In Britain, one source noted that women so dominate broadcasting that they "decide what we see and hear,"[32] while men have been relegated to role of sperm donor. The media bias in favor of the fairer sex is so great that their devotion to them often violates the parameters of common sense. Despite the fact that the average woman in the United States lives five years longer than the average man,[33] a *Newsweek* article actually had the temerity to make an issue out of the cancer rate for women falling at a slower rate than it does for men.[34] Apparently, men dying half a decade earlier was of no consequence to them whatsoever.

Winning the female vote is now the goal of every male politician, and they will do whatever it takes to get it even if it means demeaning their brothers, belittling their country, or kissing Oprah[35] on national television. Reality has nothing to do with the edicts of the Leviathan as the relentless cultural denigration of men has caused Congressmen to passively endorse every initiative that is put up for passage. Our public servants will do anything to appear female friendly and even pen pernicious Bills like the Violence Against Women Act (VAWA). This government offering to activists put a billion dollars into "into the hands of radical feminists who use it to preach their anti-marriage and anti-male ideology, promote divorce, corrupt the family court system, and engage in liberal political advocacy."[36] *AMEN!*

The same federal largesse is not extended to battered men whom feminists deny exist in the first place. An impartial criminologist reported

"...being stunned by the hostile attitudes toward male victims that she encountered at one of the nation's first conferences on domestic violence. She naïvely thought that 'we were all there to do good – for all who needed it.' Yet when she mentioned having read a brief newspaper article about male victims, many of the other women at the conference turned on her, saying, 'This is OUR issue, OUR cause. If men are battered, then let other MEN do something for them.'" [37]

Only by keeping up the ruse that women are oppressed can irrational activists like the one just mentioned ensure their own continued employment and time in the public spotlight.[38] Without the big lie of male domination they would have to go out and get real jobs, but that is not so easy to do when you happen to be a paranoid basketcase. In fact, it is a fate worse than death. My own belief, that we should have "a fair field and no favors"[39] is not one that you will be hearing out of the mouth of any famous feminists anytime soon.

The government that feminists and their fellow travelers have constructed is the farthest thing imaginable from a patriarchy. Even a cursory analysis of its laws, taxes, overpaid bureaucrats, and decision-making illustrates that it is an entity devoted to functioning as Woman's protector. The Federocracy is as matriarchal as a NOW[40] executrix meeting. The nanny state, which women continue to expand via their votes, has granted them lives as effortless as the lyrics to a rap song. The state extends entitlements to them that are wholly unavailable to men. All told, the federoracy finances 160 race and gender preference programs[41] even though they are unneeded. Washington's policy of negative action (dubbed "affirmative action" in their newspeak) makes preferring one sex over the other the permanent order of the day. This state-mandated partiality prevents men from being accepted to colleges and programs, and actively discourages employers from hiring and promoting those who are deficient in estrogen.

For women, the doors of advancement are wide-open and beckoning, yet the government believes that their occasional non-performance is always a result of discrimination. This could not possibly be true as Washington actively encourages employers to shun the direct sex,[42] and every corporation that has been in business for more than a minute has learned the hard way that the government is a force to be feared. The same can be said of the inflated egos and inherent dysfunctionality of those who serve out their time in federal annexes and cubicles.

Any arguments men make on their own behalf are immediately discounted due to the nature of our genitalia. Radical feminists are pathological and cannot be reasoned with. Occasionally, within the muddle that is their thought, they will defend their fantastic allegations by admitting that "the patriarchy" is not oppressive in the traditional sense. One even told me in an email that our country was not a patriarchy ala *Planet of the Apes*, but remained a patriarchy nonetheless. My response to her was to point out that if the patriarchy commits unseen, unheard, and undocumented crimes then it is no more a patriarchy than it is a Gay Pride Parade. No matter how they may wish to twist it, having an infinite number of rights and benefits is not the stuff of a despotic system. If it looks like the good life and feels like the good life, then it is the good life even if one's internal inadequacies and deficiencies prevent them from enjoying it. These feminists should learn to be more critical of themselves and take it easier on the rest of us. They will be much happier and more productive when they do because "The World is Yours" Toni Montana.

That being said, why then are some professions devoid of women? This is a result of their—all too human—personal preferences and choices. In a free society, people will always choose what they want to do and discrepancies will always occur across population groups. Logical types expect this and deem it unremarkable when it transpires. Our social engineers, however, are outraged. They demand that more women find their way into the glamorous professions, but say little about their disproportionate representation in the less glorious vocations. They never clog the streets of the Capitol over males taking up the majority of the nation's coal mining, sanitation, and pipefitting positions as most women hold those careers to be beneath them.

Feminists, if they really wanted to know the truth, would be wise to query boys and girls about they want to do when they grow up. If they did so, they would soon discover that a discrepancy exists between dogma and actual life. My work requires me to query youngsters about their anticipated future, and I have never once heard a girl say that she wished to be a mechanic, a bricklayer, a welder or a carpenter. Nor have I ever heard one say that she wanted to be a scientist, a trader or a Marine, but boys have mentioned all of these professions to me and many more. No one makes them do so and usually I am the only one who cares if form is filled out properly. They say what they do because it is an accurate reflection of the way they genuinely feel. The fact is that boys and girls do not have the same dreams and aspirations. One female academic observed: "Reinventing the curriculum will not make me more interested in learning how my dishwasher works."[43] She is right and such authentic reasoning defeats the collective intellectual output of an entire social movement.

Upon reaching adulthood, it becomes apparent that the girl is the mother of the woman as the fairer sex are not (generally) as interested in the minutia of politics, economics, and government as are men.[44] This is evidence of personal preference and not reflective of discrimination. Disinterest and ambivalence are a far more compelling explanation for the dearth of female politicians than are discrimination or sexism; although, it is reckoned sexist in modern circles to even make such a suggestion. Putting forth an alternative hypotheses is akin to entrenching the patriarchy.

What is essential to note here is that as far as the fulfillment of vocational outcomes is concerned, women are very much the equal of men.[45] The pay gap is entirely fallacious. Income variation is more due to divergent ambition than anything else.[46] Women are not as motivated to prioritize financial gain over other factors as are men. Often flexible scheduling and a favorable geographic proximity are more important to them than getting rich.[47] As a means of fixing a problem that does not actually exist, prominent Democratic politicians like Hillary Clinton and Barack Obama have attempted to socialize women's wages.[48] They have euphemistically termed their act of government control "The Paycheck Fairness Act."

Our elites devoutly believe that women should be inserted into every high profile position available, and that the more women we have the better off we are. This is a harebrained notion. Leadership has no correlation with whether one possesses ovaries or testicles. Despite this eventuality, society's bias was gaudily apparent in January of 2007 when Congresswoman Nancy Pelosi found herself two heartbeats away from the Presidency after the Democratic landslide in the fall. The chorus of yeas that greeted her at inauguration time was maddening—which is not even hyperbole as during the State of the Union address, Democrats barked "Yeah!" and "Hey!" after President Bush introduced Pelosi with "high privilege" and "distinct honor."[49] Had I been Commander-In-Chief the opening words would have been slightly different. My alteration of the text would have included, "We're saved! Here comes the vagina! The vagina is before us! All hail the Great Humongous!"

During the whole Pelosi-palooza I heard few pundits express any ⁓nfidence in her for what could be construed as legitimate reasons. She ⁓s to be just another party hack who achieved success by carefully the use of clear or meaningful language while she was on the clock. Pelosi's way is to criticize her opposition while presenting the people with no alternative form of leadership.[50] In other words, she is a typical politician. Yawn. Of course, Pelosi pretends to be otherwise and displays her female privilege in the process. Her sexism is undeniable: "'Maybe it takes a woman to clean house,' said Pelosi, a mother of five. Asked if her remark was deliberately sexist, she replied, 'It is. Because the fact is a woman represents what's new, because it's never happened before.'[51] Pelosi, with her overblown mannerisms and Reynolds wrapped-features, is just another superficial, self-promoting clown within our political landscape. She is just like all of her statist predecessors as she is addicted to redistributing, or transferring, the earnings of the citizenry to the coffers of the government. Apart from showing the world that sexism is a perfectly legitimate method for acquiring political power, she has accomplished nothing in her time as Speaker of the House.

The Hillary Clinton Presidential campaign has been built around one issue: she is a woman. Bay Buchanan elaborates: "Hillary is running for president *as* a woman, selling her sex as a significant asset of her candidacy. She is offering women in America a 'Madame President.'"[52] With qualifications like those, no doubt America will change her title to Emperor once she is elected.

We should also consider all the genitalia mongering that went on in 2005 when President Bush had to select a replacement for Supreme Court Justice Sandra Day O'Connor. His wife, the First Lady, weighed in on the topic and expressed a hope that her husband would nominate a woman...due to the fact that Mrs. Bush is a woman.[53] How impartial of her! Luckily, Mr. Bush did not take her opinion into account, but contemplate what the uproar would have been if a male in a prominent position had said the same thing about his own sex. The result is that he would be harridanned from Washington power circles quicker than Larry the Cable Guy. Since no powerful person would ever do such a thing perhaps the narrator should step in to illuminate the absurdity of the gynofetishists. Had I walked around Grant Park in downtown Chicago and expressed the same type of sentiment it would have been most amusing. I could have approached a stranger, shook my head, and said, "Boy, am I worried about the Court. I just hope a man gets the gig. Oh please, oh please let it be a man because the last thing we need is someone determining trust law who has never experienced an annual prostrate examination." I do not think my reservations would be well-received. Our elites crave the female accumulation of electoral swag and the only thing we can do about it is to vote the darn bums out.

All of this propagandizing and political pandering has resulted in very real misery for men. Restraining orders can now be filed against them should their girlfriends or wives tell a judge that they are merely afraid of them.[54] No actual proof of wrongdoing is needed and unproven allegations can sometimes result in the destruction of a man's professional career.[55] Most men have accepted this state of affairs either willingly or due to cowardice and a need to conform. It may also be true that the young can imagine no other way of living. Regardless of how it came about, 49% of the American population has declined to organize itself politically. Without a lobby or pressure group, our rulers will continue to mass produce anti-male legislation and their response to men who question it will be to parrot the words crooned by Eddie Cochran long ago: "I'd like to help you son but you're too young to vote."[56] Males would be wise to remember the prescient words of David Horowitz: "In political warfare, if only one side is shooting, the other side will soon be dead."[57]

Despite the accusations and recriminations of our elites, journalists, and feminists, American men are quite liberal and enlightened in their views. Most of us have internalized the notion that absolute equality should exist between the sexes. Indeed, a recent poll found that 85 percent of American males said they would have no problem voting for a female President.[58] Your narrator is among this majority as he would gladly cast a ballot for Condoleeza Rice over George W. Bush any day of the week. Those women who believe they cannot get elected would be wise to quit worrying and learn to love the electorate. Undoubtedly they will be pleasantly surprised once the ballots are scanned. Only phantom barriers bar women from advancement today.

Further exacerbating the male condition is that chivalry,[59] supposedly dead, remains a powerful force in our society. Given the state's nefarious presumption against the direct sex, chivalry has become a Hale-Bopp Death Cult for males. In the present environment, self-demeaning chivalric behaviors are both disastrous and counter-productive. Those of us who recognize this should not dismiss out of hand those who continue practicing its outdated procedures. It may be natural to feel good while aiding women and I know this to be true because I frequently Lambada upon the edge of chivalry's razor myself [believe it or not]. Perhaps the endorphin release we get from aiding women comes from deep within our biological command system. It seems that we instinctively put ourselves forward upon sensing that a member of the fairer sex is in need, and only

·ssive behavioral retraining or genetic rewiring or reading books like this one can alter our propensity to do so. Women are aware of our predisposition which can often result in serious manipulation and mischief.

The feminist Ponzi scheme of ill will has caused men to become bereft of moral authority in our society. All of us are now the presumptive offspring of those who raped women or, even worse, once denied them things or failed to speak respectively of them on all occasions. The scheme has fed into modern man's wish to feel powerful so many a brother has accepted the role of neo-oppressor. That their sisters share the same ancestors is immaterial. It is not as outlandish as it sounds because once one buys into the construct that they are shallow, sick, sex-obsessed Neanderthals then it is quite easy to make the jump to regarding oneself as the inferior of every woman on earth. The aggressiveness of women in portraying men as their ethical and spiritual subordinates is pronounced. They have to do this or else they could not keep the privileges they so value. Equity is a universal mantra of the twenty-first century and the only way to keep up the ruse of women's oppression is to denigrate men so they are too distracted to notice that they have become the masters of nothing. It is unseemly to admit a desire to place oneself at the head of the line so the best defense for women has always been a good offense.

The nature of the woman's grievance business is no cottage industry; it is a sprawling, frenetic, Steven Spielberg production. The victimology complex has its tentacles latched into every area of the public sector and will take whatever it can extort from the private sector. The politically correct majority, be they feminists or their fellow travelers, will deny their advantage reflexively just as they impose their will upon everyone else. Without the fictional oppression of the patriarchy their cushy lives within their inefficient enclaves would cease to exist so every instance of a woman being dissatisfied must be exaggerated to Goebellian proportions. Every woman's life must be embedded, or at least threatened by injustice; if not, then 100,000 advocates would quickly lose everything they have. They would have to apply for work at Harvard or the local Wal-Mart. There really is not a whole lot in between as sinister medusas do not make for effective upscale retail workers. How could they? They would only acknowledge half of their customer base. The industry allows for the legitimate venting of their rage, anger, and hate. Without this semi-official cloak, observers would take their perpetual expression of toxic emotion to be what it is: an indelible sign of psychopathology.

Activists are tied to the myth of a Spermocracy in the same way that the Nazis were tied to the fable of communists torching the Reichstag. These fanatics cannot negotiate or pretend that the status quo is even remotely acceptable. Marriage must be a death camp, and the only thing worse than the institution is when males selfishly refuse to enter into it with them. The workplace must be rife with rogues and capitalist exploiters while the myth of a glass ceiling must be promoted to ensure that women are promoted to positions which they have not earned. Without this radical-made Kultursmog, the timelessness of the Peter Principle would be proven again and again.

Case Study.

A perfect example of one such feminist is Jenny Dombrowski who recently wrote an article[60] for the *Baltimore Sun* entitled, "There's Still Plenty Left for Women to Fight For." Within the piece, she recites several positions that are fairly standard to her ilk, so her words are a suitable template from which to illuminate the tenets of the woman's anti-industrial grievance complex. She begins with a call to arms, or at least a call for more criticism and complaining:

> *If indeed the women's movement is over, then why are women still treated as objects in our society? We are inundated with images of perfection at every turn: from the check-out line of the grocery store to the movie theater to the billboards along the highway. We're informed how to slim our thighs. We're made the object of ridicule and rescue in most films. Then there's the overwhelming presence of pornography. A simple Google search for "porn" elicits more than 85 million hits. What this leads to is the most sweeping social issues of our society: eating disorders, poor self-esteem, sexual harassment, violence and abuse. Every two minutes, a woman is sexually assaulted in America. And women still make 74 cents for every $1 a man makes, according to news reports. How's that for "women's lib"?*

There are so many inanities in that paragraph that it is not easy to know where to begin, but I will live up to my burden of rejoinder and start from the beginning as crazed feminists multiply when good men pooh-pooh their charges. First off, the notion that women are oppressed is independently refuted by the very newspaper in which this piece appeared. If the mighty *Baltimore Sun* were an agent of the patriarchy then this column would have never found a home there. Furthermore, they made a point of formally rejecting my response to her positions. The exact words the male editor said to me were, "Thanks for the offer, but I can't use this on the op-ed page."[61] Obviously, my genitalia did not open up the doors of entitlement.

But what of her claims specifically? Clearly, women are not treated as objects in our society. How one could draw such a conclusion is baffling. The only thing that can be said in her favor is that often the fairer sex are treated with an awe generally reserved for religious relics. I have never once observed a man treat them in the same manner he ever did an object. My brothers affix their "male gaze" upon women in a fashion dissimilar to that of any object on the planet. Compare the average male's level of pupil dilation upon his encountering of a woman to that which occurs after he sees a computer, a garden, an oven, a refrigerator, a book, a building or a car, and you will have all the evidence you need for the refutation of this implausible proposition.

Man can become visually habituated to everything in his vista...except for women. The sighting of a novel and attractive female keens the senses. If we substitute appreciated for objectified then it becomes easier to understand how such a rancid contention came about. Men appreciate women for their youth and beauty, but their visual affinity does not result in the dehumanization of anyone. Conversely, women do not decrease the humanity of the direct sex when they appreciate men for their high levels of wealth and/or status. Objectification is such a hackneyed and weak argument that it could not maintain its shape before a puppy's breath. Here we see why political correctness is vital to the survival of radical feminism because without it they could not defend a single paragraph of their "thought."

Pleasing women and meeting their needs has become the basis of an entire culture; it is intrinsic to our domestic laws, consumer goods, and television in general.[62] Should Ms. Dombrowski honestly doubt this then she is encouraged to look up the phrase "equitable paternity"[63] or a host of other inequitable decisions endemic to our legal system. Nothing can ever satiate the activist's desire to unbalance the playing field as they have "championed blatant favoritism toward mothers in child custody disputes, often to the point of vilifying fathers" and have an outlook best described by the words "maternal chauvinism."[64]

The Duke Lacrosse case is a perfect example. PC, feminism, and anti-Caucasian racism brought about a verdict of guilt upon three boys before any proceedings or investigations were initiated. The media so accepts the notion that white males are virulent dogs that they, along with the district attorney, wrote a plot for the case based on dogma rather than evidence. They pooled their malicious talents together to craft a fairy tale based on race, sex, and class. They then refused to apologize after they discovered that a deranged stripper had made fools of them; illustrating that character really is destiny. That they ruined the lives of three innocent lads was irrelevant because their hearts were in the right place—after all, everyone did their best to railroad those three white men. How humorous it was to hear one prominent reporter excuse himself for his slanted coverage during the drama. He said something to the effect of, "Come on, they shouldn't have been there. They should have known better than to attend a party with 50 guys with two strippers." Known better? How could they suspect that the person they hired would try to frame them with the help of the media and the government? Such eventualities do not occur to the average college student who is largely unaware of the world being every bit as cruel as it is kind. Of course, the reporter would never say the same thing about a group of black males who decided to decorate a party with two white strippers. The affair in North Carolina revealed many things but the most important one was that the claims of women are given far more credence than those of men. Many women make false charges of rape but there is no shortage of men who believe them.[65] How's that for women's lib?

Getting back to Ms. Dombrowski specifically, her quip about women being inundated with snapshots of perfection in grocery stores is merely a testament to the interest that women have in such imagery. There is no question that women, as opposed to men, are the primary purchasers of publications featuring covers with the likes of Jennifer Lopez, Brittany Spears, Christina Aguilera, Paris Hilton, and Lindsay Lohan on them. If they were not interested in gazing at such persons and studying their vapid opinions then there would only be chewing gum near the cash registers.

Certainly, male taste is the last thing which drives the decision-making process of the photo editors at *Cosmopolitan, Shape, Seventeen,* and *In Style.* With the exception of feminists and those drinking from vials of lysergic acid no one would ever dispute this, yet activists are so mentally concrete and low functioning that they think a woman staring at a well-built and/or glamorous peer will bring about a host of psychological problems. This is fatuous as women are among the most resilient of all creatures and are likely to be inspired or indifferent to visual representations of their betters. Were these images as meaningful as feminists hold them to be then there would be a gaggle of suicides across the nation along with a marked decrease in our rate of obesity. In their Bizarro World, a minute after flipping through *Self*, a girl would either vow to never eat pizza again or wash down their next pie with a full bottle of Prozac. Apart from mental deficiency, another reason why feminists are as confused as they is due to their knowing no more about their constituents than they do the decade in which the First World War was fought.

It appears that with film as well Ms. Dombrowski does not like the way society's great sacred cows are represented. Personally, I have to agree with her. Women are inordinately typecast as heroines and champions when that is not in keeping with the way we know them to be. Indeed, it seems that the mission of the Oxygen and Lifetime cable channels is to present women as being empowered superheroes—a rather ironic point of view considering that their actual viewers are irritable, discombobulated, depressionacs.

Specifically, the notion of women being rescued really bothers her. Well then, I suppose that the truly female-friendly men are the ones who look the other way when their girlfriends get whacked. Although, maybe there is merit in her position as more women getting assassinated on-screen might convince impressionable minds that sleeping with the fishes is not something reserved for men alone. The bottom line here is that any discussion of this issue is completely immaterial as a filmmaker's perspective has nothing to do with the stance of the state. The only remedy for her complaint would be government censorship. This would mean wooden, mediocre bureaucrats calling Martin Scorsese to inform him of the way his films really should go down. What an odious eventuality that would be. Of course feminists would like it as they could brag that everyone was finally "listening to women." Perhaps they will consider naming their board of cinematic inquiry The National Association of Zeitgeist Interrogators as the acronym fits well with their stand on practically everything.

That feminists embody that acronym is something of which there is little doubt. We see this in their attitude towards women who stay home to raise children and thereby eschew the heady choice of working themselves to death. Fanatics attribute the decisions of these stay-at-home-moms to the spell cast upon them by the nefarious patriarchy, but the animal kingdom is the real influence peddler in these circumstances. The desire to raise and protect offspring is not a "social construct." It is a reflection of normal mammalian behavior and evidence of the way in which biology has shaped our personalities. A female's attachment to her young is hard-wired. Simone de Beauvoir knew this and that is why she said: "No woman should be authorized to stay at home to raise her children. Society should be totally different. Women should not have that choice, precisely because if there is such a choice, too many women will make that one."[66]

Feminists can modify society all they want to, but they will never succeed in taking the human out of human being. Linda Hirshman wrote *Get Back to Work: A Manifesto for Women of the World* in which she insisted that women discontinue emphasizing their needs and desires over the mandates of a leftist-socialist agenda. This is asinine because if social engineers like Hirshman are too holy to care about personal preferences then what can their self-righteous fantasies possibly offer women? Here again we see why "feminazi" is not a pejorative but a rich and essential term of description. Feminists do not care what women think, utopian visions of the future are all that matter to them. They will make their omelet even if every egg is poisoned on the way to the frying pan. The feminazi proclaims that their critics possess a "false consciousness" or that they are afflicted with some sort of deadly ism, but the last thing they would ever do is respect another person's diversity.

Ironically, their belief that women, whom feminists view as wards, do not know what is good for them is a reflection of the activist's blatant misogyny. In this way, the self-proclaimed guardians of the sisterhood are more oppressive than any male could ever be. Truly liberal persons would never try to manipulate and control others in such a condescending fashion. They would encourage everyone to make an individual decision about their own future. Political lobbyists have no idea what is best for the citizenry.

The most boffo aspect about the Dombrowski article was the author's clueless choice of words. "Rescue" should not have been mentioned in regards to women as it was unintentionally self-revealing. In the beginning of her jeremiad she shares an autobiographical tidbit that showcases just how much she is a fawn in need of saving. Thrust into the role of instructor at George Washington University, she suddenly flees her classroom after a student voices the need for a men's movement. She was ashamed that she "couldn't formulate anything in the moment but an emotional, sputtering response" so she abruptly decamped for a less stressful environ. She should take heart though as illogical emotion-plagued responses are the hallmark of academic feminism; thus, her vocational prospects are actually quite bright.

Dombrowski is a woman who denies female privilege but is so indulged that she does not think she has to give a second's hearing to those with whom she disagrees. In the university hothouse, a challenge to an instructor's weltanschauung provides them with a legitimate excuse for walking off the job. Thanks to political correctness, a coward as unstable as technetium is allowed to keep her overpaid position even after she abandons both her students and her classroom. I guess having progressive credentials alone is good enough to maintain employment nowadays. Ms. Dombrowski has it all: leisure, luxury, and the warm fuzzies which come from diminishing your students' knowledge base.

When analyzing a feminist harangue can there be any real doubt that sooner or later we will arrive at the issue of pornography? In this new millennium, the critiques are usually more subtle than what we get here. Dombrowski's reference to the P word made it seem as if Andrea Dworkin had popped out from my monitor and shouted for Twinkies. In fact, I was little surprised that the author mentioned her name at all because most feminists try to separate themselves from her late and gargantuan shadow. I guess our young instructor still wishes to sublet a bit of space on the dearly departed's syphilitic archipelago.

We find that lurid imagery is quite prevalent on the internet which means...absolutely nothing. The argument is a non-starter. Erotic materials no more oppress women than they do exterminate water bugs. Generally, the only thing clips, thumbs, and frames accomplish is to enable a man to get to sleep a little sooner at night. Purchasing or freely obtain pornography has never been linked to the pathologies she cites. There are three million normal law abiding citizens who accumulate *Hustler*, *Penthouse*, etc., and that Ted Bundy did as well does not tar them with the resin from his evil brush. Bundy probably also bought Crest toothpaste, had a refrigerator, rode a bike, and did many other things that every other person does. He was a serial killer but did not become one after seeing a few girls dress in thongs and fondle one another. If Ms. Dombrowski does not like raunchy flicks and photo spreads then I suggest that she avoid looking at them. Otherwise, she should mind her own business and spend some time studying the nature of mental illness. Furthermore, we know that porn is not anti-woman because so much of the market is tailored towards gay males. Those guys would be the first ones to speak up if their cherished steroid freaks were replaced by size 40 DD silicone queens. The plain fact is that taking off our clothes does not result in mass oppression and dehumanization.

As for the specific maladies she describes, there is no causality between those conditions and anything that has to do with men. Anorexia is a serious psychiatric condition and one that features a high co-morbidity[67] with other disorders. It does not come about from looking at magazines or understanding that fat is a cardio-vascular issue. By implying otherwise, Dombrowski demeans those women who suffer from it; the same ones in whom she pretends to take an interest. Psychopathology is present within a small minority of human beings across all population groups and countries. Cruelty and sadism are not manufactured in a printer's shop—nor are they an outcome of using "he" instead of "he/she" in our daily speech. Crazed monsters will always be with us and that is why we have a police force and a criminal code. No amount of dialectical drivel can ever change the nature of our species.

Sexual harassment has to be the one area in which feminists lie the most,[68] and this is not surprising given its subjective and illusory nature. Within the SHI, or Sexual Harassment Industry, the outrageous bias, dishonor, and mendaciousness of the feminists is prominently on display—it is a rotten infrastructure that Christina Hoff-Sommers has dubbed: "Ms. Information."[69] The appalling unfairness of their positions is evident in the response that a feminist professor gave after being accused of the dreaded crime herself. While on a podium, in front of an audience, the pseudo-scholar kissed one her students and announced that, "graduate students are my sexual preference."[70] Once caught, she then argued that the charges were unfounded by definition because "[f]emale sexual harasser seems like a contradiction in terms...feminism invented sexual harassment...[it] is a way men obstruct women from doing work."[71] Luckily for our country, semantics has yet to officially replace facts as a determiner of individual guilt.

Then we come to the "pay gap" complaint which illustrates that a lie remains a lie no matter how many times you tell it. I theoretically refuted it earlier so I will be brief here. First, no proof is offered in regards to the 74 percent figure cited which I suspect is due to there being none. Interestingly enough, at work there hangs a government poster citing the same percentage, but no evidence is cited on the poster either. It is an urban legend that becomes more fallacious with each repetition. Its presence illustrates just how much influence that radicals exert upon the government.

Second, by teasing out a few variables, the figure becomes completely laughable. When single women are compared to single men, "the gap" between them is only five percent.[72] The presence of married women in the configuration increases the disparity due to many of them deciding to put their energies into their children rather than their careers.[73] One married woman made just such a choice and that is how I obtained my current vocational situation. She declined my position due to it being ratcheted up to full-time from part-time. I was only too happy to accept 40 hours of employment instead of the 20 hours that she formerly had. In the field of education in particular, this scenario is quite common. Millions of men never consider anything less than full-time labor because we simply have no choice; we work or we die. No one will support us and there are no judges, such as those for women in our divorce courts, who will ride into our lives upon a white horse and save us. That is the way it has always been and that is the way it will always be.

Lastly, feminists like Ms. Dombrowski avoid nuance altogether when discussing the wage differential. There will forever be a statistically insignificant disparity among the sexes due to women taking more time off, avoiding posts that require relocation and travel, working fewer hours, and shunning high risk jobs.[74] The root cause of this is varying personal priorities.[75]

Not content merely with blame and castigation, Ms. Dombrowski offers up a solution more tired and weathered than Hillary Clinton: "A good first step would be standing up and demanding that Congress pass the Equal Rights Amendment, which was first introduced in 1923 and has yet to pass. Why the fuss? Because the ERA plainly states: 'Equality of rights under the law shall not be denied or abridged by the United States or by any state on account of sex.'"

Wow, what a good idea seeing as though men are the ones who find themselves discriminated against in America today. Well, it would be a good idea except for the fact that such a law is already on the books. Here we witness just how worthless a politicized education is because discrimination based on sex has been prohibited for over 40 years due to the passage of Title VII of the Civil Rights Act of 1964. Its provisions state repeatedly that it is unlawful to discriminate based on an "individual's race, color, religion, sex, or national origin..."[76] Since 1964, women have possessed exactly the same rights as everybody else. Women's lib came, it saw, it conquered, and now it wishes to remain both conqueror and victim. Clearly, Kenneth Minogue was right as feminists are "intellectuals without an intellect."[77]Although, their advocacy for an Equal Rights Amendment is not wholly due to ignorance as it is a way for feminists to receive the attention that they crave. Bandying its language about creates the impression that women remain oppressed in this country despite every piece of evidence suggesting otherwise. It creates not only a time vacuum but a reason vacuum. Facts are ignored while grievances are aired and affirmed.

Esther Villar is one of the few commentators to artfully document the discrepancy between woman's actual and presumed status in the western world. Her book, *The Manipulated Man* delineates thoroughly the nature of their eminence:

1. *Men are conscripted; women are not.*
2. *Men are sent to fight in wars; women are not.*
3. *Men retire later than women (even though, due to their lower life-expectancy, they should have the right to retire earlier).*
4. *Men have almost no influence over their reproduction (for males, there is neither a pill nor abortion—they can only get the children women want them to have).*
5. *Men support women; women never, or only temporarily, support men.*
6. *Men work all their lives; women work only temporarily or not at all.*
7. *Even though men work all their lives, and women work only temporarily or not at all, on average, men are poorer than women.*
8. *Men only "borrow" their children; women can keep them (as men work all their lives and women do not, men are automatically robbed of their children in cases of separation—with the reasoning that they have to work).*[78]

I grant that Villar's conclusions are too absolute, but that there is a societal bias in favor of women is indisputable. Our country has publicly obsessed over equality for fifty years yet the result has been to elevate half of the population over the other. The brutal truth is that in the eyes of the law and in the eyes of the general population, women are more special than they are equal. Should it have turned out to be the other way around, Oprah would have proclaimed it "A Silent Epidemic!"[79], and hauled out her band of bulging sheep to process endlessly over their predicament upon the grass of the National Mall.

Times have changed and there is no longer any reason for the media, the state, and, most importantly, individual men to treat women as a chosen people. No sex should be more "special" than the other. Females make up over half of the world's population, and are hardy, resilient, and strong. They get sick less often and live longer than men while choosing safer vocations. Indeed, they are even (formally at least) the better educated sex. It is time for everyone to accept these facts and insist that they be full and equal partners in the enterprise of civilization. Just as with men, women should be held responsible for their actions and expect only equal treatment from our government. They deserve the same rights as men...and nothing more. A woman should not be ensconced in a legal cocoon and handled like a rare artifact. There is only one Shroud of Turin, but there are over three billion women on this earth.

2

Hail to the Totalitarian Victors

If our sexuality is socially constructed it can also be de and reconstructed.
　　　　—E. Kay Trimberger.[80]

After witnessing my refutation of the fictional notions of both patriarchy and female oppression in Chapter 1, readers may now agree that feminists are incoherent buffoons and liars, but might regard my concerns as being overblown. Some of you might view these radicals as being but tertiary characters in the overall scheme of things. You might think that they are unsavory and fail to amount to much. Such a view would be unfortunate. Radical feminism is the most pernicious social movement to arise out of the ideological cesspool of the 1960s,[81] and it is not only due to their ubiquitous self-referencing and theoretical obfuscation. Their work has had very real impact upon our social structure. They have transformed the minds of many women, and massively altered the relations between the sexes. In terms of destructiveness, their impact has even surpassed their own expectations.

Radical feminism has created, in the words of Professor Howard S. Schwartz, a "Sexual Holy War"[82] between men and women. It is an altercation in which the same script is read perpetually; women are victims and men are oppressors. Just as with the country of Ingsoc in George Orwell's 1984, a once symbiotic society has been mutated into an "us versus them" battlefield.[83] The sudden transformation is most unusual and clashes with the whole of human history.

Previously, the complementariness of the male/female relationship resulted in mutual gain and never could be described as subjugation.[84] Yet the past is of little relevance to feminists as history has become herstory. Their theories are entirely Manichean in outlook. Women are to virtue what men are to vice.[85] Men are innately evil creatures[86] who routinely commit atrocities[87] while displaying characters that are, at best, morally defective.[88] Any faults that women have can be excused due to their being a reaction to male domination. Often heard is the notion that if women ruled the earth utopia would result. There would be eco-feminism, social justice, peace, and love. Once appointed, how such a society would deal with men is not generally specified...

Of course, it does not take much lucidity to know that all of this is balderdash. Women are fully human and possess most of the same faults that men do; although, on average, they may exhibit them to a greater or lesser extent. They consume drugs, drive SUVs, eat meat, commit crimes, and savage others. They even appear to be every bit as sexist as are men.[89] A cross-cultural study spanning five continents and nineteen nations found that individual women held the same view of women on the whole as do men.[90] In fact, numerous women do not like or trust other females[91] which is not consistent with the cherubim image of a "sisterhood" that activists project. Some researchers even believe that women are the more hostile sex.[92] Girls, just like boys, often ridicule one another and call each other demeaning names.[93] Women have been known to support and participate in a great many deplorable acts, and this should surprise no one.[94] I have even witnessed this play out in my own life. I was raised under the edict that I should never hit a woman, but a few of my romantic relationships have illustrated to me that women do receive the same instructions in regards to the opposite sex. I have been hit several times by at least three women I have dated over the years (admittedly a small minority). That I refused to strike them back was of little consolation— apart from keeping me out of jail.

Despite an avalanche of politically correct propaganda, some women do use violence as a means for conflict resolution. Activists always have a ready-made answer for this eventuality; female rage and irritability are a result of the way they were, or are, treated by men. I recall hearing this in regards to the murders committed by Andrea Yates. Some talking head on television wanted to know what the husband's role was in her murderous rampage. The answer was "none." Mr. Yates had no role in the executions of his children as his wife was mentally ill.[95] Regardless of how sick that particular executioner was the Huston branch of the

National Organization of Women formed a support group on her behalf.[96]

To feminists, all female discretions and sins can be transferred to the testicles of whatever men happen to be in their orbit. The wide disparity between how women are reputed to act and how they actually do act is not something that feminists will ever acknowledge. If they did, the leaky and toxic foundation upon which their hateful religion was built would turn to rubble. Their worldview is fantastic and fabricated—much like the Marxist theories which originally inspired it. With a utopian answer for every question, their religiosity sooths the faithful while labeling as untouchables all of those who criticize or defy them. That is why political correctness is synonymous with the phrase "cultural Marxism" as it is the application of Marxist economic tenets to culture.[97] In our universities, their superunified theories reign supreme and have made our academies into a dispirited zone of bitterness, hatred, and resentment.[98] Women are depicted as being victims of men and they now replace the bourgeoisie in our new dialectic. This updated version of Marxism is not much of an update as it is rife with the same old misunderstandings of human nature.[99] Women and minorities are cast as being a new proletariat, and are portrayed as groups who will save the world—provided their male oppressors are silenced and discredited.

That PC has triumphed over logic, respect, freedom, and individuality is largely a result of feminist transcendence. They are its hallowed deathforce, its Darth Vaders, and its bully boy enforcers who ensure its widespread application. A constant stream of venom is issued from woman's studies programs and the other corrupted liberal arts departments, and they have disseminated a gospel of anti-male, anti-Caucasian, and anti-American propaganda. Speech codes are a favorite weapon with which to bludgeon their opposition, and reeducation courses offer up another way to reconstitute their foes.[100] By typecasting women as victims they have managed to equate all that is feminine with all that is moral.[101] PC demands that the oppressed share their voices while simultaneously denying rejoinder to those who oppose them.[102] Hearing them chant PC conform-o-speak words like "tolerance" and "diversity" is macabre. Those who even express mild disagreement are labeled as heretics and drummed out of their ranks.

Their status as golden calves creates situations so bizarre that they are tough to parody—such as the words of the Bowling Green University professor who helped scrap a proposed class on political correctness. She said, "We forbid any course that says we restrict free speech!"[103] That she saw no irony in her statement will not underwhelm those readers previously exposed to such knuckledraggers. This is what passes for a scholar in the post-modern academy. Another humorous exchange was documented by former radical feminist Phyllis Chesler. She informed one of her peers that she was writing a book about inter-female hostility and aggression. The woman told Chesler, "You should not be writing this book. Are you ready to sell out, is that why you're doing it?"[104] A better question to ask is how someone can consider themselves "an educator" when the truth is something they wish to avoid.

A feminist education is worse than no education at all. Learning that men are to blame for everything wrong in the cosmos is not only vile, but patently false. That this is feminism's central tenet here again illustrates that the moniker "feminazi" is a highly appropriate term of description. The feminist's conspiratorial and bizarre depiction of their enemy's power and prominence is eerily similar to the one National Socialists used for Jews. One is left with exactly the same ideology after "Jew" is replaced with "white male." Feminazi is not an epithet; it is a cogent argument [of course, the feminist perspective is internationalist rather than nationalist so perhaps "Itzi" would be even better]. Insisting that activists explain to you how they differ from their jackbooted predecessors is actually a profitable method with which to deal with them. It is not likely that they will have much intelligible to say in response.[105]

That feminist speakers are often introduced to audiences as being angry or outraged is unintentionally hilarious but also quite revealing. Their purported anger is merely a smokescreen with which to hide their cancerous hate.[106] The fact is that no man has done much of anything negative to them. Largely male governors sign bills that allow public funds to be wasted on their not-for-profit organizations, college programs, and state agencies. Male politicians allow these activists to multiply and thrive. There rarely is any legitimacy to their complaints. That so many men enable them is unfortunate, but it does not diminish the intensity of their ire. Some are so deluded that they actually believe all men to be rapists.[107] Others so despise the direct sex that they regard their incarceration and trial, even when the defendant turns out to be innocent, as being of benefit to society.[108]

The feminist aversion to all things masculine is pathological and more rooted in personal deficiency and dysfunction than in real life events. No rational explanation can be found for their animosity.[109] Feminist thought is but an expression of a primitive psyche,[110] and is self-pity disguised as politics.[111] Its acceptance has harmed the nation immeasurably and enabled emotion to become a substitute for logic in our public square.[112] They have also barbarized our social interactions. Restraint, respect, and good manners are completely below them.[113] Yet, regardless of their glaring intellectual inadequacy and mental instability, feminist ideas have been internalized by our society.

Hitler often made mention of the devastating impact a small cadre could have upon society at large, and this is certainly the case with the radical feminists. Their unshakeable animosity towards men and their sword of political correctness has made the west a highly misandric place. We can define misandry as being a "culturally propagated hatred" of men,[114] and it aptly describes the current state of the Anglosphere. The misandry of today, unlike the misogyny of yesterday, has not been tempered by the chivalry of the other sex. Women display empathy towards children but fail to show similar feelings for men on the whole. Stereotypes now proliferate which enforce our culture's enmity for men;[115] whereas, in the past, women were never portrayed as Neanderthals.[116]

Hallmark cards specifically cater to misandric and sexist trends by featuring editorials disguised as greetings. These serve to poke fun at male vanity, arrogance, and mega-ego while offering no equivalent messages in regards to the fairer sex.[117] Society allows this to go one due to the assumption that men are getting what they deserve—even though most of us have never harmed or oppressed anyone.[118] Your narrator is quite hardened to the injustices of the present age, but even he was slightly unnerved to discover an advertisement for a knife set in which the utensils were housed in a man-shaped block. The idea is that, after each use, one replaces the knife and gets to simulate the act of stabbing a man in the chest. What a joy! If the creator of this item were to make a similar product featuring a block in the shape of a woman, they would face boycotts, *New York Times'* reporters, and possible hate crime charges.

Today, it is "a House Rule" that men can make fun of their own kind, but are forbidden from making fun of women.[119] We are encouraged to laugh at ourselves while women are expected to laugh right along with us.[120] There is no equanimity. Comedians like Jay Leno and Tim Allen routinely center jokes around the queer antics of men, but never extend their humor to women.[121] Why would they do otherwise? It would be like creating a cartoon about Mohammed. To make fun of a woman is a depraved act. This is lamentable as their foibles are most humorous, and excoriating feminists is absolutely divine. Jokes like this one are not only hysterical but shed considerable light on the activist's Jacobin nature:

Question: "How many feminists does it take to change a light bulb?"
Answer: "That's not funny!"

This one is almost as good:

> *A radical feminist is getting on a bus when, just in front of her, a man gets up from his seat. She thinks to herself, "Here's another man trying to keep up the customs of a patriarchal society by offering a poor, defenseless woman his seat," and she pushes him back onto the seat. A few minutes later, the man tries to get up again. She is insulted again and refuses to let him up. Finally, the man says, "Look, lady, you've got to let me get up. I'm two miles past my stop already!"*[122]

To the feminist, women, as opposed to life or death, are a life and death matter. While doing a search for jokes about feminists I came across a discussion thread that was goofier than most of the one-liners. It was at a Women's Studies academic forum[123] and concerned whether or not instructors should begin their ovulars with a wisecrack. A good many of them were not keen to do so. One favored reading a poem as a better way to start class. Another pondered, "Does it help to sense that jokes are often at someone's expense, and that someone may be a stereotyped imagined?" Another sister wisely agreed. She pointed out that humor itself is hateful. She said, "The purpose of humor which looks at specific groups is to make fun of that group and help maintain the status quo." Who knew? I thought humor was a gift from God. They better not tell Jerry Seinfeld because it would invalidate his entire existence.

Feminists are very good at attacking but turn to unstable gelignite when met with even minor resistance. Professors who question the PC line are often reported to the administration.[124] There is no collegiality for non-feminists in the academy. If their peers in the professorate should be honest enough to question their bogus statistics they will be met with pickets and verbal abuse.[125] Should any college kids have the nerve to make fun of the ridiculous clowns who man the Womyn's Studies enclaves, their jibes could end with their own expulsion.[126] To the feminist, reeducation is always the preferred form of therapy.[127] Their assaults on logic and truth are always protected, but PC's sensitivity never extends to white males.[128] A male Caucasian's freedom of speech is always in jeopardy.[129]

The needs and desires of the feminist can never be satiated due to their endemic totalitarianism. They insist on more government as the cure for every ailment. Only state sponsored coercion can bring about the feminist utopia and the Leviathan will erect for them a totalitarian hell on earth.[130] Mad with power, they pathologically despise those who differ from them. Their enemies must be denied even the smallest amount of mental space.[131] Their hatred of pornography is merely an attempt to eradicate the private fantasies of men.[132] Feminist zeal and venom has cast disapproval on the very act of being a man.[133] The only loophole in their worldview is for men to renounce their masculinity and get on with the wondrous business of acting like a woman.[134] Most feminist initiatives are but a way to get others to live lives which mirror their own. Despite their incessant complaining and gross displays of psychological disturbance, feminists insist that the mass of men will only be happy when they adopt female habits.[135] I cannot speak for all men, but their's is the type of happiness that should be quarantined; transmitting it to others should be considered a felony. Their desire for emulation is transparent and represents their attempt to normalize themselves. They hope to one day walk amongst clones and then, and only then, will their malignancy become unnoticeable.

Nowadays, gays or minority males are the only individuals with a legitimate right to appear masculine.[136] Even the word "manliness" has negative connotations as Dr. Harvey Mansfield found out when he spoke to a reporter from his university's alumni magazine. Here is the exchange they had regarding one of his former co-workers: "Responding too quickly, I said: 'What impressed all of us about him was his manliness.' There was silence at the other end of the line, and finally the female voice said: 'Could you think of another word?'"[137]

Feminists seem to have a genetic predisposition that bars them from reflection. They never consider what the consequences of their actions will be. Marriage is an excellent example. A side effect of their turning marriage into a legalistic death trap is that fewer and fewer men now get married at all. The same can be said of the sexual revolution. Women are encouraged to be promiscuous which means that male physical satisfaction can be easily obtained without subjecting oneself to a juridical matanza. No doubt that a decrease in marriages pleases lesbian feminists, but this outcome has to frustrate and depress the majority of American women. To most feminists, their goal was reconstitution of marriage rather than its eradication so the consequences of their advocacy were obviously unintended. Modern unions have become a feminist institution as most men quickly transition from bull to barnacle just a few years after their surrender to the state.

Given the political miseducation of the average feminist, it is not surprising that they understand so little about government, people, and life in general. Their political "accomplishments" have been the enactment of laws and procedures which erode our freedom, individuality, and dignity. [138] Their low-brow, self-indulgent dogma has even managed to influence the decisions of the Supreme Court of the United States. [139]

We will see in the next chapter that the media routinely promotes the needs of women over the need for the truth, and their bias results from an acceptance of feminist hallucinations. Thanks to the press, radical confabulations have leaked out beyond the academic wards and infected every aspect of our environment. [140] Their sound bytes are reproduced in daily speech and are found in our Congressional records and jurisprudence. The press and our politicians disseminate feminist irrationalizations to the citizenry who, unfortunately, do not possess the satisfactory background knowledge with which to recognize that their bank of theories are nothing more than a compendium of psychobabble.

When gazing back at the events of the past four decades or so, the only optimistic thing that can be said about the United States is that we have yet not turned into Sweden. Our homegrown feminists have not constructed an official party or pushed for bills exacting special taxes from men or publicized plans to coerce couples into acquiring gender neutral names. [141] We could easily have become Germany—a nation where devices are attached to toilets which sound the alarm every time the seat is raised—but we have not. [142] It is verboten for Fritz to stand while urinating as every unzipped twinkle supposedly entrenches the patriarchy. That we are not Europe is of small consolation as there are no psychological barriers or institutions in place which can forestall our further devolution.

The Lie of the Century.

Of course, there a great many feminist lies from which to choose from here, but clearly their biggest one is their systematic denial of the existence of sex differences. Basically, as I suggested in the Introduction, they do not think there are any indigenous disparities between man and woman, at least any that are a product of biology. They will note positive divergences, however, and by positive I mean ones that favor women—such as the fairer sex being more nurturing, kind, and good—but will carefully avoid attributing these to the hand of nature. They prefer to talk the language of "gender" and believe that many genders exist;[143] all of which are socially constructed.[144] They are quick to condemn masculinity, testosterone, men who roam in groups, the characteristics of male friendship, and man's unique interests and activities (which often do not include women), but will not accede the superiority of males in any area.

This is rather suspicious as male achievement has been quite ostentatious. We have built 99 percent of the earth's infrastructure along with practically every invention and made nearly every single scientific discovery. Saying that "science is patriarchal" is a worthless argument as feminists make use of every modern convenience and medical advancement. Camille Paglia had it right: "If civilization had been left in female hands we would still be living in grass huts."[145] I do not believe in male superiority, as we are human and have scores of flaws, but a little humility on the part of feminists in regards to our track record would be appreciated.

Feminists allege that our bad traits arise from the maniacal machinations of the fictional patriarchy. That we have a government which seeks to enslave and destroy those who oppose the rule of men[146] is a ridiculous concept in lieu of contemporary divorce law, affirmative action, and the fact that America has turned into a 24/7 Women's Workout World.

The concept of "gender" as well is complete hogwash. There are only two sexes and the discrepancies between them are, for the most part, biologically based. Sexual differentiation is readily evident and commonly known (unless one's mind has been incarcerated and divested of gray matter at a Womyn's Studies Center):

An international team of 250 scientists, conducting research first reported last Thursday in the British journal Nature, has completed a full map of the X or "female" chromosome which helps determine sex in human beings. The researchers found much greater genetic variation between the sexes than they had expected. All told, as the Los Angeles Times described the team's conclusions, "men and women may differ by as much as 2 percent of their entire genetic inheritance, greater than the hereditary gap between humankind and its closest relative--the chimpanzee." Huntington Willard of Duke University,

*one of the key researchers participating in this latest effort, told the
Chicago Tribune that by now "any of us over the age of two realizes
there are plenty of differences between males and females that are characteristic of the two sexes."[147]*

Well not everyone realizes it. The realm of incomprehension is
vast and powerful. Organizations as diverse as the World Bank[148] and the
YMCA[149] continue to maintain that gender is a social construct. Our social
engineers, who disguise themselves as being "liberal," have managed to
effectively obscure the issue. Reams and reams of recently released books
document that sex is anything but a cultural construct, but most of these
works have not yet been internalized by the general public. Recall here
what Dr. Rhodes told me about the continued transcendence of the social
constructionist position in our universities. I would not be surprised to
discover that a multitude of Americans believe that society is the chief
determiner of who we are and how we behave. A google search[150] revealed 10,200 hits for the phrase "gender is a social construct." Most of
these references, along with the diehards who created them, will not be
going away anytime soon.

Feminists manufacture a plethora of minor lies as well. The other
day I was astonished to hear the old "Rule of Thumb" canard repeated in
a B movie. Apparently, the young screenwriter was merely spewing back
the propaganda he heard at one of our fine universities. Of course, that
reference never had anything to do with women, switches or beatings. It
referred to measurements based on experience rather than those based on
science.[151]

Another lie that feminists broadcast is that married women have
more emotional problems than do single women. The truth is the exact
opposite of their pronouncement.[152] One prominent feminist in particular
unleashed a slew of amazing whoppers which received a mother-load of
press coverage. She said, in the hopes of getting women not to leave their
glamorous cubicles for the home, that females under 35 were more at risk
for having babies with Down syndrome than those over 35.[153] Almost
everyone knows the mendaciousness of this statement. She followed it up
with another outrageous aspersion by saying that there was no man
shortage for older women.[154] The facts clearly show otherwise.[155]

Lying is something that radicals must do as without deception
they would come off as the jaded cranks they actually are. Feminist leaders
have always known that women would never follow their directives if they

knew what it was they actually stood for.[156] Feminism, as with all political-ly correct disciplines, wants one thing more than any other: for their enemies to be shamed into silence. Free exchange and debate would render them powerless.[157]

It is staggering to reflect on just how much of their mumbo-jumbo is believed by the average person. A male psychologist once repeated to me a treasured feminist superstition when he said that "rape was not about sex but about power." I looked at him with wonderment as his take on the subject was no different from Andrea Dworkin's. I corrected him immediately by pointing out that rape is about reproduction and that power has nothing to do with it. Rape is an illegal act generally committed by a low status (or deranged) male who does not have any other means for sexual fulfillment. That they are unaware of their desire to impregnate their prey—indeed, he may only wish to "get off"— has nothing to do with the reality of his genes pushing him towards a particu-lar reproductive goal.[158] He may also be completely irrational and crazy and have no conscious awareness of why he acts in the way he does.

Rape is a horrendous crime, but it is not one committed in the hopes of accumulating power. We know this to be true because rapists primarily prey on women who are fertile.[159] Even a feminist source [accidentally?] acknowledged this when she wrote "[e]ighty percent of rape victims are under thirty years old; 44 percent are under eighteen."[160] Women under 18 have no power, but dinosaurs like former Secretary of State Madeleine Albright and Justice Ruth Bader Ginsburg do. They make headlines and Ginsburg even restructures our laws. If the feminist as-sumption were correct then those fossils would be the ones targeted. Prominent, high-status females are almost always over 40, and thus, are rarely victimized by rape.

As a way to counter-act truth, feminists have also put forth the absurd notion that "women don't lie about rape"[161] which I just recently heard mentioned on a television show. Obviously this is fallacious as women are no different from men when it comes to lying. Indeed, it is possible for them to lie about practically anything. One study of rape charges found that 60 percent of the accusations under review turned out to be false.[162] People lie about all sorts of things so this finding should not surprise anyone—with the exception of Prosecutor Nifong from the Duke Lacrosse charade. That a segment of the population believes that women are too saintly to engage in fabrication and deception illustrates the surreal nature of their status in our society. If the media were not so biased and compromised, then they would discount any source insisting that half of the nation's population were archangels. In the final analysis, American males should be grateful that feminists are so confused, angry, and incompetent because without those traits life would be far worse for us than it already is.

3

Deception as Nutrient

One who knows the enemy and knows himself will not be in danger in a hundred battles.
One who does not know the enemy but knows himself will sometimes win, sometimes lose.
One who does not know the enemy and does not know himself will be in danger in every battle.
—Sun Tzu.[163]

The truth is that which feels right and good and loving.
—Oprah Winfrey.[164]

I also took up residence in the self-help aisles of bookstores. I needed something to make me feel better, some book, a phrase, words to get me through.
—Stephanie Klein.[165]

We have documented the ubiquitousness of feminist lies, but the mystery as to why those lies are so readily believed has yet to be established. Is it possible that women are more susceptible to distortion and misrepresentation than are men? Do sex differences exist when it comes to deceiving oneself? Regardless of what conclusions we draw, the only thing for absolute certain is that the above inquiries are verboten in our politically correct society—which is reason enough to undertake them here.

Consider the quote from Oprah. Does the truth always feel loving and good? No, more often than not it makes us feel indifferent, surprised, horrified or depressed. The truth can be righteous but it also can be patently unfair; affirmative action is a perfect example as the government

55

of the United States has decreed that a woman's need for a job is more important than a man's. This particular truth is aggravating to me, but the displeasure it arouses does not diminish its reality.

The reason that we study Stalin, Mao, Hitler, and Pol Pot is not because of the emotional effect their murderous careers produce in us. We examine them because they were evil villains who irreparably altered the course of human events. That they were not right, good or loving is not an excuse to avoid studying them. History is an invaluable tool in every circumstance as the accumulation of information is an end in itself, but people like Oprah only want to illuminate the parts of it that self-affirm and inspire. Acknowledging only the sweet and soothing are the habits of a doomed ignoramus. Such persons will forever be baffled by 66 percent of what life has to offer. They will moan "why, oh why, oh why" whenever bad things happen, but they willingly go through their life in this fashion so there is no reason to feel sorry for them.

Are women more likely to be such persons? Perhaps, but it is impossible to ever really know this due to the media's attempts to deceive to them at every turn. The press will say anything in the hopes of making their pet projects feel better. Were journalists to initiate a similar crusade on the behalf of men then I have no doubt that many of us would also become less realistic in our perceptions of the world.

We have digested Oprah's words but let us reflect on her career. Most men regard her as being a talk show host with little to say, yet 49 million people,[166] a huge majority of them female, adore and worship her. They hang on her every word and cannot wait to emote over the topics she selects. Why? It is due to her deliberate manipulation of their emotions and that she makes a point of telling them what they want to hear. She has termed her self-absorbed, narcissistic hour of television a daily "ministry."[167] Well it certainly is, but to whom do these disciples pray? The program is nothing more than affective crack for addicts who gave up on logical thinking long ago. Indeed, a poll found that 33 percent of respondents[168] regarded Oprah's counsel as being more influential than that of their religious leaders. The sheep look to Oprah for guidance and the last thing they will ever do is question her, but she seems to know but a speck about most subjects.

In 2006, I began to notice how many women were devotees of her program regardless of their individual levels of education or intelligence so I decided to watch a few episodes for myself to see what was really going on. The results were appalling. I called the series of articles, "Watching Oprah: My Venture to Hell"[169]—which is exactly what it was.

All the irrationality and emotion that I had imagined was gaudily on display. She presented all manner of sound-byte information and analysis, but had no segments which were critical of women or encouraged them to take responsibility for their own life choices.

Most comically, the episodes even ran advertisements for a website called Depression Hurts.[170] Clearly it does, but the drug manufacturer who runs the site must know something about Oprah's audience or it would have not spent that kind of cash for a commercial. Perhaps *The Oprah Winfrey Show* has exacerbated the pre-existing conditions of its viewers or perhaps those viewers never had conditions at all until they regularly began to bathe in two decades worth of self-absorbed dreck. Her fans appear to have a greater predisposition for self-pity than the rest of us. To them, reality and history have made women the red-headed stepchildren of civilization.

The other day, as I waited at the dealership for my car to be fixed, I overheard a perspective commonly accepted in our society. It was uttered on a television program with a similar fan base called *The View*. The commentator observed: "We tried having a man on this show but it didn't work. The women want to hear what women have to say."[171] This quip was met with spirited applause and I have no doubt that her perceptions are entirely accurate. The entertainer's statement captured well the essence of the problem for women in America. The fairer sex only wants to hear the opinions of their own kind. A desire for truth is either unstated or immaterial. Legitimate genitals are deemed more important than legitimacy of message. Our society has so over-inflated the worth of women that, in some circles, possessing a vagina alone is enough to grant authenticity to one's views.

That women desire having their pre-existing attitudes[172] confirmed more than they do discovering truth is a distinct possibility. I have observed this phenomenon on countless occasions. Quite recently, I was at a conference[173] in which I, along with the main speaker, was one of the few males present. The fellow was a luminary and an expert in his field, but he definitely was aware of the audience sex ratio as he constantly played up to women throughout the day. At one point, I even heard him describe Asperger's Syndrome as a condition characterized by extreme egocentrism which he termed "a common male feature" because, for his brothers, "it's always all about me." The audience guffawed and deemed him very clever. That this was the gospel was readily believed even though, when compared to the fairer sex, the ego of the male is barely noticeable.

Women, and not men, frequently engage in directionless conversation and gossip about the people they know, they are also more likely to obsess about their own feelings, and to be absorbed in mundane affairs concerning themselves as opposed to worldly events. All of this was irrelevant on that day, however, as myth rather than reality was believed.

Before the lunch-break this same precious academic, in reference to some innocuous matter, announced, "There is a god and she's listening." Well, for his sake, he better hope so, but the important thing was that the crowd loved him. I have found that such throw away lines are quite the norm at this sort of gathering. They assume, perhaps rightly, that men in America are so feminized and dominated by women that they will not speak up for themselves. This assumption was correct in regards to the narrator who, amidst his co-workers, will not say much of anything. Without survival, I could not live to argue at a later date.

Why a man like this would denigrate his brothers is unclear, but assuredly cowardice, the need for popularity, and a wish to conform have something to do with it. That weak males act in this fashion is regrettable, but the problem of women refusing to examine reality would exist even if they did not. Society's exaltation of the fairer sex allows them to prefer redemptive conversational baths to the cleansing streams of truth. Its soak is easier, more pleasant, and—just like tobacco which also creates pleasurable side-effects—will eventually destroy you.

What is the causality behind these mass delusions? Is it a weakness inherent to all people? Well, again that is hard to say. Humans all exhibit to varying degrees a need for self-deception. A compelling argument can be made that men as well would prefer cushiony distortions to brutal truths if we did not realize, via personal experience, that the long-term suffering of such a preference always outweighs its initial benefit. If a man embraces the cult of victimology he will soon become extinct. There is no room for masculinity within the confines of the sensitivity state. He must solve his own problems or fade into the netherworld; whereas, society will always support a woman's choice to delude herself.

That all humans deceive themselves does not diminish my position. Certainly, in some instances, self-deception is adaptive. Had the microscopic minority who survived Auschwitz fully acknowledged the cursedness of their situation they would have never made it to the day of liberation, but, in the west today, there are no Interstate 75 off-ramps leading to Treblinka. For most of us, vanquishing the genuine is non-adaptive. I once knew an old guidance counselor whose favorite phrase was "name it, blame it, tame it." It is a trite mantra but it is as good a method for mild problem solving as any other, yet it has no application for the "empowered" woman—this anti-elite will name something other than the problem, blame something entirely unrelated, and eventually become lost in a maze created by their own distortions.

There is symbiosis at work behind the pipe dreams of women. They have a need to be deceived and civilization is only too happy to assist them in their endeavor. Whatever myth the fairer sex pines for is actualized by the culture at large. A cycle then forms wherein society weaves magical explanations for female difficulties in the hopes of giving them a glossy explanation or discounting them entirely. The massage and catharsis makes everyone feel good, and the cycle can last forever provided that both parties are willing to keep up the charade.

Let us look at some specifics.

Feeling fat? Ah, men tell you to feel that way. Do not listen to them as they are evil and hateful. Do not worry at any rate. You just be you.

Your doctor suggested that fat is shortening your life expectancy? Well, he or she is wrong. Fat is a feminist issue as opposed to a cardiovascular one.

Spending money frivolously? Well, what choice do you have? In our unfair society women have to spend a fortune on makeup and fashion just to get the attention of the opposite sex [the fact that wearing a ten dollar tank top is more than adequate to ensure male favor will never be conceded].

Cannot do your job? Sure you can. Regardless of your inadequacies, you are a goddess simply for managing to get up everyday. Who else could do that? You are Super Woman!

Yes, the excuses are endless and by this means the privileged sex never has to examine their decisions with a critical eye. Nowhere is the destructiveness of the "truth as an alternative lifestyle" approach more deleterious than in the rare case of a woman who attempts to make sense out of sexual differences. The first thing that such a person would need to acknowledge is that their own perceptions on the subject are lacking, but it would be hard to find many women who believed that to be true about themselves in our society. Women are powerful creatures by birth so there is no reason for them to solicit the opinions of men or scientific publications in regards to sex disparities. If you reign supreme what you know already is more than satisfactory. Valid information on sex disparities can be obtained with a minimum of effort, but most women confine their searches to endless sheaths of publications generated by the women's self-help industry. Women consume reams of articles written exclusively for the fairer sex concerning love, dating, and romance. Here, the questions are always met with magical answers. This blunts their desire to obtain intelligence from unusual—or non-self-help—quarters. Due to the rate at which these materials are consumed it creates a demand for more "advice" pieces to be written. Continue this process ad infinitum and you arrive in America in the year 2007.

Such journalism is explicitly or implicitly anti-male in its orientation. We might call its point of view: Women are from Heaven, Men are from Hell. Several female writers have noted the inherent dysfunctionality of these narratives, something which Laura Kipnis does here: "What's problematic about women's scorn for men isn't that it's necessarily undeserved, it's that it's so steeped in disavowal. Disavowal not only takes a lot of useless intellectual effort that could be devoted to other things, but is self-deceiving. Self-deception is deforming."[174] And there are few people more deformed than those who spend their entire existence gazing at their own navels. Rather than discuss serious issues, women's media keeps the discussion to their reader's lives alone. Viva la difference is a notion no more accepted than the presence of neo-Nazis at a Bat Mitzvah.

The advice pushers confirm that to be a woman is to be divine. This medium depicts men as a horde of primitive hominids who soullessly wander the plains in search of flesh, money, and blood. When the recipients of this radioactive counsel make their own attempts at "male behavior modification"[175] they find that the results are not always what they had in mind. You can get a man to agree with you that he prefers older women with established careers to the young and fertile ones, but once you leave such a fellow will never ask a Ms. CEO out for a date; in other words, he will lie right back at you. Hectoring, lecturing, and demeaning men makes them resentful and causes them to gradually disappear from relationships and family life.

Intellectual rigor is not a highly prized trait in our society, but ignorance is more dangerous when present in females than in males. This is particularly true in regards to human reproduction where many women are familiar with menopause, yet few have a solid idea of the point at which it actually begins. Having children is never a given and "putting them off" until you are ready can accidentally result in your putting them off forever. Despite what feminists claim, many women yearn to raise children, but do not exert the necessary curiosity which would enable them to uncover their own expiration date. Why bother with such boring tidbits when you can watch another episode of *Friends* or *Dancing with the Stars?*

Due to a refusal to research issues for themselves, most women passively accept the edicts of journalists and television personalities in regards to topics of paramount importance to their lives. This is a mass personality flaw and not something that can be excused away. Self-proclaimed gurus like Oprah and Rosie O'Donnell display unshakeable confidence and expertise about every subject with which they are queried, but such a bearing is an immediate indication that they have no idea of what they are talking about. No one, no where, in any society knows half of what these ladies pretend to. It is a hallmark of an educated, rational, and wise person to admit that they do not know everything, but humility is not something you will find in either of those two blowhards. They are but entertainers despite their being fully vested in appearing otherwise. That so many listen to their prattle is both frustrating and damning.

That intelligent women would respect the views of celebrity buffoons may be due to an all-powerful need to conform or an indigenous disdain for hierarchy; the latter is evidenced by their refusal to draw a distinction between an informed opinion and an uninformed one. The possession of these proclivities makes them ripe for the duping. Laura Kipnis poked fun at the self-help cabal's counsel: "Wasn't that what happened the last time, when you got all goopy over Mr. I Need My Independence, who basically treated you like Booty-Call Betty? Not having had a date in a year and a half is no reason to act like a doormat; remember, you're hot! Here are ten bedroom tricks that really turn a guy on. What about an edible thong? But remember that hotness comes from within. It comes from self-confidence and liking yourself."[176]

Confidence is a very important trait…if you are trying to attract a woman, but for men it is a non-starter [more on this later]. Such a truth is not likely to be mentioned in *Cosmopolitan,* however, and the same can be said about a woman's innate lust for male status.

For a man, it is a real challenge to go through life steeped in denial and self-deception. The man who thinks the rules of attraction are the same for both sexes will quickly discover the error of his thinking. In his dealings with women he will observe a bevy of behavioral differences. A major developmental milestone for the teenage male is the realization that girls are not as obsessed by sex as you are. Further, regardless of what their teachers and adult role models might say, girls love bad boys and it is not an urban legend. Indeed, for many women, their fascination with antisocial males is something that will continue, with slight variation, until the day they die.

A man's height, wealth, and status are more essential for the procurement of girlfriends than his personality, and most men slowly realize this over time. During the mating ritual, should a youth be misguided enough to emulate Alan Alda or Woody Allen and adopt the trappings and disposition of a New Age man, the absoluteness of the rejection he will experience should quickly convince him that the approach is futile (hopefully!). Unlike members of the glitterati, the average guy is neither famous nor rich, and cannot succeed when hampered with New Age baggage. Doctors, criminals, lawyers, sports stars, and coke dealers all have a decided advantage over the run-of-the-mill Joe when it comes to picking up chicks. It will not take long for Mr. Touchy Feely to discern, even if he refuses to publicly acknowledge it, that women are entirely different from what he thought them to be. Yes, pronouncements in women's journals about members of fairer sex craving "girlfriends with penises" are utter hogwash.[177]

On the other side of the hill, no such realizations will likely occur. Women will continue to delude themselves with bunkum like "only shallow men" desire gorgeous and youthful women because no man is going to take the time to set them straight. He would realize that the girl probably would not listen to him anyway. These ladies, regardless of the dwindling business that correlates with advanced age, will remain true believers in the idea that someone somewhere will come along and rescue them. This man will love them for who they are regardless of their abundant flaws. It is something that is destined to happen. It is written in the stars.

Should she suddenly be seized by adaptive self-doubt then she can consult the mainstream media who will echo her basic opinions and administer bromides to polish her self-delusion. When the weight of her personal experience becomes too depressing to ignore, the media will acknowledge her tragedy by blaming the country on the whole. They will say that men in the United States have too many hang ups. We are a superficial and puritanical lot. They will assuage her by suggesting that life really is different elsewhere. Trainwrecks like her are welcome in France so she better grab Alec Baldwin and find her way over as soon as possible. There, she will discover that the Gauls revere bedraggled and promiscuous women as being the saints they actually are. Besides, a talking head may posit, what kind of a country is it anyway that allows its male inhabitants to have their own preferences in mates? Journalists will not tell them what life in Kabul, Khartoum, Riyadh or Pyongyang would have been like for them, and the last thing these ladies would ever do is consult works by infidels such as your kindly narrator. Why would they bother when they can dismiss entire volumes of thought with throwaway quips like, "what would you expect a man to say?" Due to the misfortune of their paramours' benighted births, men will always be blamed—either at the personal or national level—for the romantic difficulties that women encounter.

Even sources once deemed informational, like *Newsweek* and *Time*, now disseminate lies. These glossies have shed their former "just the facts" orientation to become psychological analgesics for the right kinds of people; a grouping which always includes women. A couple of years ago, I came across a *Newsweek* cover story[178] concerning the increased infidelity rates of American wives. Every aspect of the article horrified me. The reporters seemed to revel in the development of mass infidelity among members of the fairer sex. Their glee with this trend of interpersonal treachery should have caused them to re-title their piece, "You Ho Girl!"

Newsweek thinks that by taking a slant on this topic that they are empowering women, and in a way they are right because they are empowering women to eradicate love. They hope to convince women to act just like men; that is their version of equality. By normalizing infidelity they hope to erase, what they misconstrue to be, a sexual double standard between men and women. Should women become as promiscuous as men it will therefore be a win/win situation for them—even if it produces results that please few women and advance none of their biological imperatives. What the magazine's reporters do not realize is that a man's distaste for female infidelity is biological and deeply ingrained. Our revulsion for wives who cheat is highly adaptive and increases the odds that the family we end up devoting our lives to is actually our own family. When a woman strays she robs her husband of his genetic future. No part of him will continue on past his own days. He will never reproduce and he will spend the rest of his life supporting the child of another man. The adulterous wife's actions are psychologically akin to murder.

In contrast, when a man commits adultery the stakes are not so high. No woman—in a natural setting that is—has ever given birth to a child that was not her own. With the exception of those cuckolds who are married to porn stars, having a whore for a wife is a dishonor that all men wish to avoid. There is no double standard here because the physiological rules are totally skewed. The real standard is, "mommy's baby, daddy's maybe," but that is far too perspicacious a quotation to ever appear in *Newsweek*. Reprehensible advocacy journalists have considerably more power and they just might change the world, but it will not be to their liking. Reports like this one make men increasingly uneasy about taking vows.

These magazines do not confine their lying to sex alone, they will print absolutely anything in the hopes of lifting women's spirits. The probability that their fables produce interminable despair for their readers is a risk they are willing to take. The same outfit also ran a cover story on professional women and their prospects for getting married. Its bias was as staggering here as it was with infidelity. They initiated the article under the auspices of "setting the facts straight." It seems that two decades ago, back when *Newsweek* was not as ideologically predisposed as it is today, they ran a piece concerning the pitiful chances white professional women had of ever getting married.[179] Many of their readers did not feel warm and fuzzy from skimming it so they assigned some reporters to rewrite their journalistic history. Lo and behold, they found out that their previous conclusions were incorrect. They constructed a fairy tale disguised as news and dubbed it "Marriage by the Numbers."[180] The fact that they shared few meaningful numbers or facts with their readers is not surprising as their conclusions have more to do with purging past doctrinal error and fulfilling wishes than with the sober appraisal of truth.

Their report concluded that the previously published information was wrong as 90 percent of baby boomer men and women have been married over the course of their lifetimes which means...absolutely nothing. What happened with the baby boomer generation has no impact on the future relations between the sexes. That cohort of citizens was raised in an era nothing like our own [and its present toxicity is largely due to their pernicious influence]. Most of those folks were married long before the sexual revolution was won so isolating their outcomes makes no sense whatsoever. In terms of our own arbitrary cultural distinctions, three generations have already followed them so it is spurious to focus on baby boomers as a method of gauging the future trajectory of this nation.

Suspiciously, no mention is made of what has been happening with generations X or Y along with what the prospects for Generation Z will be. The reporters also cite no sources for their conclusions, and no explanation is given as to why males would suddenly abandon their time-proven and effective preferences for finding mates. If they chose women who were favored by modern society—those with little or no fertility left— men would only manage to ensure their own extinction. Most of us will not make this choice, and no amount of cover stories will ever change this eventuality. Men will continue to select the best possible specimens, and avoid fruit that is obviously spoiled which is the same thing that our predecessors did.

Other than seeing one's name posted on a sucker list in the announcements section of a newspaper, there is little payoff for men who pursue older professional women which is why *Newsweek*'s original story managed to capture the truth. They sounded the alarm that male attitudes were changing, but now, in this new millennium, the editors prefer mollification to education. Instead of acknowledging that male tastes exist for the soundest of evolutionary reasons, the media continues to stroke the fairer sex. They would rather send the message that everything will turn out for the best...regardless of the choices they make. This then empowers women to become impotent. They must now await events, and most women will not like how those events turn out. Women have become infantilized by our laudatory culture, and seem smitten with its faux therapeutic approach to living.

Another instance of spinning falsehood into truth comes from the fashion industry; specifically, with the sizes of female clothing. Here, women are being lied to and are fully aware of the fact. They also appear to be reveling in this eventuality. The existence of this sham was unknown to me until November of 2006 when I asked my girlfriend what she wanted for Christmas. In keeping with her nature, she would not tell me so I followed up my question by asking her another. What dress size did she wear? I then threw out some very small numbers in the hopes of getting a response. She laughed after I did so and said, "All of those and more." I did not get it. She then explained to me the recent phenomenon of "vanity sizing." It sounded so bizarre that I looked it up on my own as I thought maybe she was having a bit of fun at her Uncle Bern's expense. She was right though. Here is how one source described it:

> *While Americans have statistically gotten larger, women's clothing has gotten smaller -- that is, if the numbers on the size labels are to be believed. It's no secret that retailers have been playing to women's vanity for years by downsizing the sizes on garment labels, but the practice has reached an extreme in recent months with the introduction of the sizes "double zero" and "extra, extra small." If vanity sizing continues on this path, analysts say, it is only a matter of time before clothing sizes are available in negative integers...The downward*

*evolution of sizes illustrates the extent to which retailers, apparelma-
nufacturers, and designers are conforming to American women's obsession with wanting to be thin -- even if it's only in their minds...*
[181]

What a weird, but absolutely comical, passage. It should also be
the stuff of ridicule, but criticizing women is not something we do in
contemporary America. Hence, part of the nation will soon be buying
clothes stamped with negative integers. What is so priceless about this
happenstance is the way in which the cycle of falsehood is so transparent.
Clothiers lie to women about sizes, and women, cognizant that they are
being scammed, reinforce the clothiers by buying more of their wares.
This then encourages the designers to deceive them further.

Manufacturers would never try this with men. If Champion or
Dickies began calling a XL a XXXL they would have a lot of irate customers on their hands and a ton of refunds to process. They would never
try it and the jerk who suggested it would be fired.

The Exquisite Example: The Male Preference for Younger Women.

What would men be without women? Scarce, sir, mighty scarce.
—Mark Twain.[182]

The media's attempt to transform male sexuality is as dogged and
tenacious as were the defenders of Stalingrad. Their tactics generally begin
with the questioning of whether male sexuality exists at all. Some hold our
desires to be strictly a product of an unjust society, and that, barring our
inherent suggestibility, we would look for the same things in women as
they do in us. I guess we should call this the "moderate" approach as it
clashes with the male as oppressor model. That take on men implies that
our choices arise out of malicious intent. Between conformity and antipa-
thy there is another interpretation which indicates that our tastes stem
from our intrinsic shallowness and inferiority. Nowhere is this belief more
gaudily expressed than with the subject of the male fascination for young
and beautiful women. Pop culture is devoted to this approach as society
simply cannot accept that there might be a biological basis behind our
enchantment with nubile ladies. In turn, it also cannot accept that there is
a biological basis behind our aversion to the older, snaggletoothed variety.

When it comes to the nature of male selection, my personal favorite media contortion is the rationalization that we like younger women due to a need to recapture our youth.[183] What a hoot. If I wanted to recapture my youth all I would have to do is put on some Ocean Pacific shorts and play a couple of CDs by The Smiths. The last thing I would do is follow some 25-year-old all over town like a lap dog hearing odd questions addressed to me like, "Why don't you want to go out? It's Tuesday." It would not be long before I would have no job, no prospects, and painfully enlarged testicles. Believe me, most men would rather not deal with women whose presence causes us to have no control over our hormones, our cash flow, and our lives. There are easier ways to relive those electric years than to fall in love with a younger woman. Voluntarily entering into an arrangement that could lead to our own destruction is never consciously in a man's plans. This explanation is rooted in fantasy...and misandry.

A close second is that we avoid intelligent and successful women due to our insecurity[184] over our own intellectual limitations or out of a need to dominate and control others. Well, I can point out the flaws in this perspective with little difficulty. There is no control to be found with a person you want to lick from head to toe because there is little doubt that she does not feel the same way about you. With such women, one must be a lobbyist and never a dictator.

Another baseless claim is that we prefer younger women because our same-age peers can see right through us.[185] This might even be more risible than the first explanation as most older women cannot see past themselves for even a few moments; let alone see into the mind of another person.

What all of these excuses have in common is that they emanate from an ardent belief in male inferiority. Witness the words that a disillusioned female medical student said to John Townsend in his *What Women Want–What Men Want: Why the Sexes Still See Love & Commitment so Differently*. Her response to getting rejected by a fellow doctor-to-be is rich with self-righteousness and self-massage. She said, "They don't want a woman who can challenge them on medical knowledge."[186] I guess that is it in a small ampoule. Actually, her statement tells us much about female confusion in regards to men. Is intellectual commonality the principal mechanism by which men are attracted to women? Never, granted it certainly helps, and it makes one take a girl a lot more seriously provided that one is already attracted to them, but it can never take the place of physical allure. If it did, most men would go after girls based on their board scores. Besides, in this age of gross superficiality, that medical student has it all wrong. Meeting a woman who mirrors any of our passions immediately qualifies her for the bonus round. This is a time of fluff and circumstance. Most males have expectations which are suitably low. It is disappointing to observe that so many women believe cathartic canards over truth when it comes to men.

All of these verbal gymnastics are a total waste of time. The plain fact is that nearly all men prefer younger women over older ones.[187] Youth always heightens our enchantment. A man may like a 45-year-old female but he would like her twice as much if she wound back the odometer to 30. The media refuses to believe this, but most scientists have never doubted it or the corresponding truth that women seek out men who possess abundant status and wealth.[188]

Our tastes have evolved for cogent reasons. A man's desire for feminine youth and beauty is never shallow. Indeed, it is actually quite deep. Both attributes correlate positively with fertility and reproductive potential."[189] Furthermore, at age 22 a woman's estrogen levels are the highest they will ever be which is also the exact point at which she is most attractive to men.[190] The female characteristics men most admire are their eyes, lips, body symmetry, and slim waists. All of these directly correspond with a woman's level of fertility.[191] A woman's youth is intimately connected with a man's ability to fall in love with her.[192]

Dr. Helen Fisher noted that our love has little to do with societal mores and values. The state that we call love is chemically triggered: "When the time is right and a man *sees* an attractive woman, he is anatomically equipped to rapidly associate her attractive *visual* features with feelings of romantic passion."[193] This is an incredibly effective courtship device. That a woman is capable of having babies is of paramount importance—whether men are consciously aware of it or not.[194] Our daily opinions are irrelevant as our biology propels us in the direction of the most fertile specimens. Fertility can be summed up as, "sex is the route, reproduction [is] the destination." [195] In fact, as men age, a woman's youth becomes more and more essential, and we practically make a fetish out of it.[196] Men who marry a second time select, on average, a woman five years younger than themselves while those who marry a third time opt for wives eight years their junior.[197] The man's bias against older women is due to a need to find the "maximally fertile woman."[198] Those men who did not conform to these biological mandates—and chose spinsters or ones in terrible shape—never reproduced and have, thus, disappeared from the gene pool and our planet.[199]

Are men concerned about menopause? Absolutely, says Robert Wright. He explains: "The last thing evolutionary psychologists would expect to find is that a plainly postmenopausal woman is sexually attractive to the average man. They don't find it. (According to Bronislaw Malinowski, Trobriand Islanders considered sex with an old woman 'indecorous, ludicrous, and unaesthetic.') Even before menopause, age matters, especially in a long-term mate; the younger a woman, the more children she can bear. In every one of Buss's thirty-seven cultures, males preferred younger mates (and females preferred older mates)."[200]

The reality of male preference may be far bleaker than what most women or mainstream media journalists suspect. Writer John Derbyshire even complained about starlet Jennifer Aniston's age and appearance after he saw a considerable amount of her in a *GQ* pictorial. He believes that even "...at age 36 the forces of nature have won out over the view-worthiness of the unsupported female bust."[201] Perceptions like his are not the sort of thing one finds at a university nowadays, but they reflect more truth than a thousand Womyn's Studies syllabi.

There can be no doubting that male tastes are not "shallow." Without them, our species would never have made into the twenty-first century. Rather than deride men, the media, along with women in general, should be grateful for how driven we are. For their own good, women must accept that man's devotion to younger females is not a societal construct; it is a biological predisposition which will never go away. The optimum means of handling the tendency is to adapt and adjust. Women should find the best guy they can when they are young and on top of their peer hierarchy. Those women who fail to do so will face rapidly diminishing prospects as they age. We will see in a later chapter that their egos will, in all likelihood, prevent them from "trading down" when their position is still salvageable. Those in their thirties and forties who are just hearing this information for the first time would be wise to select men of acceptable, and not spectacular, quality as a means to compensate for their own decreased worth—that is, if marriage is a serious goal them.[202] Whether they like it or not, it is time to settle.[203]

Given the obvious merit of women becoming proactive and taking ownership for their own destiny, it is a wonder that so many of them continue to blame men for not adopting female prerogatives. The media assists them in their folly by perpetually unleashing a "make men realize they are wrong" strategy.

Our slanted journalists were undoubtedly pleased to discover the results of a recent research study in Uganda. It documented that a troop

of chimpanzees featured some males who preferred to mate with older
females than with younger ones.[204] This brought many an activist journalist to wonder if the example the chimps set were transferable to humans.
Could Bonzo be recruited to aide in the societal war against male sexual
preference? Does he prove that our predilection for nubile females is
socially constructed? Luckily, Bonzo does not. What the media conveniently forgot to mention in regards to this story is that chimpanzees in
the wild have a life span of between 30 and 40 years[205] so their preference
for "older females" has no meaning when applied to the human condition. The older females in that particular troop could well have been only
25-years-old. Furthermore, that sub-species of chimpanzee eschews
monogamous relationships[206] which again makes them an unsuitable
yardstick for comparisons with humans—particularly if one happens to be
a rapidly oxidizing spinster on a quest for marriage. Another complication
is that the females in the chimpanzee study group were all observed
entering into estrous[207]—which means that they were fertile, and that is
definitely not the case for many a post-menopausal women initially
enthralled by the news which came out of Africa.

A most perplexing media counter-offensive has been launched
around the notion that women should adopt male sexual preferences. I
guess the argument here is that lusty desire is not so bad if men are the
ones who become the objects of it [sounds good to me]. Today's women
are being encouraged to actively search for younger mates even though
this strategy is diametrically opposed to their own biological interests.
High status and wealth are traits rarely found in younger men. Journalists
have dubbed these blessed women "cougars."[208] The cougar, predictably,
is an older lady who covets younger men and it is hoped that the idea will
catch on with every female in America. Thus, presumably, a 23-year-old
girl will now date an 18-year-old boy. Such a notion clashes with the
whole of my dating experiences, however.

As a freshman in college, we were shunned by practically everyone
including female freshman whom we could have easily gone out with the
year before. None of the girls would have anything to do with us because,
at John Carroll at least, only the upperclassman could drive on campus
and get into the Cleveland Heights bars. We had nothing to offer those
girls and were effectively non-persons. That we were at our sexual peaks
was indisputable but our randiness was not a point in our favor. Well, I
am sure somebody somewhere will find an easy answer to the women
love status conundrum; just as I am sure they will also find a way to
convince people that sleep is wholly unnecessary in our high-tech century.

Whenever reporters come across a Cougar-loving man, they are quick to publicize his outlook. Take these guys for instance: "Self-described cougar hunters, 29-year-old Jeremy Mape, who works in commercial real estate in San Francisco, and 28-year-old Mark Lobosco, who is in software sales there, say they like the confidence and sexual experience of the cougars they know — and the fact most are not looking for **commitment** [my emphasis]."[209] Ah, well, that is the real subtext to the story is it not? The women do not look for commitment because they know that they cannot get it. One of the great joys of sleeping with an older woman is the comforting realization that there is no chance that you will ever fall in love with one. It is all about sex and that is that. None of the unpredictable and unsavory emotions that foment when dealing with a young chick are present in one's interactions with a cougar. Older women are like Barcaloungers; they are soft, effortless, pleasurable, decadent, and if they suddenly break you can always obtain another. I guess I have to admit to being a fan of the cougar after all.

According to one source, the trend is taking off due to the habits of a couple of female characters on a television program.[210] Wow, what can we say about people who base their decision-making on the plots which emit from the boob tube? We should ask television personality Brooke Anderson about that because she described cougars as "turning the tables"[211] on men. How sad it is that so much of what we regard to be female is no more than a reaction to what is male.[212] Perhaps Anderson does not realize that human nature is something unaffected by the Nielsen Ratings or public relations spin. Our sexual desires are derived from biological need and advantage. They have not evolved from a longing for revenge and/or emulation. Women do not turn the tables when they adopt male mating preferences, but they do ensure their own misery. All the cougars' phenomenon really proves is just how much women are manipulated by society. If social engineers initiated a hardcore reeducation campaign to convince men to "go after" older women with ornate resumes they would quickly discover that their efforts were as fruitless as the womb of a cougar. No amount of advertising and propagandizing can sway us. Status and wealth are non-starters for men. It does not matter how you spell a woman's title: CEO, CIO, or CFO a grandma is still a grandma.

Movies, and not only the news and self-help media, cajole men in-to adopting female sexual strategies as well. Their main goal seems to be getting men to part from their predispositions. Recall the horrendous film, *Shallow Hal*, for instance. The plot is built around Hal (Jack Black's character) being a "shallow," beauty obsessed fellow. One day, thanks to the magic of Tony Robbins' neuro-linguistic programming, he suddenly discovers that he can no longer notice the external attractiveness of the fairer sex. Only Woman's internal beauty is discernible to transmogrified Hal. The result is a politically correct fairy tale that is as predictable as it is boring. He is freed from biology and falls in love with a boar of a female, but what the filmmakers do not realize is that the new Hal is more featherbrained than the old. Previously, he categorized a woman's worth based on their physical fitness and beauty. In doing so, he was following a method of mate selection that has enabled us to become the most successful species on earth. His former tactics gave him the best odds of obtaining a fertile woman and also one who was strong enough to survive childbirth.

The new Hal can now copulate based on personality attractiveness alone. This is very bad for him, but great news for the lazy, overfed members of the sistahood. It is well known that obesity correlates with mental disorders like depression and OCD (obsessive-compulsive disorder). It is unremarkable that corpulent individuals cannot control their own behavior, but there certainly is no reason to think that they may have more picturesque "insides" than the rest of us. Only under the dictates of political correctness would we dress up weakness as being an asset. After Robbins casts a spell on him, Hal's reproductive chances quickly evaporate because a porcine woman is less likely to be fecund, and more likely to contract gestational diabetes, hypertension, preeclampsia, and fetal and neonatal death.[213] She may also produce babies afflicted with omphalocele and various other birth defects.[214] No, there is nothing shallow about avoiding rotund women; it is a wise and intelligent strategy. That we have progressed to the point where we castigate those men who are desirous of healthy mates is a sign of our own devolution.

The real "trend" has nothing to do with cougars, farm animals or convincing men to prize fat chicks. The main problem is that women refuse to see the world as it actually is. They would rather hook their mouths up to a fire hose of lies than slug down a few spoonfuls of truth. Yes, the media's influence is great and nefarious, but individual women must learn to resist on their own. They must say no to misandry, and reject the myth of female superiority. Taking life and people as they are is a challenge, but it is better than finding out at age 60 that every single thing you ever believed in was a total lie. No amount of short-term pleasure is ever worth that. If women continue to shun everything that makes them feel bad then they will prove true the scandalous words of W.

L. George which were stated back in 1915: "She can seldom carry an idea to its logical conclusion, passing from term to term...This comes from a lack of concentration which indisposes a woman to penetrate deeply into a subject; she is not used to concentration, she does not like it. It might lead her to disagreeable discoveries."[215] Today, we regard men like George as Neanderthals, but what is clear is that the search for truth should not be one confined to men alone. Hopefully, women across American and the west will realize that the stoical acceptance of reality is a pillar upon which all of our futures can be built.

4

Empowerment, Feminist Style

Inordinate self-love is the cause of every sin.
—Thomas Aquinas[216]

There is hardly a practical psychologist who has anything to say about it that is half so illuminating as the literal exactitude of the old maxim of the priest: that pride is from hell.
—C.K. Chesterton[217]

One could make a compelling argument that the word known to all women is empowerment. Empowered, empowerment, empowering are all weighty combinations of syllables which provide background music to our times—as if they were the "wonk/wonk" in a seventies porno flick. Empowerment in our culture really means but one thing: Women Rule. If you type the words "women" and "empowered" into a search engine you will find a great magnitude of links. My query, at the time this was written, yielded 1,260,000 results, so it is fair to say that empowering women is a common topic of conversation. According to *Wordnet,*[218] to be empowered is to be "invested with legal power or official authority especially as symbolized by having a scepter." To empower is to "give or delegate power or authority to" another.

The brilliant mock news organ, *The Onion*, crafted a hilarious satire with this trendy word in mind. It was entitled, "Women Now Empowered By Everything A Woman Does." Here is an excerpt:

"From what she eats for breakfast to the way she cleans her home, today's woman lives in a state of near-constant empowerment," said Barbara Klein, professor of women's studies at Oberlin College and director of the study. "As recently as 15 years ago, a woman could only feel empowered by advancing in a male-dominated work world, asserting her own sexual wants and needs, or pushing for a stronger voice in politics. Today, a woman can empower herself through actions as seemingly inconsequential as driving her children to soccer practice or watching the Oxygen network." Klein said that clothes-shopping, once considered a mundane act with few sociopolitical implications, is now a bold feminist statement. "Shopping for shoes has emerged as a powerful means by which women assert their autonomy," Klein said.[219]

This passage is only discernable as satire because I identified it as such. Advancing the cause of women is now a synonym for justice, and whatever lies are told in the endeavor can be gleefully rationalized away. Helping women is thought to be good for the country. Lauding their every act and breath is not only good form, it is a requirement for those wishing to run a company or get elected. Chief Executive Officers must have a representative number of women on staff and enact rigid rules for respecting them or else they will be accused of creating a hostile environment for the fairer sex. The government's punishment for "gender" infractions can bankrupt an entire corporation. Laws and social stigma mandate that we treat a woman with far more respect than we would a man. Were this not to be the case, the rotten edifice of female superiority would crumble into post-modernist dust.

Speaking of the government that is the entity that bestowed power upon the American female. The scepter that women now wield is backed by the full faith, credit, and, most importantly, force of the United States government. Women are ascendant by virtue of the state actively favoring them over men [for the reasons I cited earlier]. Their newfound status has been granted rather than earned. Empowered may be an understatement, however, as the Federocracy's privileges are all-encompassing. Woman's new, and frankly extraordinary, legal powers are quite foreboding. She can send a man to prison, possibly forever, should she claim that he forced her to have sex with him even if they are married. The same is true of single women who can claim than an excessive amount of alcohol prohibited them from remembering what exactly transpired on a date. As men we should be grateful that women do not brandish these disproportionate powers against us more often. The sanity and normality of the average woman is the rationale for their not doing so. Just as with men, they generally refrain from acting in ways that purposefully destroy others.

Government's grand coercion is but half the story as affirming women is a major goal of our culture. To get around the inconvenient fact that the world was not created by those who nursed, cooked and cleaned,[220] extensive lies have been told. The past is sculpted until its shape fits into the corrupted lens of our modern interpretation. Activists, in the guise of scholars, deconstruct any event until it gives women the voice they feel they deserve. New storylines are inserted into past narratives so that they too reflect the outstanding qualities of women.[221] The worship of self-esteem has necessitated this outcome.[222] Women of the present now swim in daily baths of affirmation and acceptance. They hear, "You can do it! You can do it! No, we're not kidding, you really can do it."

Author Cameron Tuttle has some advice for any women who missed the admiration train. They too can find a way to be full of themselves if they try: "Most people have this crazy idea that you need some special reason, skill, or power to be confident. Ridiculous. Can't remember the last time you felt confident? Just strike a pose. Your body will remember and the feeling will spread. The secret ingredient in your bad girl 'tude is confidence."[223] What more needs to be said? Women should feel confident regardless of the actual qualities they possess. They can show off their bodies to passersby (as one professor did),[224] and happily sing the words of Christina Aguilera: "I am beautiful no matter what they say/ Words can't bring me down/ I am beautiful in every single way/Yes, words can't bring me down/So don't you bring me down today."[225] Well, I will try anyway Christina because I think you are a little too skinny to be beautiful, but I realize that young divas do not care about my opinion.

Like the brainwashed fanatics who carried standards reading "The World Belongs to Us"[226] in Guy Sajer's *The Forgotten Soldier*, today's women are encouraged to possess a bizarre and deadly form of self-esteem. It is the type of self-regard that evaporates upon encountering the slightest challenge and whose ensuing absence only becomes known after the decision has been made to bulrush a tank. This kind of pride never lasts because it was an apparition to start with. One encounters a considerable number of these prototypes nowadays. Empowerment has made them experts about practically everything. Most of them are undoubtedly smart enough to learn all kinds of things if they put forth a modicum of effort, but their bloated self-esteem prevents them from doing so.[227] They have been taken in by the "everyone has a valid opinion" mantra, which is merely an excuse for the ignorant to ramble on endlessly. Of course, everyone has a right to their own opinion, but there is a difference between a view that is informed and one that is not. I recall a time when I was out with my old roommate Bo in LaSalle County. We met two waitresses who decided to make a psychological guinea pig out of Bo. I heard them call him a hypochondriac for worrying about where he had parked his car. Being the hairpin that I am, I then asked them for the definition of hypochondriasis. They said it meant a person who worries too much. They then looked at me like I was a moron for even asking them the question. "Well, there it is," I said. Yes, there it was.

One can barely walk out of their house nowadays without encountering some sort of testament to the holy female. My gym recently embarked on what I can only describe as a breast cancer crusade. The two locations at which I work out[228] are currently festooned with pink ribbons showcasing their dedication to the fight against breast cancer. One can even buy t-shirts sporting the coveted pink ribbon for a mere $10.00. Conversely, there are no gym shirts devoted to fighting prostate cancer. We hear about breast cancer constantly despite there being fewer cases of it diagnosed in 2005 than there were of prostrate cancer [212,920 cases versus 234,460].[229]

The ungainly, perhaps even immortal, expectations of empowered and privileged women are highly evident in the very title of a major not-for-profit organization: "Y Me National Breast Cancer Association." Why me? What a strange question. A more accurate one would be, "How could it not be me?" Cancer of some kind is the second leading cause of death in this nation,[230] so what would make anyone think they were above getting it? Apparently no one has yet explained to these empowered creatures the nature of a malignant neoplasm.

While looking up information about prostrate cancer I noticed something rather extraordinary. I have been told before that the purple ribbon is supposed to symbolize one's support for those suffering from prostrate cancer but this appears to be an incorrect assumption. Various sites reported the purple ribbon as representing patients with Lupus, Huntington's Disease, or pancreatic cancer. I then came across a site for The International Purple Ribbon Project which did not correspond with any of the above afflictions. Its stated goal was to end "interpersonal violence."[231] I quickly discovered that it was dedicated to helping women victimized by men. One of the books in their "Recommended Reading" section is called *Why Daddy, Why?* Another is titled *The Dance of Anger, A Womans Guide to Changing the Patterns of Intimate Relationships.* The editor of the page describes it as "[a] fantastic tool to cease putting oneself into inappropriate situations and relationships, and to remove oneself from current ones. Anger is reduced to its true nature."[232] Suspiciously, there is nothing here which describes women's anger outside of the context of men. This is unfortunate as it is well-known that the most violent relationships are those which occur between two females. Dr. Allan Carlson and Paul Mero outlined this phenomenon in their excellent book, *The Natural Family: A Manifesto*:

> *Contrary to the predictions of feminist theory, domestic abuse (verbal, psychological, and physical) occurs significantly more often among lesbian couples than among heterosexual pairs. Surveys indicate that women who have been in both lesbian and heterosexual unions received significantly more abuse in the lesbian relationships. Nearly one-half of lesbians surveyed reported 'being or having been the victim of relationship violence.' Almost two-fifths of lesbians surveyed admitted having used violence against a partner. The researchers suggest that 'the academic community…shares some of the blame for ignoring same-sex domestic violence,' likely because of 'a reluctance to challenge feminist frameworks.*[233]

Quite similar to the universities wherein Womyn's Studies programs and Men's Studies programs both focus on male oppression, the purple and pink ribbons now both symbolize the physical plight of women.

Notwithstanding the cult of women's health and the way the public is encouraged to ignore certain kinds of violence, there is an undeniably manufactured feel to women's empowerment. Despite the excessive entitlements and deafening fanfare, the average woman does not seem to have noticed her own paramountcy. One would not think that this would be a problem as confirmation of supremacy resounds from every quarter. Television shows, pundits, magazine articles, and politically correct speech serve to remind women that they have made it, that girls rule while boys drool, that they are on top, and that they are the chosen ones. Yet all of these accolades merely underscore an obvious dilemma. Historically speaking, aristocrats have never needed to be reminded of their noble birth but it seems that women do. That they have not fully internalized their transcendence illustrates its inherent illegitimacy. Women with integrity know that rhetoric is never a substitute for aptitude. That one urinates from a sitting position has no correlation with talent, skill, or leadership ability. I would not be surprised if a great many women found bewildering their newly acquired authority. Their situation calls to mind the final scene of the movie, *The Candidate,* wherein Robert Redford has won the governorship. In the midst of his triumph, he turns to his staff and wonders aloud, "Now what?" No one seems to know. I will state it again: found privilege, like found money, is never comfortably handled.

Females being given jobs in what were once the male domains— politics, the military, the trades, and sports—has only heightened their confusion as it will not take long for them to notice that they, and not the feminists who hype their "careers," are the ones who are subjected to drudgery, death, disability, and character assassination. The fact is that most feminists will have nothing to do with any type of hard labor. They chiefly lobby, write, and waste time in non-profit institutions. They simply are not talented enough to occupy the positions in which many career girls find themselves.

Feministas can only compete upon a tilted playing field. Their capable and skilled sisters have become the conduits for their dreams as activists could never outperform trained seals, let alone the average man. This realization is a major reason why feminists are so vehemently anti-corporate and pro-socialist. They could never thrive or excel in an arena in which hyper-emotionality, irritability, and hysterical delusion are not prized commodities. Without the socialist dominions of our schools, bureaucracies, political associations, and charitable organizations they would starve in the street. That is why they love taxation in all its forms; the more money that gets stolen from private citizens the better. The cash gets lifted and funneled into state financed bureaucracies that form the base of their power. Were it not for these environments, in which productivity is generally frowned upon, they would have to be nice to people, relate to others, and actually respect another person's diversity.

Ironically, despite the boasts of feminists, radical activists do not empathize with their empowered high IQ peers. Those women who ascend the corporate ladder may well learn to respect the pro-family choices made by their predecessors. Compared to the rat race, spending time with friends, family, and children is not so bad. Emotionally, it certainly is more empowering than hanging out with complete strangers who care nothing for you. Since the beginning of time, most humans have labored for the purposes of survival alone; working for the sake of empowerment would be a most alien concept.

Sooner or later, the female pawns poisoned by feminist propaganda look up to see that a job is not salvation. Indeed, their only real advantage is the right to work themselves to death. Then they may have a "click moment" of their own, and decide that human sacrifice is something that really should have gone out with the Aztecs. The result is a freeform bitterness which dares not speak its name. No amount of sloganeering can replace a wasted life. Without all the constant bolstering, celebration, and accompanying shame that goes with underachievement, many professional women would drop out of the empowerment game and choose less stressful careers. In response to this possibility, feminists spew forth more and more hyperbole in the hopes of getting women to ignore their own desires and carry the flag of the sisterhood.

5

The Woman's "Real Man"

When most women get together, all we talk about is sex and how awful we treat you just because we can.
　　　　　—"Sandy" from North Carolina.[234]

I can be very demanding at times, but I also like to feel like I'm not demanding. So pampering me without my realizing it is always a nice thing. Without me saying, 'I want this.' You know what I mean. I want a mind reader, basically. That's the best kind of pampering.
　　　　　—"Trixie" from Philadelphia.[235]

Some issues in life are only temporary annoyances and are quickly forgotten. This is true of many sources of friction between the sexes such as the rumor that men's bathrooms would be modified due to the wishes of feminists in Germany, Australia, and Sweden. Luckily, despite the urinals being helpful to men, "and by extension, degrading [for] women,"[236] it has yet to happen and probably never will. Yet the definition of what traits, apart from biology, embody masculinity and manliness is a topic for which discussion will (hopefully) rage eternal. The moment in which society is silent on the matter will be the moment in which the troglodytes have won as the direction in which we are currently headed is far from encouraging. In the future, there is no way to know what type of person will be considered a "real man." He could be a metrosexual in Capri pants who loves to shop and shimmy about town on his moped. He could also be a variation of the Sensitive New Age Guy who deeply understands women, and is never wholly content that he was not born one. Perhaps by 2050, the word "man" might describe little more than a bipedal primate no different from a woman except for his having more body hair.

In light of what may be, it is imperative to commemorate the essence of manliness and masculinity for the benefit of future generations; although, what makes one a man is a rather ethereal concept. Dr. Harvey Mansfield sought to define these traits[237] in the book, *Manliness*. The author views it as being "a quality of the soul,"[238] which hinges upon the possession of confidence and the capacity to command.[239] The manly man is one who excels at getting things done. He is skilled in the art of productivity. Action is favored over reflection.[240] He quickly grasps the nature of a problem and solves it. A manly man leads; he does not follow.

On those occasions when his actions do not achieve the desired effect, such an individual accepts responsibility for his misjudgment and is not afraid to take ownership of disaster. He reflexively protects his family, and does not need to prove his authority to others because they already sense it.[241] One of Mansfield's examples was Theodore Roosevelt, and I would add to the list the names of Ronald Reagan, Winston Churchill, and Vince Lombardi. There are many other such persons among us. The exquisite traits of these individuals give them not only the ability to lead but the ability to instill confidence within others. Those seeking to diminish men claim that fear is something males are programmed to deny, but Mansfield takes exception to this. He offers up a different conclusion. Fear in itself is not unmanly, but what is unmanly is for one's trepidations to paralyze them in the face of crisis.[242] Weighed risks are not to be avoided as assuming them is integral to competent leadership.[243]

Mansfield's arguments do not appear controversial on their face, particularly due to his concession that many women possess these same characteristics. Yet his resuscitation proved highly unpopular because the attributes he described are not often found in what makes one a "real man" today. The new man eschews competition in favor of coordination and consensus building. He does not "tell it like is" because it might cause others to feel pain. He is tolerant and sensitive. Even when his associates are wrong he is attentive and affirms them. Millennium man empowers, consoles, glorifies, and defers—particularly towards those individuals he deems to be part of an "oppressed" group. His docility pays off a historical debt which was never his to begin with. In his spare time, he advocates for social justice which sounds quite benign, but is, in practice, a glossy evil. The Marxian construct amounts to little more than the government stealing the resources of the people for the betterment of the government.

Romantic relationships are the region in which the ideal man[244] is in his glory. He customarily puts the needs of his lover above his own. He knows, and will accept, nothing of the biological basis of human behavior. He has internalized Woman's reproductive strategies as his own and castigates his brothers when they reveal an obsession with female age and beauty. He is deluded into thinking that the physical is a realm for only shallow men. The new man is so steeped in faux depth that he regards hormonal urges as being beneath him. Fertility, an unconscious concern that drove the decision-making of his fathers, is inconsequential. When selecting a mate his priority is to find the "perfect person." Director Kevin Smith presented this perspective in his film *Chasing Amy*; a debacle in which he had the female lead parrot this cancerous philosophy. She could not confine her quest for romantic nirvana to the region of one sex alone as inner worth was all that mattered to her.

Despite Smith's advertisement for love and lust as a social construct, the sensitive man generally avoids homosexuality as a side habit, but, in other areas, he will assume that he is the one in the wrong whenever he uncovers a difference between his desires and what society tells him he should desire. If he pursues women as an avenue to physical satisfaction, shame will ensue, but it will not reduce the rate of his doing so. His lack of control may humiliate him and he will forever wish that he could extinguish his obsession over female body parts—even as he deletes their phone numbers from his cell phone and tosses their business cards in the trash. With lament he will wonder when the day will come in which he will be freed from his base and animal instincts as his being an animal is not something that he can ever accept. He will feel self-righteous indignation whenever he sees strangers turn to savor the bouncing of a derriere, yet, just as he grumbles his disapproval, his eyes too will delight in the same view. He is devoted to society's politically correct mores so he will avidly deny caring about a woman's age and claim that weight is not an issue for him. The sexually promiscuous past of his mate will be of no importance, and he may even describe her previous behavior as being "liberated." With her career, he is totally behind her, and he will beam with pride whenever she gets a promotion.

After a while though, despite his outward allegiance to all of these ideals, when the time comes he probably will not marry a modern woman. The new man will undoubtedly blame himself for this failure, and point to his own immaturity as being the reason for why he could not "pull the trigger." The fact is, however, that somewhere deep inside him he knows that marrying a skank is an act of which he is incapable.

Should he get suckered into tying the knot anyway it will generally prove a temporary and painful interlude for both parties. The lucky groom will be forced to match his preconceptions with his actual behavior, which is something he cannot easily accomplish. He will have to accept the traditional role of family cash-o-matic while effortlessly swallowing the unique indignities of our age. Soon he will notice that the benefits bestowed upon his fathers will not be bestowed upon him. His turtledove may have no intention of taking his name or be interested in anything more than the "economic" aspects of their union. She will not defer to him about any matter and the extraction of privilege and advantage will always be on her mind. It cannot be otherwise because her individuality and authenticity are of paramount importance. Should his wife continue to work she will work for herself as chivalry bars him from taking an equal share of the profits. His new wife may reject the idea of domesticity, and regard her continued fidelity as something for which her husband must earn. There will be no revealing of any this beforehand as deception is intrinsic to the marital ceremony. Few men marry virgins, yet, invariably, every bride I have ever seen has dressed in white. On the weekends, his job will be to entertain and enable as he spends eternal and vacuous hours in the company of her friends and relations. His wife's expectations will be bottomless, and, without his constant effort, he will quickly become just another schlep who failed to meet them.

Yes, today's "real man" is a totem of sacrifice. He exists to earn, befriend, please, garner, and adore. When my peers express the fear that men might be replaced by dildos and vibrators I laugh as no such device can free women from debt, allow them to live in luxury, increase their free time, heighten their status, and act as a bulwark against poverty.

Next, we come to a most crucial question.

I. What Do Women Want?

Well, you can tell by the way I use my walk, I'm a woman's man: no time to talk.
    —The Bee Gees.[245]

Answering such a question is quite arduous. One needs more than a thousand monographs to tease out all the necessary variables and assumptions. It remains daunting even when narrowed down to one specific subarea, such as that of desire. Olga Silverstein, of *Vogue* magazine, confined her query to the subject of men alone: "Women don't want to be dominated and bullied, but neither do they want a man to be a baby. They want him to be a 'man.' Then, when he's a man, they don't like it because he's too controlling and they're afraid of him. They all want heroes, but they want warm, tender, loving heroes. Oh, what a fantasy that is!"[246]

Fantasy is an apt description for it. A husband is not a magical elixir that will cure his wife's every known ill. Besides, men have their own interests whether they mention them or not. What we should conclude from Ms. Silverstein's summary—along with what many men know from experience—is that the answer to the question of what women want is "Everything!"

A century ago, wealth, status, and attractiveness were universally prized in men and remain so today, but now traits like physical youth, the capacity to be a soul mate, and an inclination for becoming the sorceress's apprentice have been added to the list. When this myriad of attributes is considered, it seems rather unlikely that anything woman born could fully satisfy the requirements of the modern woman. They have been conditioned to believe that if they have a need, somewhere, somehow some abnormally lucky guy will fulfill it. Should one fail to do so, his woman will regard him as being an inferior specimen—that is if she does not already regard him as being an inferior specimen due to the genitalia with which he was born. Their opprobrium and displeasure is then internalized and causes their man to question his own worth. That he would do so is his own fault. He should have refused to imbibe from the noxious concoction of political correctness and chivalry from which is ordained the nature of the woman's real man in our society. Listening to her criticism is foolish because what women want varies on a daily basis— sometimes even within the same individual. For that reason, one cannot place too much stock in their words. By the time they get around to telling you their perspective it may no longer apply. Their discontent "was so yesterday." Well, you get the point. Tying one's self-concept to their views is similar to boarding a steamer for England and then discovering that the ship's navigator randomly determines your course each morning by the rolling of two dice.

Therefore, a woman's opinion regarding who is, or who is not, a real man should be completely discarded. Should one do otherwise it would result in a maddening micromanagement of personal behavior with the end result being neurosis. The man who grafts his self-esteem to female conjecture is doomed to resentment and bitterness. That is not to say that those who are subjected to this brand of non-sense should make their contempt known. Coming out and saying anything is not recommended. Semi-detachment is ideal because, as I will explain momentarily, women love it when their pronouncements are cherished.

The example of the woman's real man helps us understand why prostitutes are so often addicted to artificial euphoriants like cocaine, heroin, and alcohol. Just like the street walker, this poor drone must thwart the pain and emptiness that permeates his soul. He flies the flag of another and responded to the freedom God gave him by voluntarily entering a state of bondage. A content man thinks for himself and recognizes that ulterior motives lie behind his paramour's digs at his character—which she often mislabels as constructive criticism. Due to their girlfriend's or wife's stake in his mental life, it is vital for him to realize that intimates are automatically incapable of honest, disinterested criticism.

Nowhere is this more evident then in regards to his confidence. Women have a clear and conflictual stake in the way men see themselves. Preventing self-assurance is an unstated goal of many a woman. They are fully cognizant that male pride—even if it is legitimate—can endanger their romantic relationships. Indeed, any sudden increase in his self-worth could price their girlfriends out of the market. Thus, characterological insults like "you're not a real man" must be placed in their proper context and demystified. This invective is but a pathetic and cruel attempt to manipulate a "loved" one. Those men who accept the rants of biased reporters will soon be buried in an avalanche of misery.

Given this eventuality, why then do so many men morph themselves into exact replicas of what women want? There are but two explanations. The first is very, very, obvious. "Chicks dig it" is not just an advertising mantra. It is a phrase believed by every single, heterosexual man. The need to find out what women want and then give it to them is what makes us reliable workers, climbers of corporate hierarchies, and the purchases of overpriced stones. By our twenties, the need to meet women's expectations becomes burned into our neural pathways as we associate their gratification and excitation with our own.

Yes, sex sells. The desire to please the fairer sex fuels chivalry and every other imaginable sacrifice. Pathology only becomes evident when one pledges allegiance to a woman's wishes over every other constructive concern. When this occurs the man accepts a mission impossible in which the only objective will be to gain approval from those not vested in

according it. Soon the man's past will be forgotten along with his friendships; although, such concessions could amount to nothing as pawns are
rarely prized by their masters. These fellows have deciphered only the
explicit, rather than implicit, messages of women. What women imply,
rather than what they state, is more reflective of their true needs. Taking
their every word as truth is the wrong approach. They may say that they
want men with distinct genitalia and female brains, but this is seldom the
case in practice.

Dr. Ethel Person clarified the discrepancy between female word
and fact in her excellent book, *Dreams of Love and Fateful Encounters: The
Power of Romantic Passion*, "Moreover, as some men probably correctly
intuit, many women, despite what
they say and consciously believe, are attracted more to macho men
than to 'feminized,' soft, intuitive, and liberal ones (perhaps as earlier
suggested because such men may too closely resemble the 'nurturing
mother'). And, in fact, while some men who appear to be liberated from
gender stereotypes actually are, still others are simply masking gender
conflicts and dependency problems with a rhetorical overlay."[247]

The pronouncement of solidarity with women's issues by the
woman's man and his adoption of female grooming habits reeks of
illegitimacy and contrivance. Shopping at fashionable boutiques, throwing
out perfectly good clothes in the name of fashion, and becoming addicted
to women's television shows may well form the basis of a primitive bond
with the fairer sex, but often the fruit of this bond is the mere stroking of
head and ego rather than the stroking of the more crucial body parts.
Many women refuse to have sex with a man who acts as their wife.[248] That
they would do so is only natural. What possible evolutionary advantage
could come from a woman marrying her identical twin? I cannot think of
any. Consider the converse for a moment. Would any of my peers lust
after a woman who looked just like them? Would unshaven legs, Carhartt
bibs, five-o-clock shadow, and a bristly brushcut titillate us? In a
word…no. To men, viva la difference is the order of the day as it is with
women—whether they admit it or not.

The man who seeks to become a woman's echo not only has no
ambition but is also not a man. Incessantly repeating "that's right" and
"you go girl" might get you a seat in a talkshow audience, but it will not
result in sexual or psychological fulfillment. Furthermore, the distrust
these men show for their brothers is but a projection of their own emptiness. As a response to their inadequacies they choose to celebrate "the
other" which happens to be a women in this case [of course, it could be

any entity within the politically correct troika of race, gender, and class]. They regard themselves as being weak, compromised, and selfish so they tattoo these attributes to the biceps of their fellow males. Society would be better off if this rabble confined themselves to saying "I am a pig" or "I am an oppressor" rather than projecting this description upon men on aggregate. Consider this quote by Sacha Guitry: "If I were a girl, I'd despair. The supply of good women far exceeds that of the men who deserve them." Really? How could that be? He should tell[249] that to the suckers who unknowingly get hitched to the pseudo-actresses of the *Girls Gone Wild* video series. Should these men happen to be full-fledged masochists[250] then they well could achieve ecstasy by taking on a female overlord, but their example will result in agony for non-deviants. Relationships can never be built on one-sided sacrifice. Mutual interest and mutual temperament are the basis for any successful union.

The last subset of men I would like to mention are those who defer to women because they regard them as being their inferiors. Although never branded as such, these men are the real sexists and misogynists among us. Ironically, the media often calls them "liberals." These boys emphatically support the myth of women's oppression but for the most selfish of reasons. Their actions stem from seeing women as little more than insects in need of their rescue. They are so convinced of their own superiority that they are incapable of assessing any aspect of the contemporary world. To them there can only be one plot: man as powerful criminal with woman as his gentle victim. Not all men are oppressors in their minds, however. They would concede that a rare breed of seraphim exists among the incubi; one who, like them, possess goodness, righteousness, and nobility. These males must therefore defend the honor of women due to the female's lowly ability and status. Undoubtedly, they shut their eyes each night with deep satisfaction realizing that were it not for them the fairer sex would be confined to brothels or even blasé, poorly decorated homes in Utah or Kansas. But regardless of whatever hellacious fate awaits the average woman, these jack*sses, and they alone, will save them. Former president William Jefferson Clinton is the perfect embodiment of such a charlatan. Should any of the rest of them become politicians they too will introduce, back and/or clamor for all sorts of cockamamie government "solutions" to problems which were never problems in the first place. The women they supposedly liberated were about as in need of liberation as members of the U.S. Senate.

These egomaniacs respond to every crime women commit by instinctively transferring the blame to whatever man was in their life at that moment. Currently, the media is abuzz with the case of a crazed female astronaut who tried to abduct and kill her romantic rival. It would not surprise me in the least if one of these self-appointed female guardians attempted to insinuate that her act was somehow the fault of the man with whom she was obsessed; although, their universal love for women does not extend to every individual. Should a particular woman fail to express gratitude or deference to their magnificent person then their stance will quickly change. Moments after wishing the offending party dead or breaking off relations entirely, these saints will resume championing "women's rights" across stylish tables and publications all over the world.

In my opinion, a far more practical way for a man to garner the devotion of women is to just be himself. One could do worse than to follow the edict of a writer who penned a series of articles entitled, "What Women Want: Who Cares."[251] Flying your own flag is always preferable to being a woman's real man. By doing so, it is not much harder to sleep with them, and has the added advantage of making it easier to sleep with yourself. It is certainly better than spending a Saturday morning with a manicurist or undergoing electrolysis for the removal of your leg hair.

Finally, as I alluded to earlier and as a warning to male readers, it is heartily recommended that this particular part of our ongoing discussion go unmentioned with your significant other. Silence is mandatory. The decision to mentally escape female control is one which cannot be advertised. Women want to be appreciated for their every attribute, and this includes their intuition along with the advice they so eagerly give. One should always pay lip service to their attempts at male modification. The best tactic is to gaze into their eyes and initiate several head nods during each soliloquy, and then go back to doing whatever you were doing beforehand. Yes, this is a passive-aggressive approach, but there really is no other way of handling one's mate when female supremacy is the law of the land. Unless your name is Scott Peterson or that of another "famous" villain, the aggressive-aggressive response to conflict resolution only exacerbates the situation. It would be nice if one could be truthful and kindly tell the woman to mind her own business, but, like skipping a course during a meal at a Parisian restaurant, that sort of thing just is not done. There are some problems in life that you cannot fight city hall over and this is one of them. Acknowledging the value of their suggestions is a requirement and it is the quickest way to get their focus off you and back onto their weekly installment of *Dancing with the Stars*. Reversing the inequity existent among the sexes is not likely so men should make use of their ingrained penchant for logic and strategy.

II. Is the Real Man a Wolf to Men?

These are cardboard cut-out men who gush with empathy whenever their wives and girlfriends need to dump their professional stresses and female angst on them: weak and soulless men who haven't the guts to make a mark themselves, who take the passenger seat in their women's juggernaut journey to post-feminist Nirvana.
          —Nirpal Dhaliwal.[252]

Theoretically, the ridiculousness of a woman outlining for a man the nature of his inner qualities is readily apparent, but such proclamations, should one lack the proper mental machinery for disarming them, can still manage to wound. Thus, before leaving this subject, I will proffer insight on the ways in which a man can assert himself when ambushed in such a fashion.

As I alluded to in the Introduction, after I began writing about these issues my overall level of enemies increased exponentially. I received numerous nasty emails that all had a common premise. Indeed, it seemed as if my foes were cutting and pasting their retorts from a single Microsoft Word file. The rhetoric uniformly included something about my having a small penis or feeling insecure in my masculinity which was why I said the things I did. After noting the universality of this piffle, I began to suspect that there was more to their denunciations than a disagreement with me over the idiocy of The Equity Pay Act. Despite there being no merit in either put down, I could not resist baiting them a little. I emailed back to say that a male appendage of any size contained enough sensory neurons to pleasure the whole of China, so its length would be entirely immaterial to its bearer. Alas, to this they did not reply.

My feigned ignorance aside, it is common knowledge that many men consider the pleasing of a woman to be a potent indicator of masculinity, and, despite its obvious absurdity, the view remains a popular one. Female satisfaction as a barometer of manliness is about as logical as placing a Sudanese General in charge of a slavery awareness campaign. It is rather comical to think of how this came about amidst claims of our society being a patriarchy. That men would make women the arbiters of their own worth is a strong indication of just how seriously the views of the fairer sex are taken. Female gratification should have only a vicarious relationship with a man's identity. Men should be judged by what they do and who they are, and never by the quality of their pay-as-you-go service to women.

Rather than "real man," the proper name for those reveling in personal subordination is "b*tch." Sadly, the amount of women who question men regarding their masculinity is pronounced, and the tactic has to be effective or else they would not keep doing it. Often the slur manages to cow men. Those who take issue with it and stand up for themselves are then maligned further. Their attempts at self-vindication have a counter-indicative effect. Their passion is morphed into aggression, and they are accused of aggressing, or picking on, women—the same individuals who started the conflict. It is not long before these men learn that defending oneself against women is a dishonorable act in itself.

What an amazing trick this is as reversing the tables makes its irrationality quite clear. A man would never question a woman's femininity, and if he did, a bewildered silence would ensue as both parties stared at one another nervously. She might think, "How can this guy, who buys his clothes at Wal-Mart, question my femininity? What a basket case!" While he might wonder if it was a mistake to have released the entire bottle of ether from the ceiling before the night's festivities had properly began. Yes, a woman would have every right to be mystified in such a circumstance but the important point to remember is that, in our society, only men are placed into such irrational situations.

The deconstruction of a recent tiff with a female reader showcases the hidden meaning behind insults concerning masculinity. A charming individual said of your narrator: "If Mr. Chapin had a pair, he wouldn't be so threatened by 'feminists,' and we would be spared his misogynistic rants."[253] I see, so if I were a big tough guy then I would act like one—by letting people push me around and lie about me. Hmm, such a stance does not seem consistent with having "a pair." This lady regards the real man as one who lets people say whatever they want about him and who happily accepts whatever punishment comes his way. If that is true, then the real man is nothing more than an object of female domination.

How could such an outrageous state of affairs arise? Everyone in America is supposed to be equal so a man should be no more inclined to ignore offensive remarks than anybody else. Here we find that being a real man is antithetical to feminist interpretation. Accepting guilt when you are innocent is the act of a weakling and a coward. There is nothing manly about becoming a masochistic whipping boy. My father was not an oppressor and my grandfather was not an oppressor so I will not be accepting that label for myself. My genitalia should not force me to play "The Gimp"[254] during my ongoing relations with women.

There is nothing in western tradition which bars self-defense. God did not destine the narrator, or any of his readers, to be a slave on this earth. Both spiritually and politically, one must never assist or enable others in their attempts to subjugate you. We must act in a manner that ensures our survival. Of course, this is categorically different from being vengeful. A life filled with wrath is something to be avoided as clinging to resentments is a slow form of suicide. Clearing one's name is not a reprisal. In the case of the feminists, if I could magically get my critics and enemies fired from their not-for-profit positions I would decline to do so. I have no interest in making them suffer. All I want is for them to leave me, my fellow males, and the political process alone. Bullying and intimidation are their tactics; they should not be ours. We will forgive and forget after we make known the false and malignant nature of their claims. If these liars are willing to put down their weapons of emasculation, I will be happy to forgive them. What I will not do is encourage and perpetuate their evil by submitting to their will. We must speak truth to liars.

The claim that a real man is one above feminist opinion is but a thinly camouflaged expression of misogyny. Its underlying message is that men are so mighty in comparison to women that they should not care what they think, but this could never be the case in the United States of 2007 because men have less power than women. Those men who answer feminist fabrications are the ones who treat them as equals. They hold women accountable just as they would anyone else. If a feminist is a peer then it is only natural to refute the lies they tell. The National Organization of Women has 500,000 members[255] who preach a devoutly leftist, anti-individualist, and socialist anti-gospel so why should not we fear them? A force of a half-million zealots is surely one to be reckoned with. No, it is the cowards who acquiesce and the noble men who resist. The manly man does not remain silent when others impugn his family, his ancestors, his race, and his God. A real man does one thing when threatened: He stands and fights. It is all a farce, but Marx was wrong. This one is becoming history.

III. Counter-Test: Defining Oneself Outside of Women.

Sometimes a man must be alone and this is no place to hide.
—Bob Dylan.[256]

If the opinions of women are not to be trusted then from where should men look for validation in life? To alternative sources of course; chiefly those that come from within. In the present environment, objective definition is essential, and, should a man feel the weight of society upon him due to his not fulfilling the desires of others, I will offer up independent tests or proofs of masculinity. All of these exist outside of female jurisdiction. Hopefully, they will act as a palliative in his time of need. With this criteria, he can evaluate the quality of his own psychological infrastructure. Meeting all six tests is not to be expected, but I applaud those who do. They are as follows:

Proof One: In all but the direst of circumstances, I think logically and do not let my emotions corrupt my thinking.

Proof Two: I understand that my personal life and my vocation are separate entities. I remain professional in my dealings with others whether I like them or not.

Proof Three: I am interested in topics outside of my own experience. I find value in mental pursuits that have no direct bearing upon my own life.

Proof Four: I do not alter my beliefs, interests or values as a means to conform to a peer group or society at large. I am not afraid to embrace unpopular truths.

Proof Five: My friends are just as important to me as my romantic relations. When my friends are in trouble, I work to get them out of trouble even if the decision jeopardizes my welfare.

Proof Six: In my personal life, I treat people differently based on my feelings towards them. I avoid being two-faced in my relationships. People know it when I like them and they also know it when I do not.

These tests were approved by my friends, Thomas Varnelli and Steven Wills. The former observed, "Unfortunately with the androgynization of the country, a lot of men no longer meet such criteria."[257] The latter summed it up with a phrase of his own: "Being a man means one thing, and that is doing the right thing when times are hardest."[258] Hopefully, these conditions will provide a level of comfort to those hectored and cajoled into taking a second job or impoverishing themselves for the "manly" purpose of funding a wedding or a ritzy, high status vacation.

In the final analysis, men should not be too concerned about a woman's opinion regarding their masculinity. The direct sex must realize that their views are biased and self-serving. A man should be every bit as skeptical regarding their pronouncements as he would be those of a dentist who claimed that Hershey's Syrup made for wonderful toothpaste. Questioning one's manhood is a method of control, and I am sure that those practicing it will be more infuriated by this portion of my book than by any other. My words are bad for business—very bad for business.

6

The Fundamental Theorem of Women

Little red wagon, little red bike, I ain't a monkey but I know what I like…
—Bob Dylan[259]

She cut her hair and I stopped loving her.
—Billy Bragg.[260]

Never judging anything or anybody is a mark of cultivation and refinement in the modern age. We are expected to be situationalists; we should modify our morality and values to match the changing opinions of our time. Or at least whatever the mainstream media reports are the opinions of our times. We are now ruled by euphemism rather than logic. Respecting diversity, [261] tolerating difference, and refusing to judge others are the keys to being a happy and healthy citizen.

Under no circumstances must we greet the dysfunctionality of others with condemnation or even accurate observation. We must not burden our friends and relations with our own "value systems." If our indifference allows others to destroy themselves then there is nothing that we can do about it. The most socially appropriate response to seeing an acquaintance giddily career towards the abyss is to say nothing as your hand waves a sentimental goodbye. Departing from this practice would necessitate our non-judgmental peers judging us to be bad persons. The best thing to do is to bump through life like a sleepwalker and never awaken to the realization that the combination of judgmental intelligence and constant experience is what allows us to make sense of our world.

Much could be said about relativism in all of its nefarious forms, but, for our purposes, I must note that romance may be the one remaining area in which relativism has not triumphed. Despite its never being officially acknowledged, with love one can still have a discriminating palette. Notions like the need to find true love and the need to find a soul mate are widely accepted, and this means, by definition, that many are met but few are chosen.

As with all things, in practice, females are granted more latitude in this arena than are males. Males can remain fashionably choosy provided that they offer explanations rooted in the language of romance as opposed to those rooted in truth. If he expects not to be castigated a man must not cite weight gain, materialism or a complete lack of morality as a reason for dissolving a relationship. By separating the contenders from the pretenders with politically correct language he can remain quite judgmental and selective throughout his lifespan. Saying that girls lacked the will to settle down or possessed the proper levels of ambition [hah!] are fairly safe ways to publicly describe failed trysts. Even more effective is to blame a rift on hard drug usage, an ex's love of animal torture or that she currently resides in San Quentin.

Subtle factors for prospective mate dismissal are perfectly legitimate when enunciated by women but this is not the case for men. It is recommended that the nauseating particulars of a non-heroin using female not be shared. Other women will not understand and they will sympathize with her plight. As I have already stated, society's standards for what men should look for in women have little to do with biology or reality. As we know, many a liberal male is quite pleased about his wife being "liberated," but this term excuses the display of a multitude of flawed traits. To the woman's real man being liberated means that his wife is mature and sees the world through a twenty-first century prism. Unfortunately, that particular prism functions as a Presidential Pardon, allowing her to remain self-absorbed and narcissistic, due to matrimony wiping clean the disgrace of her personal history. That so many guys marry such women is puzzling, but to brag about it to others is ghastly.

In juxtaposition, the direct sex has no pat moniker which vindicates the need to find relationships which are intrinsically advantageous. Men are supposed to be perpetually on a quest for women who will act as their muse; who can guide them, inspire them, motivate them, and, most importantly, correct them. In dating, as we know from the Deception as Nutrient chapter, this means that only female reproductive strategies can be fully acknowledged and officially celebrated. Male strategies are denigrated or denied entirely. What was once "viva la difference" is now an unholy mess. Our relations are encased in hypocrisy and irrationality. Let me now describe a few emblematic stances of society when it comes to the differences between male and female mating prerogatives:

When A Woman Desires...	*She is Deemed...*
A Man with Ambition	Deep, Meaningful, Sensible, and Fair.
A Successful Man	Wise, Forward thinking, and Intelligent.
A Man with Intelligence	Intelligent.
A Man with Wealth	A woman with a false consciousness. No real woman would care about a man's worth. They can make their own money and doing so is one of life's greatest joys.
A Young Man	Heroic. Then, when he leaves her for a younger model, the existence of the patriarchy, along with male inferiority, will be proved once again.
An Attractive Man	Honest, Sincere, and Empowered.

When A Man Desires...	*He is Deemed...*
A Young Woman	Immature, insecure, egotistical, and on a quest for his own lost youth.
A Beautiful Woman	Shallow, superficial, insecure, intellectually deficient, and of redneck lineage.
An Intelligent Woman	A Liar.

A Pleasant, Friendly Woman	A dominator bent on conquering all those who come before him. As we will soon see in the next chapter, the quest for an amiable mate equals the quest for a submissive. It is widely acknowledged that such desires are a red flag. This type of man wants to adorn his woman with a red latex suit and insert a rubber ball in her mouth.
A Supportive Woman	Crazy, insecure, weak, and not a real man. The man who craves a supportive woman is a needy, reactionary freak. He will be too self-absorbed to ever adequately serve as her valet, key grip, best boy, and/or husband.

Yes, these are the genuine double standards endemic to our romantic relations. The best of men laugh them off while the majority of us are somewhat stunned to find that our biological inclinations have no place in the world into which we were born. The worst of men buckle before this social stigma and adopt for themselves the female perspective. They will live out their lives as blighted orcs afraid of the sunlight. These are the women's real men that we just discussed. They described getting married as being "the right thing to do" even if their destiny means living out their days as cuckolds. Perhaps they do it as a cleansing act to extirpate their sins or maybe the plots aired on the Lifetime Channel are the only one they have ever really known. Regardless, we must turn our backs on them as it does not matter what made them accept such a role for themselves. They are charred figures who no more resemble men than the Chihuahua does a wolf.

Apart from a few confessing Hamlets who wish to be equal brides with their partners and are duly celebrated in the pages of *The New York Times,* societal attempts to craft legions of new men have largely failed. Most of us refuse to meet the politically correct standards for sexual attraction regardless of how often our tastes are denigrated. We happen to like what we like and do not see ourselves as being in need of reconstruction. Most men say nothing in response to allegations of inferiority or insecurity but do continue to date as they please.

What must be remembered here is that neither sex is served when the boundaries between them are erased. Men and women have separate agendas, and we should never expect that our mates will be our Mini Me's. The process of finding a mate involves patience, courage, and, most importantly, the healthy ability to know that perfection can never be found. We must tailor our desires to what is available. We must obtain the best person we can at the least cost to ourselves and our individual identity. No one, not even Barack Obama were he to be single, is capable of finding a woman who embodies every trait that he seeks. There always are trade-offs. Utopia means no place and the people who hold out for it will end up alongside communism upon the dustheap of history. There will always be something tarnished, unfinished or lacking in whoever we find, and accepting this eventuality is a prerequisite for happiness. Nothing on this earth is exactly as we would like it to be. To presuppose that there is someone out there who is a replica of ourselves is to believe in our own divinity. Flaws and limitations are what separate us from God.

We should consider ourselves incredibly lucky to find someone we like, love, and respect. Finding commonality and compatibility is of paramount importance when winnowing the field. Personality similarities should be our main concern, as Dr. Jared Diamond explains: "The more similar a man and woman are in political views, religion, and personality, the smoother will be the negotiation. The match in personality traits is on the average closer for married couples than for dating couples, closer for happily than unhappily married couples, and closer for couples who stay married than for those who get divorced."[262]

Commensurate traits depressurize relationships and create comfort for both persons. Their interactions are sincere and they "can be themselves." When this is not the case, a mate leads us to Golgotha rather than to catharsis. The lust for a clone does blur essential distinctions, however. I concede that personality differences attract divorce lawyers, but sex based differences form the basis of attraction. Man and woman are independent but complementary. We are not interchangeable persons like the characters of Samneric in *The Lord of the Flies*. Brainwashing the population into thinking otherwise will not eliminate disparities.

Sometimes the lust for commonality can take on comic proportions like in a scene from the movie *Diner* in which one of the characters forces his fiancée to take a test assessing her knowledge and devotion to the Baltimore Colts. This was quite humorous in the context of the film but highly ridiculous in the context of actual existence. If a man searches for a woman who possesses his level of fanaticism for sports he will forever be doomed to disappointment. The same can be said of women who long for a man interested in shopping and home decoration.

A few years back I went out on a date with one such a person. She was completely confused in regards to this matter. She looked crestfallen after I told her that I did not like chocolate. She looked so distraught that I had no idea how to proceed from there. Was it a deal breaker for her when a man said that he did not love chocolate? Man and chocolate aficionado are as incongruous a pairing as woman and welder. I tried to move on from there but made little progress and that was the last time I ever saw her. Selection by minutia is selection gone mad. The healthiest among us comprehend this truth.

Given that we only encounter the archetypal mate in our imagination, should we completely purge our minds of its representation? No, that would be too extreme a reaction, and one which I do not think is possible anyway. Somewhere in our perceptions the ideal always remains in some form. It functions as a tape measure by which we categorize all others. It is the distance from this ideal—and yes, there will always be a distance—by which we determine who is right for us.

How this image of the quintessential first entered our heads is not clear. It is my belief that the shadowy vision of the person we pine for became instilled within us from a variety of sources. Our own upbringing plays no small part. The optimal could be a glorified form of a relative, a friend of the family, or a stranger we met when we were very young. Somehow the apparition enters our cranium and cannot be forcibly removed thereafter. No doubt that our genes had an impact on the image as well. Our inherited predilections direct us on our search. Society is unquestionably another determinant. Its verbal, visual, and auditory authority influences our receptivity and desires. In the case of men in particular, our internal makeup—personality, drive, and ambition—is altered to various degrees by the women we wish to impress and obtain.

With men in particular, at a certain point in our development, our minds complete the process of compiling the precise characteristics and form of our paragon woman. Thereafter, her haunting presence affects our judgment of every female who follows. The mythic woman hovers within us at all times. She forms a shrine whose purity can never be violated. Glimpses of her in new women will be noted and serve to pique our interest. She begins to take ethereal form not long after the first time we see *Sesame Street* and is finalized at some point during our adolescence. Soon thereafter, the abstract is merged with the corporeal as her essential traits become known and internalized. Her final representation is an extensive product of thesis, antithesis, and synthesis by which we soon discover who she is, **and most importantly, who she can never be.** While a man knows that the sublime will always be confined to the realm of fantasy, he also knows that females who radically depart from the mythic woman's image are persons that he could never love. Her unspoken, lingering, and largely unacknowledged presence has a major impact on all of our future decision-making.

The optimal woman is the catalyst from which arises a law I term *The Fundamental Theory of Women.* I will outline its underlying assumptions below:

> *The more the attributes of a man's prospective mate correspond with those of his ideal woman, the more likely it is for him to form a sincere, passionate, and long-term attachment with her. Contrarily, the more divergent a prospective woman is with his ingrained representation of the ideal, the less likely it is that he can form a permanent attachment with her.[263] The absence of a physical and psychological correlation between the mythic female and an actual woman precludes the possibility of romantic love entirely.*

With modern women being flimflammed into regarding themselves as superior to men they will never learn of this of theory nor will they recognize its effects. If women studied men in the same fashion that we study them their lives would blossom with a prairie full of victories.

The theory explains why men are happy to have a plethora of women visit their beds, but are dead-set against their remaining in them for more than a few nights. These females lack the qualities that we envisioned in our first few decades of life, and there is no denying their total disharmony with the exemplary. Many women will find that there is no shortage of men to escort them on dates, fool around with them, and have sexual intercourse with them, but that a healthy majority of their suitors are decidedly against a long-term commitment. The men who play with them understand that their relationships cannot be permanent, so there is always a time limit to their affections that they will not acknowledge. They will avidly provide such women with physical satisfaction (or at least attempt to), but their spirits will be forever closed off to their lovers. The vernacular of such relationships is well-known. The man will speak of the woman in a predictable fashion: he cannot marry her because of the things she did in the past or that she has too many miles on the odometer or that she is not the kind of girl that you marry. These are clichéd male snippets which symbolize well the dysfunctionality of our society. Women often express the same sentiments, but with far more verbiage, in regards to men who are devoid of ambition and resources and with whom they could not possibly settle.

That men continue to advance their own interests in the face of perpetual cultural pressure and assault is nothing short of amazing, but poisonous criticism has never yet overpowered nature. Our prerogatives were shaped by forces that no dogma or propaganda can erode. An offshoot of The Fundamental Theory of Women is that a hyper-powerful mental filter exists within every man that ensures that he will not be derailed from his reproductive quest. This filter separates out much needed information from the vapid verbal noise which surrounds us. It is ensconced deep within our cognitive structure, and, thus, is not moved by a studio full of Oprahatics or the social engineering messages of *Time* or *Newsweek*. Thanks to this intermediary, when it comes to mating, most men march with the certainty of Alexander regardless of the way in which they are later received. This theoretical apparatus is something I term our Emissary of Essence (hereafter referred to as EoE). Its most important function is to weigh the worth of prospective girlfriends and gauge the way in which they correspond to our concept of the mythic female.

It may surprise readers to learn that the famous person with whom I have assigned the structure's appearance has little in common with Clint Eastwood, Robert DeNiro, Arnold Schwarzenegger or anybody else who could be remotely described as manly. Our EoE is an psychic ambassador from an earlier and simpler time and is therefore devoid of muscles, riches, splendor, education and masculine features. He is small but earnest, soft-spoken but incorruptible. I envision him as being none other than the character of Christopher Robin from *Whinnie the Pooh*.

I grant that it is odd to imagine that the protector, ally, and guiding force for an adult male could be found in the person of an undeveloped boy. Admittedly, young master Christopher is a rather unorthodox candidate for this role. He is a small child whose previous qualifications amounted to little more than wandering in a forest with a goofy set of companions so he is not the typical stuff from which a guardian is made. He knows nothing of modern life and would showcase zero insight in regards to business, technology, fashion, politics, or professional sports. How could a simple boy upend the agenda of shrieking feminists, government apparachniks, and intellectuals who believe that male characteristics positively correlate with mental illness? My answer is that he can and he can do a far better job than the rest of us.

The strengths of Robin, our EoE, can be found in his very naivety, artlessness, and clarity. The only things he knows about are the ones that really matter. He is unworldly but possesses a pathfinder's knowledge of the 100-Aker Wood that is our essence. His unwavering comprehension of our identity along with his intimate understanding of our drives is why he excels at his work. He knows which women are in keeping with our objectives and which ones are not. On this subject, and on this subject alone, his voice thunders like Danton and he persuades like Churchill. He is the father of the man. Knowing the truth and reminding us of it is the best antidote to the emotional anarchy of the present day. He is our best defense.

As with all boys, there is nothing politically correct about him. In our youth, we said what we felt and we never afraid to describe the world as it actually was. We never feared being branded with an ism or the cacophonous censure of social engineers. Life was uncomplicated and that is why Robin has the power to call us back to those unclouded days. The woman's real man is expected to communicate via obfuscation and diplomacy but our EoE is only capable of uttering the truth. He can only be judgmental and thank God for that! Without such candor many a man would be lost forever.

Our emissary is prized because his perspective is pure and virtuous. One adheres to his admonitions because his words negate the artificiality of our frivolous and debauched age. His efforts are detected in our diminished esteem for girlfriends who better resemble soldiers of fortune. He encourages us to cut off relations with women who are no closer to dear old mom—or any other female who walked the planet before the last century—than they are to red snappers or Mongolian gerbils. Our cultural arbiters may exalt the glories of sexual liberation and experimentation, but Christopher Robin can defeat them with the lucid muttering of a single sentence. "If she loved you then she would never act like that." Like Hemingway, his words are concise and Spartan, but they allow us to move continents. The questions with which he would reproach us are practically impossible to answer: "Why would you ever marry a person like that? What are you expecting to get out of this deal?"

The boy endures so that we may live. A boy could never understand the fallacious tricks which mandate our viewing promiscuous and selfish women as liberated. To him, a woman who has slept with numerous men is not free and wondrous; she is communal and bears the mark of Cain. This boy has not been miseducated into dispelling his own interests. Such women would provoke his condemnation and damnation. For him there would be only one legitimate response. The man he represents must avoid this girl and forget that he ever met her. She is below his sympathy and understanding. To Robin, a whore is always a whore. If this person demanded marriage, our EoE would not engage us in mental gymnastics. His only answer would be a plain one: "Never!" There is no way that a boy could justify attaching his name and reputation to the person of a prostitute.

The loneliness and incompleteness of some men causes them to form pair bonds in situations that deserve only air and open space. They are saturated and steeped in the edicts of our new dispensation, and young Christopher might be the lone rational voice they ever hear. Our EoE is the only barrier preventing their mistaking a swindle for a deal. Robin's presence is absolutely essential particularly for these "peace at any price" fellows.

Yet all men occasionally teeter along a line of irrationality in regards to women; especially when immorality and unreliability are combined with receptivity and a lustrous figure. It is at this point when we all become susceptible to disaster. Our lust can carry us to places that only Robin knows we should not go. It is at that moment in which his persistence can restore us even if takes several weeks and months to act on his advice. It is hoped that we act before finding ourselves in a rented Hummer at the gates of a drive-through wedding chapel in Las Vegas. Then only our EoE can convert us on the road to serfdom. He can preserve us from servitude and prevent the scribbling of a signature to a government contract that will leave us beholden to an unstable monarch.

Lastly, I should note that there is a bit of unintentional irony in my choice of Christopher Robin to play our Emissary of Essence. In the course of writing this, I discovered that A. A. Milne's treasured character, based on his own son, has also been ravaged by our social engineers. It seems that the Disney Corporation decided to do away with him[264] despite his integral role in the original story. They planned on writing him out of future scripts and replacing him with a girl sporting a bicycle helmet named Darby. What is even more satirical is that she wears the type of helmet that most of us would have thrown in the ditch back when we were kids. Eventually, Disney relented and yielded to an outrage seldom expressed by the non-deviant members of this nation. They reinstated young master Christopher and gave him a cameo role in their *My Friends*

Tigger & Pooh.[265] Well, all I can say about this scandal is that it does not really matter. Should he lose his job with Disney we will always have important work for him to do.

Thus far, I have only described how our EoE functions within a particular individual. What happens when an entire host of women, a gigantic subset of the whole, wildly clashes with man's mental representation of the ideal? This actually is our present condition within which fewer and fewer men consent to get married and have come to regard women in the physical sense alone. We currently have a society-wide dilemma by which one sex is increasingly incapable of making a commitment to the other and is reluctant to form long-term attachments.

Of course, as I outlined in the last chapter, there will always be men who marry women and who will do anything for them because the good graces of the fairer sex are integral to their identity. There will be fewer of these sacrificial prototypes around in the future, however, even if the number of metrosexuals, New Age men, and non-specified males who forswear masculinity swells. The reason for this paradox is that these anti-hormonal men can never extinguish completely the influence of their own EoE's. No matter what they outwardly may say their own Christopher Robin's are fully aware of the modern woman's corruption and decadence. They realize that these females are of exceedingly low quality when compared to those of the past. Women who exist for the purposes of self-indulgence, empowerment, and 80 long years of entertainment are worthless as wives. Even to an ubersexual, this is not a suitable mortar upon which to lay the bricks of his future. Many of these women are simply not marriageable, and The Fundamental Theory of Women explains why this is so.

Our relationships in the west have taken the form a permanent middle game in which the most likely conclusion is stalemate. The complexity of the moves are not worthy of a Kasparov or Karpov, and are wholly computer generated. They are as unimaginative as they can be: two people meet, the man has his own desires which he does not express, the woman shares her own desires and/or the desires society expects her to have, man voices no objection, a courtship begins, man obtains physical satisfaction, female obtains conflicting levels of physical and emotional satisfaction, woman makes an ultimatum concerning marriage, and man duly leaves while offering up a variety of excuses and justifications that do everything but reveal the truth. The match is then repeated with a new series of challengers. Draw after draw is recorded in the decades to come.

Who exactly benefits from this arrangement? The obvious answer is man as he receives short-term satisfaction without the penalties that accrue from being vested in the process. Yet, his victory is a pyrrhic one. His life and social relations have unquestionably changed for the worst over the course of the last century. The sexes, once complementary entities that fostered life, are now alienated from one another. The self-inflicted debasement of women has inevitably resulted in our own defilement as well. Man is born of woman and her sickness cannot be quarantined. Man should not be a mercenary roaming from one tent to another in the middle of his life. Our days are filled with perpetual exposition and are devoid of resolution. The birthrates of the west are in free fall. Can there be any doubt of the pathology inherent to a society which fails to reproduce its own citizenry? After all, "is there any denying that the future belongs to the people who show up for it?"[266] Regardless of the frequent electric pleasures that man may receive from the fairer sex, their denaturation will bring about our own extinction.

As Mark Steyn convincingly argued in *America Alone: The End of the World as We Know It*, there are other peoples in this world who will inherit the lands we once fought for. They will replace our value systems with laws and practices which really are patriarchal and the result will be the enslavement of women.

7

Woman as Master

It's better to have a lazy bossy, than a bossy lassie.
—Old Scottish Saying.

Pills and potions and ether air, that girl has rockets in her hair.
—Orbit.[267]

One trend that men have been grappling with: Figuring out their roles in relationships as women have become increasingly financially independent, increasingly sexually liberated, and increasingly determined not to let their biological clocks dictate their relationship status.
—David Zinczenko[268]

Regardless of the long-term implications that our decadence has for the west on the whole, for the present time our culture is as radicalized as it ever has been. Women are more dominant today than ever before. With women controlling the public domain either overtly or covertly, there seems to be little rationale for their not doing the same thing in their personal relations with men. For the woman searching for a man to be her footnote, these are bully days indeed. Never has there been more malleable clay from which to mold a human being into an accoutrement. There are numerous psychological rewards available for those who wish to become the page of an alpha female. These males are often described as being liberal, equitable, sensitive, and just. Of course, those of us who are repulsed by such fellows have different names for them. My own favorite is "parakeet males."[269]

First and foremost the motivation of these men must be considered. Why do they wish to submerge their own identity with that of a woman's? I happen to know someone who is the perfect example of one such non-entity as he used to be one of my best friends. Should a trade guild ever form which caters to the submissives of ballbusters, I am sure that old Fred will quickly obtain membership status there. Since I first met him he has spent all of his free time following one girl after another. To the ladies whom he pours his affections he is more of a groupie than a boyfriend. His friends were quick to discover whenever he latched onto a new girl as his annoying coffee klatch phone calls to us quickly subsided. We also witnessed his lightning acquisition of the habits and interests of his paramour. If she liked sailing then he liked sailing, if she pickled her brain with mindless television then he pickled his brain with the same levels of "must see TV." He would begin following *Boston Common, CSI: Bethlehem* or whatever other idiocies happened to invade his living room. Most recently he has decided to take up running because…his new girlfriend does it. He leads the life of a straggler.

Despite his frequent infatuations, Fred has always maintained a continuing attachment to his male friends as he tries to insist on our being a party to his folie à deux. He tries to recruit his pals into being co-groupies of his girlfriend. If they went to dinner, a movie, a bar or a street festival, Fred would always lobby for us to accompany them. It was as if he wanted others to share in the guilt of his self-obliteration. He used to brag proudly about being a chameleon but there is no pride to be had in altering one's opinions and habits to suit those of another. His subservience has purged his body of confidence and now he floats listlessly about Chicago like a glider someone tossed from the top of the Sears Tower.

Well, Fred is not too engaging or memorable a person but there is one lesson that he can teach us. His approach to women happens to be a highly marketable one. Fred, due to a unique combination of reflexive submission and psychological malleability, is in heavy demand among females. His desperate need for their approval has forced him to throw nothing away regardless of the way in which a particular woman may treat him. He has gone out for two year spans with women who took thunderstorms personally and who made fun of him in front of his friends. I recall one ex-fiancée informing me and a girl I was seeing that Fred was no more than a "bellhop" (which he was not) while another girl of his I saw give out her phone number to two other guys while ostensibly on a date with him. If you ask me, that is the kind of woman who belongs in the landfill alongside Maureen Dowd, but Fred takes all comers. His relationships have provided him with endless distraction from the poverty of his inner-life. He seems to relish the role of sidekick. The last time I saw him he boasted of flying off to California where he chauffeured his girlfriend and her friends all over the vineyards of the wine country. He shared that he functioned as their designated driver for the trip. Oh Hurrah!

Yet his popularity among the fairer sex never fails to disturb. There seem to be no shortage of women looking for a "little buddy" of their own. They wish to play the Skipper to some poor sap's Gilligan. What does this mean for our collective future? Will society soon brim with Ferrignoesque females hulking over men and insisting that members of the direct sex function as their aides-de-camp? The trend points in that direction but the fact is that such relationships are not sustainable. The union of dominant woman and bootlicker man is a historical, psychological, and genetic aberration. At its heart, it simply cannot work. Women rarely respect men who are wimps and an alpha female offers a male no possible reproductive or physiological advantage.

The key to recognizing this is in the nature of dominance as a personality trait. We can define dominance as a method or disposition by which one obtains resources through intimidating their rivals either psychologically or physically.[270] The dominant person makes sure that their own needs are filled before those of others. They may make use of force, coercion, threats, manipulation, verbal abuse, social standing, or refined mental game playing.

Traditionally, due to their physical strength, it has been males who were most dominant in tribal structures and hierarchies. Throughout our history, the more that a man has been able to dominate in a group the more access he has had to life-sustaining resources.[271] This truth was not lost on women who, for thousands of years, have relied on males to provide them with meat and sustenance. This was especially true when they were pregnant and/or fragile as their capacity to gather was limited. High status males received more resources than others and more capably protected their family from harm. For women, their own social ranking in a group surged via their association with such fellows.[272] Thus, by mating with the most dominant male they could find, they ensured their own survival.

Due to this cascade of positive benefit, women have acquired a strong taste for socially dominant males. They also have become highly competent at separating the contenders from the pretenders.[273] Women deduce dominance through individual attributes such as physical size, popularity, body language, aggressiveness, and confidence.[274] A testament to the usefulness of dominance in our own day is that it is a fairly reliable predictor of which men experience vocational success and go on to become leaders in the business community.[275]

A hybrid personality affectation, surgency is also greatly revered by women[276] as it reflects the level of extroversion and dominance that a man possesses. Women can discern this in the man by the way they are treated by others.[277] Their level of admiration for their mate is greatly influenced by his standing within the community. The importance of a man's status is readily evident when one listens to the words of women. I have written about it before, and I believe it to be the rationale as to why so many of them, without fail, make initial inquiries about how one knows their friends, how long one has lived where he does, and what the dynamics of one's family are.

At this point, an essential distinction must be made regarding dominance. The trait does not imply that women desire men who will "dominate them." That has nothing to do with it; although, we should not be surprised that such men fail to always be diplomatic in their conversation and daily interactions. What I am strictly referring to here is the way in which men are socially dominant and manage to rise above their peers in the eyes of society.[278] While an affinity for dominance may be the best way for a woman to find the worthiest and fittest mate, unintended consequences may arise. These men stand atop social hierarchies but they are also less kind and tender than their reserved and reticent brothers.[279]

Given what we know about the female fondness for dominance, is it safe to conclude that it is a factor that when displayed by women manages to impresses men as well? It is not and this answer may surprise members of the fairer sex. When it comes to attraction, dominance is always valued more by women than men.[280] In experiments, researchers have found that manipulating a woman's dominance levels does nothing to influence male mate selection; whereas, while doing the reverse makes men more attractive to women.[281] Women artfully apprehend nonverbal displays of dominance, but they go practically unnoticed by men when they are exhibited by women.[282]

For the direct sex, dominance is at best a non-starter. At worst, it is a serious turn-off. A partial explanation for this can be found in our biological past. No possible advantage could have accrued from a man mating with a dominant woman over the course of the thousands of years in which we evolved—a period known as the Environment of Evolutionary Adaptation. The disadvantages of such a union are readily evident. A dominant woman would have eroded a man's sense of well-being and decreased his chances for survival. The ascendant female would have dragged her swain into plenty of conflicts that he normally would have had the good sense to avoid, and, once thrusting him into these fights, she would have been of little use in resolving them. A dominant woman would decrease her man's physical security along with that of their brood. Her posturing would start many a conflagration while leaving others to extinguish them. Most likely, the dominant female as mate would have been a guarantor of early death.

This is a valid reason for why the alpha woman's caricature of dominance remains repugnant to men. Indeed, the present circumstances are not much different from those of the past. Unlike our lust for fatty foods and salt, a distaste for dominant women remains quite adaptive and helpful. Woe to the non-masochist male who ends up welded to such a person. Their conversation and expectations make them as unpleasant to be around as starving crocodiles. Crocodiles, in fact, are to be preferred as at least with a reptile you can always call animal control and have the offending party removed when you have had enough of them. Men who find themselves trapped in a "partnership marriage," which is supposedly rooted in equality find that it undermines their masculinity[283] but how could it be otherwise in a society that defines equality as female supremacy?

Increased socio-economic power has no correlation with female attractiveness and this is for the soundest of reasons. An authoritative female is a hindrance and not an advantage to a man. If they become rich, their money remains theirs to spend as they wish and a husband is considered unmanly when he spends his wife's money. Women will not have a sense of noblesse oblige towards their lower earning mates. Powerful jobs and positions will serve to heighten their own status and cause them to regard their partners as being inferior. The more cachet a woman acquires the more she thinks that she deserves a mate of even greater distinction than herself.

Apart from the chirpy parakeets among us, there are many men who become yoked to domineering women out of necessity as they could not procure anything else. Sadly, these victims of randomicity will never be able to reconcile themselves to the arrangement and will resent their wives[284] both for the way they are treated and for their dependence upon them. They will become passive aggressive husbands who lack the courage to flee but who still maintain enough pride to undermine the commands of their overlords. They will sign up and tune out by engaging in pathological forms of freedom seeking such as gambling, alcohol or pornography. Over time, even a woman who succeeds in getting her man to become a servant will never wholly purge him of his own needs along with the missives of his Emissary of Essence. Certain characteristics cannot be shamed or needled away. Regardless of the way that our elites portray the alpha female as a Lexus or a Mercedes, she will always be a Chevette in the minds of men.

Here, as in so many other areas, males are maligned for prizing personality traits that differ from those esteemed by women. The direct sex is blamed for their lack of appreciation for the Woman as Panzer Leader. That man fails to pine for a Ludendorff of his own can be attributed to his insecurity. If he were confident then he would cherish such a female as she would save him from the quagmire of having to think for himself.

Rather humorously, not only do men dislike dominant women[285] they are disdained by their sisters as well.[286] This is rather obvious as no one gains from having a power-drunk leader who eschews responsibility and accountability [for added insight in the years to come see the specifics of the 2008-2012 Hillary Clinton Presidential Administration]. These women will not fight for the people they dominate as they expect their wards to fight for them. Women also share with males an aversion to mother-in-laws who are excessively judgmental, controlling, and manipulative.[287]

Although in retrospect it seems unlikely, your disheveled narrator has had scores of encounters with dominant women. Perhaps this is due to God's belief that suffering builds character but whatever the reason I have become mired in frequent battles with this ladies. I shudder at the amount of times I have woken up to find myself sharing a pillow with an absolutist. The one thing for certain is that it has not been due to luck as I appear to appeal to these women despite the mandates of logic, self-interest, justice, order, and what I previously thought was an ubiquitous human need to follow the path of least resistance. To this day, these types of women remain my constituency.[288] What makes them tough to refuse is that they are often in vastly superior shape than their peers and less likely to be obese due to their being over-served in the testosterone department. This eventuality makes physical contact with them extremely pleasurable; although, the same could not be said in regards to their conversation.

That I do not now flee from them on sight can also be attributed to my own lack of status. I have never been an alpha man either in word, deed or appearance. My lack of eminence does not allow for the effortless dismissal of women who are both attractive and receptive. At this point, I have become fatalistic about the issue as—barring a winning lotto ticket—it will always be this way. Like the poor, dominant women will always be with me. All I can do is expand the parameters of my shrinking patience and accept that a fixed expiration date is stamped upon our affairs. As soon as my lust fades and my voltaic fascination dissipates, I conduct a fighting retreat while hoping that my psyche survives the maneuver relatively intact.

In 1998, I had a very memorable relationship with one such Viking princess. I met her in a pool hall which is exactly the kind of place that one would expect to find such a hyper-competitive person. She was a southern transplant to the Windy City who was stunning, fiercely intelligent, but lamentably dominant. Three weeks into our assignation, I was so taken by her beauty and interest that I said little in response to her apart from, "Yes, mam." Her allure so completely captivated me that I deferred to her about practically everything, yet it was not long before it became clear that practically everything would not be good enough. She was seeking a level of submission that I could not possibly provide. Her requirements in a man could best be summarized as "slavery or bust."

Our first skirmish occurred after a Thursday night dinner as we strolled down Belmont Avenue together in the direction of her apartment. I eagerly anticipated the AC/DC moments which we would soon be having in her bedroom. My mood was euphoric so it must have struck her as a good time in which to start an argument. In the midst of our jaunt— amid a late night assembly of Goths, stoners, gays, hoodlums, and the occasional yuppie—she shared with me her plans for the future. Specifically, the designs she had for her husband-to-be. The conversation went as follows:

Kindly Narrator: Your plans for a husband? Umm, gee, what might those be? The purchasing of a timeshare in Clearwater?

Viking Princess: No, I'd like my man to do something for me that demonstrates his quality.

KN: His quality?

VP: Yes, well, once we, now I hope I'm not freaking you out, Bernard, by talking about marriage this early on am I?

KN: Of course not, you're referring to "husband" in the abstract.

     This was not a lie on my part. I meant it. Practically nothing she was capable of doing or saying would have freaked me out at that point.

VP: Exactly, anyway, I'm going to insist that he get a tattoo with my name on his flank. For me, that would totally symbolize our bond along with his devotion to me.

     I made no answer. We kept walking and she began talking about something else but I could not stop ruminating about what she said. Unbeknownst to me, young master Robin had awakened and began reminding me that he was never going to condone these orders. When I attempted to ignore him he began to wonder aloud about the nature of my birth. He wondered if I had been switched with another family's baby at the hospital because none of my ancestors would have been so pusilla-nimous as to accept being branded by their wives. Clearly he thought this was a distinct possibility as he had heard of fellows like me at school before. As he recalled, they were given a nickname which rhymed with "bussy." I knew he was right. After a quarter mile I could remain silent no longer. We were headed for a showdown. I had been a swell guy for nearly a month and had still not ruled out the possibility of marrying this fit and remarkable girl, but this provocation was too much. I was emo-tionally vested in her already so my reaction came out of nowhere. I suddenly exploded in mid-pace.

KN: Wait a minute. Let's go back to the tattoo idea. I have to be honest with you. I think that forcing your husband to get branded reeks of evil. It's straight out of an S&M movie. What the hell are you thinking about? You don't have the right to do that to another person. Only a sick power freak would do something like that. Now, I'm sorry but you don't want a man you want a prison b*tch. There is no way in Hell I am going along with that sh*t.

VP: I'm not surprised you'd say something like that. It just shows how much of a boy you are. Since you feel that way why don't we just call it quits then. You're not the man for me.

I was stunned by her reaction. She drew a line in the sand and I was not yet ready to cross it. I folded quickly before her mighty re-raise. I kept walking alongside her but sulked for several minutes. She stared back at me while we declined queries from beggars for dollar bills. Shortly thereafter, I apologized but at least did not say that I would ever consider coloring my skin with her name. In spite of my submission, I knew from that moment on our relationship was doomed. It lasted for a few more months, but our time was important because it marked the first time in my history that I became aware of my attracting the wrong kind of woman.

In the hopes of gaining some sort of understanding of this phenomenon, before we broke up I asked her why she was ever interested in me in the first place. She was gorgeous and we both knew that I was under-qualified for the position. As always, she had a ready answer. With a heavy twang she explained: "I don't respect men who worship me. What am I going to do with some—what's that obnoxious word you say all the time—pussy? What can a guy like that do for me? I admit though that sometimes you can be a real dick…and I do mean that, but at least you're someone I respect. After all, I wouldn't b*tch at you if you I didn't think you were worth b*tching at. Besides, the way you always get mad at me is sort of fun. I like pressing your buttons…and it also proves that you care about my opinion."

I said nothing in response. I did care about her opinion but not for much longer. I appreciated her explanation and her sincere prospective tells us much about the great expanse which exists between the sexes.

Ironically, those women fortunate enough to land a sucker are rarely satisfied with their swag. A parakeet excels at eating seed and making noise but is not worth much else. Not content to suffer alone, these women often wish to make everyone else every bit as miserable as they are. They even encourage other women to make the same mistakes that they did. These dominatrixes will not be satisfied until a Battle of Cannae rages in every home.

I recall an old boss of mine who used to try to talk our girls into shopping for their men at a eunuch shop and also of the way she tried to convince our boys to accept female domination. I often heard her tell our oversexed lads—who got it on a more regular basis than the adults that worked with them—that they should always consult their prospective wives before making decisions. She seemed oblivious to the fact that the demographic group to which she was preaching rarely got married at all. She must have hoped that one day those boys would learn to systematically subvert their own desires in the same way that her poor and wretched husband did for her. All she managed to accomplish, however, was to make them more leery of marriage—assuming that they even listened to her at all.

It is not overstating the case to say that the emergence of the dominant female is one of the greatest threats to romantic love. They exert a corrosive influence upon our inter-sexual interactions. Some of them seem fully aware of this fact so they euphemize their characteristics in the hopes of camouflaging their destructive tendencies. Instead of admitting to being controlling and passionate about placing people under their thumbs, they describe themselves as being "independent women." Yet they are not even that. In fact, independent is the last thing they are. Their every breath is taken under the auspices of finding another person to subjugate. Without pawns to push around the board of life they feel empty and worthless. They need lackeys like a church needs parishioners. They are afflicted with a ceaseless lust for power. These individuals only feel content when they are surrounded with bodies to nag, micromanage, and dominate.

Only the unwell can fall in love with a woman whose business is control. The pathology of these despotic females is so evident that it even forced one of their own, Oprah Winfrey, to address the eventuality on her website. Perhaps she was unnerved by all the excessive competition from her peers and the uncomfortable realization that she cannot remain top dog for long in a landscape littered with millions of alpha females. Whatever the cause, Dr. Phil seems to have been recruited to explore it. He did so by making practical suggestions to both parties locked in a relationship wherein the woman is master.[289] To the wives, he gave this excellent advice: "When you wound somebody's soul, it takes a long time to heal. Ask yourself, 'Do you want relief from this control problem?' If your answer is yes, make a life decision that you are through being a control freak. Control you." An excellent suggestion but one they will never follow for the reasons given above. Governing others is often the only way for them to feel safe in their environment. However, what pleased me the most about this article were the words he had for their husbands. Only a guy like Dr. Phil with his impeccable mambi-pambi credentials could get away with saying, "You need to stand up and be a man." Bravo! Unfortunately, few men watch daytime television and even fewer men ever surf the Oprah website.[290]

The true tragedy of the wife as Chieftain is that no sooner do they obtain the serf they always dreamed of than they grow to despise him.

Here as well, what society recommends is not really what anybody wants. Consider their ideal husband...the peasant who hides behind the foliage. This is a fellow who, by definition, never possesses the characteristics that most women value so I suspect that their own EoE's have made them aware of this fact. Their version of Christopher Robin [perhaps nicknamed Darby?] will whisper in their ears and steadily increase their internal sense of dissatisfaction. The sucker they have tattooed to their flank is generally one barren of wealth, courage, high status, strength, and ambition. Those traits are never present in one who compulsively licks the boots of another. Indeed, his appalling deficits were precisely the reason why he let her lead him about in the first place.

An association based upon one person trampling another thrives in few circumstances. Slaves are useful, but rarely loved. The servant is a conduit to other ends, and never an end in himself. Conversely, those who treat others as deities mock themselves, the object of their worship, the entirety of our species, and God himself; as it was the Lord who granted them the life of an independent being, a gift which they now disown. In the final analysis, the fulfillment of the Emperoress's dream only serves to solidify her perpetual bitterness.

Marriage already features a high level of systematic and structural transcendence for women so there can be no justification for their dominating every facet of a couple's private life. The notion of a wife running the home is widely accepted—even by anti-feminists like the narrator who has never argued with past mates over furniture or other household decisions. As with most other men, my sole reservation has been in relation to cost. I never have had any input regarding color schemes or feng shui or whatever other malarkey they come across in the pages of glossy publications. I have never cared about such matters and never will. Most men are the same way; although, such confessions will not satisfy the uberfemale. A husband who is only burdened by slight inequality would not be one who appeals to them.

In order to establish harmony within the home, many husbands adapt to injustice by taking a spineless stance in regards to their wives. Lawrence Henry, generally a most sensible person, believes that the key to blissful matrimony is the ability to say, "Yes, Dear,"[291] in response to spousal requests. No doubt that such an approach will be wildly cheered by female control freaks and gay master sergeants all over the world, but the truth is that love and subordination are mutually exclusive concepts. That becoming a yea saying robot would be preferable to rounding out one's days in solitude is absolutely frightening. Such an emasculated husband would be better off if he joined a cult. No matter what the level of attachment is, boundaries must remain standing between two people. Without entrenched boundaries, it is not long before a man's free time becomes devoted to ballroom dancing lessons, shoe hunting, and sitting in the fitting areas of mall boutiques. The trinity of "There is You, there is Me, and there is Us" is far more just and fair that the one embodied by the modern mantra of "Me, Me, and You're Now Part of Me." A partner should never be an autocrat. A controlling, domineering woman is a sick woman. Her requests should be denied and her company should be avoided.

What would a dominant woman think about this chapter if she got drunk one night and accidentally mistook it for an exposé in *Whip and Candle Wax Weekly*? Well, she probably would not argue with my positions but would instead attribute my views to jealousy. This emotional state is all-too-often cited by radicals in the ether within which so many foul ideas collide. Perhaps she would claim that I was envious of her finding a mannequin for a life partner. To her, my opinions stem from an unstated desire to obtain a slave for the purposes of licking my toenails. This response is predictable as deviants usually are convinced that everybody else is secretly just like them. The allegation would prove just how firmly such a woman is pinioned to the axis of domination and submission, and also how little she knows about the average man. My experiences and studies have convinced me that the great majority of men have no wish to find a woman they can control. Most of us want little more than to be with a person who will return our love.[292]

I have been in about 50 relationships of varying intensity over the years and I never once recall trying to control a woman even though most of my girlfriends were persons in whom I was emotionally vested. If their pursuits involved serious partying, infidelity, or drugs I simply broke off our affair at once. I did not waste time castigating them, harassing them or, far worse, attempting to change them. They made their choices on their own and there was nothing that I could do about it. Que Sera, Sera.

Many women seem to regard their significant others in an entirely different light, however. This makes practicing the Golden Rule in regards to the fairer sex rather futile. I have never once insisted that a girlfriend escort me on mundane errands such as shopping, getting an oil change or even moving from room to room. Unfortunately, I have found that such requests are routinely made of me. The most offensive one I ever received was when an ex asked me to go the stylist with her. It would necessitate my waiting for her in the lobby on a Saturday morning until her barber was finished. I laughed heartily and assumed that she was kidding. She was not. The stylist was only a small stopover in a day that she had taken the liberty of structuring for me.

I strongly believe that males in general are far less likely to desire a mate they can attach to their hips than are women. This is due principally to our being more solitary creatures.[293] Generally, women are more sociable and extroverted than are men.[294] Men have a much greater need for space and physical isolation,[295] and quiet times could never be had with a scampering Jeevette issuing forth a stream of constant advice. Men naturally do things on their own and are less likely to be concerned about what "people" think. Yet for women, a man is an object of status so sending him out on errands and adding him as an accoutrement at public events is of great benefit. Women are infuriated by men who avoid public displays of affection and association. They want to be included whereas men often just want to be left alone. Women are also far more suspicious of their spouse's friendships, associations, and non-sexual activities than men are of their's. They often reserve the right to approve or disapprove of their significant other's friends and this is all the more true when they possess few friends of their own.

The libertarian, or freedom loving, impulse will always be more prevalent among men. That we are far more likely to be Libertarian is an objective fact, and one that is unlikely to ever change.[296] One female writer even joked that she liked going to Libertarian functions because the ratio of males to females was "100,000 to 1."[297] For must of us who possess these inclinations, their effects are pronounced on our political and personal outlooks. To us, "Don't Tread on Me, Liberty or Death," and "Mind Your Own F*cking Business" are not merely rhetoric; they are a way of life. The problem is that when you hold such a mindset, it is very difficult to maintain a romantic relationship with the average woman. This is calamitous as a firm sense of self should never be a barrier to getting along with the opposite sex.

The fact is that nowadays, regardless of a woman's age, appearance, intelligence or supposed acceptance of equality, many continue to believe that in romantic relationships "their man" exists to serve them. This outlook is catastrophic for everyone. For the woman, their personal secretary will soon become an object of derision. The fascination she initially had for him will never last. For the aggrieved male whipping boy, a taunting, trash-talking welterweight is not a person whom his Emissary of Essence can ever accept. Even frequent sex, that quintessential tool of male motivation, cannot wholly satisfy as there are not very many men who wish to drift off each night alongside Sub-Commandante Marcos.

Dominant controlling women are a plague, and will generally be readily abandoned whenever their afflicted mate's prospects happen to brighten. That these women confuse dating and marriage with an open air experiment to morph a mature, high functioning adult into a lemming is a regrettable feature of the modern age. In the final analysis, Cardinal Richelieu had it wrong, dominance, as opposed to intellect, is the trait most unbecoming in women.

8

The Sexiest Thing a Woman Can Wear

Southern belles always get what they want. Watch and learn, grasshopper
Men love happy women. Act happy and you may discover how to be happy. Limit
yourself to five complaints and demands a day. If you're not counting, you're over the
limit.
                    —Vox Day.[298]

Life is hard and lonely; it's only natural to want someone to share the misery with.
                    —Susan Jane Gilman.[299]

What is the sexiest thing a woman can wear? Is it a jet black thong with fabric provocatively protruding from the waistline? Is it a lace Victoria Secret product that most men wish women would demand for a Christmas present? What about a human adornment such as the narrator himself fitted about them ala leotard?

All of these are legitimate guesses but they happen to all be totally wrong. There is one item that universally heightens female appeal and it is has nothing to do with apparel. A simple, but exquisite, smile upon their face is all the embellishing that they need. A smile is superior to anything else one can bedeck, bejewel or tattoo upon a female. This enhancement is a Godsend and we should thank Him for giving a little something extra to those already richly endowed. The grin is the apex of their appeal and is more enthralling than anything they can slip on in a changing room. It is something available to every woman and was available to them at birth. With the pulling back of a few facial muscles their personality can become electric. Their exaltation is a semiconductor which enlivens like a shot of amphetamine. Nothing enriches a man's spirit more than the pleasure which comes from an attractive woman actively enjoying his company.

More impressive than scanty attire or silicone implants, a smile symbolizes a good—and more importantly stable—disposition which vastly bolsters a woman's reproductive worth. It is a better proponent of her interests than diamonds. Frequent smiling increases the likelihood of her finding a man who will commit for the duration. Nothing signals "life partner" more than a content affect. Regrettably however, pleasant women are slowly becoming as rare as Oldsmobiles.

Women who possess the traits of affability, kindness and joy have practically an unbeatable advantage over their sullen, agitated, and pestilent peers. To be fair, kindness is a characteristic highly prized by both sexes.[300] In Dr. David Buss's famous cross-cultural study, the attribute was never rated lower than third in importance by both men and women.[301] From an evolutionary perspective, the advantage of kindness is obvious. Benevolent spouses contribute far more to relationships and family than do their surly counterparts.[302] No one wants to spend an eternity with a Rosie O'Donnell.

One must be realistic about their expectations in this area, however. Apart from a few mentally retarded youngsters I have encountered, few people are happy everyday. Life is a challenging and sometimes frustrating process so the person who is perpetually euphoric is downright abnormal. He or she may well be afflicted with a hormonal condition (and one that most of us wish we could acquire). Men must be aware of this as finding a woman whose countenance matches that of Glinda the Good Witch in *The Wizard of Oz* is about as likely as waking up on a cold February morning to discover that the Detroit Lions have won the Super Bowl. It will not happen.

Perfect women, like everything else rumored to be perfect on this earth, do not exist, but what a man should search for is a woman with a stable mood and an appropriate affect. The quest for these traits may seem rather pedestrian, and not the stuff of *Penthouse Forum*, but they are best strategies a man can adopt. Girls who are consistent, anchored, and respectful are the real gold in a market marbled with pyrite. Yes, such women are uncommon today but only a bona fide misogynist—unlike the ones generally labeled as such in our culture—would say that they do not exist. Those who exhibit characteristics of high reliability along with physical attractiveness are the evolutionary equivalent of Her Majesty's

Coldstream Guards. They are powerful, majestic, confident, elite, and, in contests with their peers, utterly invincible.

Of course, part of the reason these women are so sparse is that they are not single for very long. They marry early and undoubtedly choose their husbands well. These females are on the other side of the divorce rate—the lynchpins of enduring relationships that the media dare not name. I have met many such persons and the thing they usually have in common is that their last name is unfortunately preceded by "Mrs." Single men usually come across them far too late. Their fleeting apparitions serve as a reminder of what might have been. They came into this world with sturdy emotions, stalwart minds, and immutable rationality which are the finest of human gifts. These are the traits which caused us to rise from the sea and made us the rulers of earth.

We often call these women low maintenance which is an accurate description in every sense. Their pride is never sinful. They do not descend into narcissism. They understand that civilization was not created exclusively for them, and realize that one day they too will become dust. They are conscious of their humanity and do not expect others to treat them like holy artifacts. The low maintenance woman is content to lie upon humanity's historical continuum as opposed to thinking that it stopped at the precise moment in which they were born. To the men who know them, they are easy on the blood pressure and never create drama out of daily events. If one is lucky enough to be bonded to such a creature they will infuse your days with dopamine and joy.

Of course, I do not mean to imply that these women are nothing more than men in designer clothing because clearly they are not. They flamboyantly display their femininity and the way in which they differ from us is both inspiring and uplifting. In turn, they expect their men to act like men. In this way they are traditional, but modernity has soaked into their essence just as it has everyone else's. When dealing with men, they expect an equitable deal and not are interested in becoming anyone's chambermaid.

The bottom line here is that these women should be venerated and corralled as quickly as possible. The circumstances of twenty-first century western man are not ideal, so achieving a bond with a loyal, fair, and just woman is obviously the best case scenario. They are an end in themselves. My illumination of their ostentatious merits is so uncontroversial that readers may now be turning the page in anticipation of what will come next, but not so fast. Alas, there is a great deal more to discuss as content women are often besieged by their peers and our society. Here is yet another area, in which feminists and the media have joined as one – perhaps we could call their union delusionnugen—to craft a ridiculous myth about the modern woman's most lethal competitor. It seems that the male appreciation of the low maintenance woman is in dispute. Some societal commentators would argue with my view and claim that such an opinion was only held by weak men. They would counter by saying that normal men are bored and turned off by pleasant, kindly, and vanilla women. They would hold that a man's stated preference for such a person is but another indication of his endemic inferiority. Our proclivity for stability is really but a ruse. We only pretend to want a mate we can get along. What we really want is a patsy that we can subjugate. If radicals said this alone it would be unremarkable because, as we already know, they deem all male proclivities to be misguided, inappropriate, and linked to domestic violence (either in act or in fraudulently compiled statistic). Yet there appears to be a black corps of women who believe that men "like a challenge" and only respect girls who are difficult. Some even feel that we have an internal need to be trained by the women in our lives.[303]

In this regard, the deliberate skewing of logic, history, and psychology has caused me to feel more than a little sorry for those women who have been so thoroughly misled by the self-help industry. After devouring some of their books I got the distinct impression that these authors were members of an ancient race of primitives who had descended upon New York with the express purpose of occupying the offices of the major publishing houses. Once ensconced in their swivel chairs they then decided to rewrite our mores and customs with the aide of borrowed Crayola markers.

The woman's advice writer seems to have only one guideline for her fictitious nonfiction: to increase a woman's self-esteem by any means necessary. No amount of lying, schmoozing, stroking or dogmatizing is too great if it is done with the goal of glorifying Woman. As we already know, male sexuality is anathema to them; so, on those occasions when they cannot ignore our obvious tendencies or realize that they cannot be summarily dismissed with the tossing of a few isms, they respond in a predictable manner. In the four points below I describe the method by which they frequently discount a man's perspective on mating:

1.   A man's opinion does not matter as we are too corrupt
      an animal to know what we want in women.

2. We have been socialized into liking what we like and our tastes are but a reflection of patriarchal society. We are not independent agents.

3. Even if male tastes are cross-cultural they remain pathological. Just because male attitudes are ubiquitous across the species does not free them from guilt. Men should change their beliefs along with their practices.

4. "A Real Man" does not think that way. Only fascists have politically incorrect yearnings. [The unstated assumption here is that a real man likes women for the same reasons that women like themselves.]

To these authors, having a rude, crude, and bitter personality should never be held against them. They excuse their nauseating demeanor with the claim of being real. Conversely, they depict as fake the women that men easily get along with. Their unwavering displays of anger merely serve to illustrate their breathtaking authenticity.

My libertarian inclinations generally prevent me from pointing this out to strangers, but a few years ago I broke with standard practice and stuck my nose into someone else's business while waiting in line for a ticket to the movies. The girl that accompanied me left to use the facilities so I was, ala *Annie Hall*, bored and subjected to the conversation of the couple in front of me. The young lady was quite incensed and kept turning to her beau and saying, "What is the problem with men? Why can't they handle a woman's anger?" He had no answers and mournfully shook his head. He was probably just pleased that her anger was not being directed towards him on that occasion. After a few more rants I could take no more of it so I spoke up. I tapped her on the shoulder and announced, "Miss, I think I can answer your question. The reason that men are repulsed by irate women is that free-floating anger is a sign of mental instability and mental illness. That is it in a nutshell. Normal people don't get mad about nothing." I smiled after speaking but the guy gave me a dirty look and the girl immediately turned her back on me. Vignette aside, there is no reason why anyone would want to spend even a few seconds with an antagonistic, acrimonious person. For a non-desperate and non-masochistic man to accept such a woman is inexplicable.

One of the most pernicious self-help guides that I had the misfortune to read was Susan Jane Gilman's *Kiss My Tiara: How to Rule the World as a Smart Mouth Goddess*. This book was a showcase of everything wrong with not taking the opposite sex seriously. The author pretended to be devoted to furthering the interests of women but her counsel was both counter-productive and counter-intuitive. Gilman comically recommended for women to complain and b*tch more than they currently do because it gets them what they want while increasing their longevity.[304] Hmm, wrong on both counts.

Even more ludicrous were the documented fantasies of Elizabeth Hilts in her text, *Getting in Touch with Your Inner B*tch*. This sage falls squarely in the men are helots camp. Her book was a real howler and I hope that one day Barnes & Noble decides to place it in the humor section. The ramblings are supposedly a response to the "toxic niceness" that women regularly practice, but toxically nice is not the way most of us would describe the modern female. Hilts' case is made by the equating of social diplomacy with hardship and suffering. The author thinks that b*tch is a misapplied term because usually it is foisted upon women who are merely successful. Hysterically, for proof she cites the persons of Hillary Clinton, Barbra Streisand, and Gloria Steinem. All I can say in response is Q.E.D. For women, Hilts does not think there are any rules in relationships, but for men the only way to acquire intimacy is to "know and respect every aspect of [a woman's] personality. The '50s proved that." Actually, the fifties did not.

We should thank Ms. Hilts though for committing to paper the "Fueher" approach to dating. I am sure that her idea of the princely man will have no shortage of admirers among her peers as he is a piece of chattel. He will take care of the kids, cook, and conduct mate therapy in his off hours (while also being offended by sexist beer advertisements). Here he is, the woman's real man in a sparkly tampon casing.

As history has shown, the bigger the lie the harder it is to refute. So, perhaps in keeping with this eventuality, Sherry Agrov released *Why Men Love Bitches: From Doormat to Dreamgirl-A Woman's Guide to Holding Her Own in a Relationship*. For a legion of dominatrixes in waiting, Ms. Agrov has truly delivered the good news. Just in case her readers are confused by her methodology, upon finishing it they can then buy the sequel, *Why Men Marry Bitches: A Woman's Guide to Winning Her Man's Heart*. I do not know Ms. Agrov, but if she is stumped for a title for part three I think that *Crate Training for Males Both Young and Old* would be salable.

How the fairer sex could be superior to men, let alone their equal, after a few decades worth of being subjected to the woman's self-help industry is very much a mystery. Sooner or later those who follow the edicts of propagandists will be mighty depressed while all the rest of us will have to handle the fallout. And fallout there has been as one of the defining characteristics of our zeitgeist is the palpable anger that many women possess in regards men. A resentment deficit exists at this time between the sexes. The ire that women feel is not one shared by men.[305] Anger is part of the reason why so many of them invest in the dissertations of these tinfoil hat relationship theorists. Women are now the masters of their own fate, but this eventuality is unsettling. Pulp fiction disguised as psychology encourages them to blame men for whatever lonely, desperate, or deflated condition they find themselves in. And as long as men are available for blame, women are then freed from the burden of having to take responsibility for their own lives.

Of course, men have practically nothing to do with what happens to them. In their latter years these women will hopefully realize that they were the generals and that they are the ones wholly to blame for any Waterloos they blundered into. The sexual revolution, along with a gloating refusal to accept mortality and biological imperative, practically ensures that many western females will become bitter and resentful. For men, there are no easy solutions to this quandary. All we can do is navigate through their rage and hope to find the best terms for relationships that are available. Unfortunately, the process of learning nothing and forgetting nothing means that there will be no recovering from the past for most of these women. Yesteryear's disasters will carry over into the present,[306] and this development will doom all of our collective prospects.

With the boundaries between the sexes being steadily eroded and the wisdom of the past disavowed, wrathful women are more prevalent in our culture than ever before. Part confused, part depressed, and part dominatrix, these ladies can be found sulking about the landscape in our schools, businesses, streets, and shopping malls. The mega-maintenance female is one who self-destructs at the end of the day should the proper homage not be paid to her. Indigenous to her character is the need to blame external forces—generally men—for the cursedness of her daily trials. When the environment enflames her, as it so often does with every unexpected raindrop or pothole, the fool sharing her bed soon becomes the receptacle for her angst.

They search for men to act as their dogsbodies who will toil endlessly in the hopes of propping up their plummeting self-confidence. These women turn men into hunted antelopes. They have a bottomless need for emotional support and validation so any man dragooned into their service is rode hard and put away fried. Entire seasons are lost in the making of phone calls, the typing of emails, the pecking of text messages, and the uttering of reflexive compliments (which invariably fail to be appreciated).

What all men must do is to take the necessary steps to avoid getting saddled with one of these ogres. This is not easily done because, as illuminated in the last chapter, our sex drive sometimes interferes with the selection process. What should be remembered is that perfectly formed legs rapidly lose their appeal when the police show up at your door in response to a sudden and one-sided argument that the mega-maintenance female initiated with you in the middle of the night (while you were asleep).[307] No brief physical high is ever worth the grief they inflict. These ladies are roaming radioactive clouds and are beyond our help.

Narcissism cannot survive honest appraisal so genuine self-reflection is the one thing that these women will never do. Their mental states would improve dramatically if they pondered vital questions like "why do I act this way?" or "did God really make some of us for the purposes of ruling everyone else?" Their answers to these queries would be more cathartic than a morning slate of talk-shows. There would no longer be a need to charge up the entire contents of the self-help wing of the local Borders if they could meld their Me-view into a worldview. After all, one only wastes time digesting books that celebrate b*tchery and harridanism when they are incapable of acting any other way. Soon, the imbibing of *You're a Woman! Hurrah!* materials will become an ingrained habit. They will return to their pulp dealers repeatedly and slurp down a palliative distilled from self-absorption, materialism, and arsenic.

Somewhere deep within them a small bit of conscience realizes that something is very wrong with their personalities so they suppress this realism with the aide of whatever materials they can get their fingernails around. What better prescription for such anxieties than *Kiss My Tiara: How to Rule the World as a Smart Mouth Goddess*? Is not erroneous news better than the truth when the truth makes you feel you bad?

The low maintenance woman is the nemesis of these neer-do-wells. Their presence unnerves and threatens the viability of the uber-maintenance female. Non-complaining and non-delusional sisters undermine their competitiveness which means that war must be waged upon them. The mega-maintenance woman assumes that the disposition and countenance of their sunny peers is but an act. Those girls are just pretending to not suffer in the same way that they do. It is a function of their being submissives who crave the domination of men.

The women who hold out against these jaded, disconsolate attackers are quite brave in fact. Only in an atmosphere of unrelenting political correctness, in which to argue with a single woman is tantamount to arguing with all women, could such a pitiful and weak accusation be made and believed by anyone. Friendliness and optimism are not the traits of a submissive. They are live-affirming qualities and an irrefutable sign of confidence and mastery. I offer thanks to the women who reject the cult of victimology and its accompanying misery. To them I recommend the modified words of Virgil: endure, and preserve yourself for better days.

9

Zero Effort...Zero Reward

In nine cases out of ten, a woman had better show more affection than she feels.
—Aristotle.[308]

Back in the hungover and halcyon days of 2003, my friends and I used to embark on a little ritual before we entered a party, street fair, bar or gathering. Evil Chuck, Duke, and I would form a circle and bellow out the word "work" at the top of our lungs. We would turn it into a 10 syllable chant while hitting notes of every imaginable pitch. I am not sharing this recollection for the purposes of self-indulgence, but instead due to it describing aptly the attitude that we brought into social situations. Work was what we were there to do, and if the place that we entered did not contain any women then we went somewhere else. Work was an ideal description of what we did. Often, the entire endeavor was more frustrating than it was pleasurable, but we regarded meeting women to be of paramount importance.

We did not go places to people watch; we went places to woman watch. We planned on capitalizing on whatever opportunities were available. Others were networkers at events, but we were laborers. We did not quit or feel sorry for ourselves. We got done what we could. No excuses were allowed, so shut up and punch the clock. In those days, women were the cause of our every superfluous expenditure, such as new shoes, sport coats, cab rides, cover charges or the ever-increasing price of alcohol. The need to procure women was always our main concern. We all wanted someone for the long-term, just as we do to today, but if the relationships ultimately "went nowhere" then that was alright too.

Did the women we met have the same mindset? Any random female could tell you that they did not. Motivation is but another area in which the sexes diverge. Here too men are the direct sex. We go from A to B without the construction of unnecessary roadblocks. In romantic relationships, regardless of what is claimed on cable TV specials, men continue to be the ones who do the approaching and the laboring. Man proposes; Woman composes. Common sense, experience, and science all confirm that women are the coy sex. That is the way it has always been and that is the way it will always be. No amount of media features on modern dating can alter this fact. Men woo and women get wooed. No man I know believes it to be otherwise. Therefore, it is to be expected that no women would chant or make up guidelines to assist them with task fulfillment.

In dating, the labor gap between the sexes is severe. The process of picking up women is always balancing act. Men must decide who they want and then determine which of these individuals want them. The man who vanquishes self-doubt and braves rejection on a regular basis becomes an artist. The Lothario is highly esteemed by both the opposite sex and his own.

Even for the world's greatest studs, being rejected is endemic to the process. It is a business cost and intrinsic to one's dealings with women. There is no point in complaining about it because, in the words of a famous fictional Mafioso, "This is the business we've chosen." Quite so, we have chosen [and been biologically predisposed] to pursue women and will pursue them until the day we die. Only starvation or prison can derail us on our quest.

As a means to make the most of our time and energy, we predominantly seek out situations in which we are most likely to succeed. Receptivity in females is something for which most of us have become highly attuned. It is the path of least resistance but also spares us from excess pain and rejection. In my opinion, receptivity is a trait in women that is every bit as important as youth or beauty. Personally, with over three billion women on this earth who do not care about me or even know me, permanently installing one of them in my bedroom is the last thing I would ever do. The ambivalence of women is well-known to men. Girls who do not know that you exist are...well, girls who do not know that you exist. There is nothing titillating or intriguing about someone who could not care less. On a scale from 1 to 10, a 6 who loves you is worth far more than a 9 who refuses to acknowledge your presence.

In practice, most of us primarily use non-verbal factors to gauge a girl's level of interest. If a woman does not look around or ever look in our direction then she is not a good person to approach. Energy and morale can be spent better elsewhere. Waiting for a sympathetic woman and then working to obtain her is a time-proven strategy, and it is one that most men follow. Some writers on dating strategy refer to girls like these as having an "on switch." When it is in off position, in regards to relationships, one should not take it personally, but they should waste no more time on the individual. As the years go by men increasingly learn to dwell in the realm of the obtainable. Objectively speaking, no possible advantage accrues from a man liking a woman who fails to like him.

This outlook can be juxtaposed with the intuitions of the fairer sex who seem to be considerably less practical than are men. Women are far more likely to be spellbound by celebrities and others found in the ranks of the completely inaccessible. Worldly considerations are often absent from the worldview of some women. I recall meeting one who told me that "the guy I want will not worry about getting rejected. He'll walk right up to me and talk regardless of whether I pay attention to him or not." Well, good luck to her because she is going to need it. Apart from bona fide masochists, most people, indeed most mammals, consistently select the less painful of any two options. It is my guesstimate that at least 90 percent of my peers agree with me concerning their preference for receptive women, and the ones who do not will more likely resemble the Dark Prince Manson than Prince Charming.

For most of us, the "does she dig me or does she not" dilemma is not easily answered. It is a constant hurdle as women try hard to signal that they have a very, very, busy life. These messages are totally counterproductive. Unless one is an alcoholic, there does not seem to be much of a reason to date a woman who goes out every night or is busy all the time. One understands such demerits in a twenty-two-year-old, but when a woman is in her thirties there can be no justification for it. They are either party animals or neurotically fearful of being alone, and this eventuality makes them about as appealing as Gloria Allred.

If they are an outstanding prospect due to something you know about them then the only thing to be done is to put one's head down and charge forward. Only then can you find out where you stand. One learns eventually though that if every non-verbal indicator is negative then it is best to forgedaboutit. The real snafu comes when the girl is attractive enough to meet your criteria, but happens to be ignoring you. If they continue to intensely talk to their friend about absolutely nothing, most of us tend to do nothing…and the cycle repeats itself night after night.

One often espies girls out traveling in huge wolfpacks, but there is only guy I have ever known who routinely approached such roving sororities. It was none other than my ex-friend Evil Chuck who is no longer an acquaintance due his psychopathic tendencies. Always funny, always engaging, and always vicious, Chuck did things that few other men were capable of. He was the type who would wander over and tap a girl in a convoy on the shoulder and say, "Not to interrupt, but are any of you going to be talking to people outside of your clique tonight? Because if so I'm available and I give great conversation." Often he would be met with total hostility, but occasionally a woman would break and away and speak to him. Generally, despite his bravery, the tactic did him little good as someone else in the assembly would become jealous of the attention her friend received and do her best to knock Chuck out of the box.

I suppose that some girls might be tempted into thinking that Chuck was the real man among us, but he was a false god. It is not uncommon for psychopaths to take more risks than the rest of the population so his bravery was tempered by the fact that he was a devoted user of human beings. Like many anti-social personalities, he was bored and listless when he could not start trouble or be the center of attention. One of his great amusements was to call up the women he knew, set up dates with them and not show up. He found their frantic calls to him throughout the night scintillating. Many of times in which he obtained phone numbers he was near-annihilated with liquor so by the time he got around to taking them out he no longer had any idea what they looked like. His solution to the problem was to walk into the restaurant in which he was supposed to meet them and then bolt if he did not like what he saw. He also greatly enjoyed having f*ck buddies who mistook their relationship for being one of boyfriend/girlfriend. He told them anything they wanted to hear provided that they kept coming over to his apartment on the weekends. If Chuck is the epitome of modern manhood then women are in far more trouble than they know.

When a horde of men are careful to avoid psychological torment and a host of women look to put forth no effort in appearing receptive to their presence, the net result is a multi-billion dollar porn industry along with lesbian chic and online dating companies that are financially more powerful and viable than the automobile industry.

The mechanics of this dynamic—between a man searching for signs of interest and a woman devoted to not displaying them—have brought us to a very real societal impasse. In the last chapter I spoke of a rage gap, but here we have a receptivity gap.

Here too, the fissure is chiefly a result of women believing that the behaviors they prize in mates are universally shared. Our repugnant social engineers have ignored a planet's worth of evidence and misled women into thinking that men and women desire the same thing (with the obvious exception of those males who shallowly covet youth and beauty).

A man is much quicker to be disabused of the propagandistic notion that women's desires are indistinguishable from his own. Even if he is initially brainwashed for a decade or two and adopts the trappings and personality of a New Age Androgynist, he will soon fathom that his socially approved persona is completely ineffective when it comes to impressing women. After repeatedly being offered friendship instead of sex and discovering that prospective mates have rejected him in favor of what appears to be a rabble of hoodlums, he will slowly realize that he has been tricked. What women want is totally different from what they say they want.

For a woman, such an awakening is not likely. Nature will not be so obvious with its truths. The fairer sex experiences rejection less often, and, as I made clear in the preceding chapter, they have a greater propensity for being addicted to the lies of the media and self-help industry. This has caused receptivity to be a major area of discrepancy between the sexes. As a general rule, men prefer chicks that dig them while women [the rank and file at least as opposed to aspiring dominatrixes] seem to prefer men who do not know they exist. Perhaps this is an inevitable outcome of the iron law of supply and demand as women, inundated with male availability and interest, are drawn to those who give no indication of being "into to them." By definition, such men are unusual and wrongly deemed to be a notch above the rest. Soon, they seek those who will present them with a challenge and higher status is assigned to them. The television show, *Sex in the City*, featured this theme in one of its subplots. The shallow and self-indulgent main character fell head over Blahniks for a high status, high powered alpha male she dubbed "Mr. Big." His indifference to her was a major factor behind his allure. The desire for the unobtainable is a reason why so many women fall in love with married men or men who have girlfriends. The affections of these fellows are divided, and their lack of availability makes them all the more appealing.

Such prioritizing will strike men as bizarre, however. Giving extra value to the disinterested is a non-starter for the direct sex.

One influential source of guidance perpetuates this misunderstanding and actively coaches women to ratchet up their indifference. The infamous work, *The Rules: Time Tested Secretes for Capturing the Heart of Mr. Right*, advocates that women should intentionally act aloof towards the men they wish to ensnare. Even though this is the most self-defeating behavior imaginable, the authors compound the damage further by recommending that women not call their suitors back. In a society brimming with anti-stalker laws and restraining orders, this is sheer madness, and the fastest way to ensure that their readers are doomed to a monastic lifestyle teeming with cats and empty packages of Virginia Slims. Considering the incredible popularity of *The Rules*, I have often wondered how many women had their futures scuttled by its half-baked edicts.[309]

With such notions permeating the ether, it is a wonder that any men are able to detect anyone being interested in them at all. A few centuries ago, women dropped belladonna[310] into their eyes before they met men who they wanted to impress. This increased the size of their pupils, an effect which unconsciously indicated their high level of interest. This proved an effective, but physically dangerous, strategy. Women would never do the same thing today. In fact, due to the strangeness of female tactics, sometimes mixed signals have to be interpreted by men as legitimate signals.

Abandoning reciprocality as a courtship method is undoubtedly due to many women believing the "good news" rather than the truth. The opinion that, "if I like myself men will like me," is pure delusion and a recipe for slaughter. The average man sees scores of women everyday and most display little concern for him so there is no reason to notice yet another specimen fully absorbed in her own life. Like the construction barrels he sees or a fleet of gridlocked automobiles, a disinterested woman is not someone to pay any attention to. In our urban centers, one gets habituated to the sight of such creatures and there is no need to approach them.

Men and women also have a different timetable for their relations. I have met a multitude of women who think that males expect sex on the first or second date. This is patently false. What most men merely look for in their early encounters with women is that their date is interested in them. That is about it. No one expects life to mirror *Animal House*—at least, most guys do not. Again, I acknowledge that famous celebrities have an entirely different set of assumptions, but only high school guys keep score by obsessing about what "base" they have reached. The one thing we must know is that the woman likes us and that is the end of it.

Women are sometimes very hard to read, so I usually make a point of observing and listening for personality clues while I am out with them. I have jokingly referred to myself as having a Chapin Intelligence Service which feeds me a constant stream of information on the women I know, but even a guy like me, who spends an inordinate amount of time contemplating female behavior, is sometimes at a loss concerning the exact nature of their thoughts.

In a recent situation, my agents proved totally ineffectual with a girl I met at the gym. I took her out on a first date and it went rather well. I enjoyed talking to her but did not get much feedback one way or another. When I called her during the week she agreed to a second date and we went to a restaurant of her choosing. There I followed my usual strategy which is to let my date talk all night. Yet, when it was over I still did not know what to think. I walked her out. She got into her car and dismissed me with a wave of the hand. No kiss or peck on the cheek was proffered.

This meant that it was decision time. I reflected back on the evening and could not detect anything in her conversation that was revealing. I thought then of something I call "The Compliment Test" which used to be an outstanding indicator of whether or not a woman likes you. The test was a great exclusionary procedure because it is easily performed and easy to score. Basically it amounts to whether or not any of the compliments you give a girl are returned. After realizing that none of the voluminous commendations I forwarded to her were redirected back my way I knew that I had to drop the position. Two dates, two bills, and no display of affection equals an endpoint. Continuing to go out with a person like that would reduce one to the role of quartermaster.

Unfortunately, with the girl from the gym, all the leading indicators turned out to be wrong. Two weeks after our last rendezvous, she approached me on the StairMaster and asked why I had not called her. Her honesty caught me off guard. Usually, both parties play the "I don't think I know you" game after dates go awry. I stared at her vacantly and said, "Well, because I didn't think you were you interested."

"Why not?" She countered.

"I just didn't think you were." I said. I could not very well go into an explanation of the Compliment Test with her so there was nothing more to say. We were two people occupying the same physical space on two different mental continents.

Another of my favorite stories regarding this matter also comes from the gym albeit a gym that I no longer frequent. It occurred back in September of 2002 at a place called Quads—which we teasingly called Loins because it was rife with gay guys like the rest of the neighborhood where I used to live. The scenery there was horrific. Other than a few delectable post-college girls, the place was bereft of women. The only reason I went there was that it was three minutes away from my apartment.

One day, as I read on the Precor machine, I happened to see a very pretty blonde with a tantalizingly perfect body. While her curves were exceptional what really caused me to over-emit my daily quota of hormones was that she was looking at me constantly. With what followed I had little choice. I knew that I had to go over and "take a beating" or I would never forgive myself. This was no time for strategy or deep reflection. I got off the machine in a somewhat contrived manner and jumped across the ten or so yards that separated us. I immediately displayed my tremendous wit by asking, "So, did you just join up here?" My lack of "game" did not matter though as a 20 minute conversation ensued. In keeping with my basic strategy, I let her do all the talking. She relayed to me that she had just moved to Chicago from California and I remember little else that she said. All I can say for certain, based on 30 years worth of experience, is that if that girl did not dig me then nobody ever has. I asked her out at the end of her spiel and she said yes. I left that night with her phone number and the material for a month's worth of fantasies. This was textbook...or was it?

That weekend, just as I said I would, I called her. I said hello and introduced myself. She said nothing in response. I repeated "Hello! Hello!" thinking I had lost the connection. Eventually she responded and asked, "Bernard? Umm, where do I know you from?"

Now, I try not to let people see me sweat. I have a good poker face, and even have a good poker voice. How proud I would be to tell readers that her answer did not phase me but I would be lying. I waited for her to say she was kidding but she never did. I was rather stunned. Not knowing my name was not a response I expected—ever. I mumbled back my disbelief. "Really? How many Bernards does one meet in a week? How many Bernards do you know?" I wanted to hang up right away but she soon figured out who I was and proceeded to tell me about all the drinking and partying that she did the night before along with all the fun that she had had since she moved to the land of Lincoln. What a freak, I thought. Here I had gotten myself all worked up over a Paris Hilton prototype. I could tell already that she was a complete train wreck. After a half hour of her horrendous regurgitations, I got off the phone and was rather despondent. Well, maybe it was textbook because with women events almost never turn out how you think they will. This was a little too unpredictable for me though. I felt both deflated and embarrassed but knew that nothing could be done. I never called her again.

Yet that was not the end of the story. My apologies to Hunter S. Thompson, but the going got weird and I failed to turn pro. Over the next couple of weeks I saw her at the gym and made a point of waving a greeting but that was it. I never stopped to talk to her and stopped lusting after her because I was no more likely to know her in the Biblical sense then I could have known a *Playboy* centerfold. The spandex she wore continued to entice, but, like nicotine, it was a pleasure best not to consider.

By the time I had completely forgotten about her she suddenly appeared bearing gifts. It seemed that she worked for an alcohol importer and had access to free customer samples so she brought me a fifth of Polish vodka. I was astonished but thanked her warmly. We then talked for a few minutes (about her). It seemed that her life was still going swimmingly, and she told me about a few more drunken escapades. For my part, I pretended to listen and even avoided yawning. After we parted, I walked around the gym with the unopened bottle at my side which undoubtedly confirmed to many a gay fellow that I was just another obese straight man with a drinking problem.

What was I to make of her offering? There were only two possible conclusions. First, that she had liked me all along and was merely pretending to not know who I was when I called as part of some misguided and primitive strategy in which to rouse my interest. It did not work as my associations with her had, by that point, turned entirely negative. All the babbling about the Led Zeppelin lifestyle and a ton of random dudes did not help either. Perhaps all of her rock-and-roll memoirs were but a ruse to suggest to a suitor about how in demand, or high status, she was. If that was her plan it was a very dumb one. I already knew just by looking at her body how in demand she was. No clarification beyond her exquisite hips was needed. Besides, men do not care about female status, and, as a rule, we prefer our women on the inexperienced side. There are tons of strippers and prostitutes who are quite popular but nobody in their right mind wants to go out with them (for more than 15 minutes).

Her tactic quashed my interest and created a canyon of negativity from which I could not escape. At that point, I wanted nothing more to do with her. Nowadays, of course, the situation would have ended differently. I am nowhere near as proud as I once was, and no longer have the same level of expectations from women. I never apply to them the standards of honor I have for myself.

The second possible conclusion is that she did not really like me until the moment in which I stopped paying attention to her. Initially, she could have seen or felt how much I liked her and then been completely turned off. Well, this too is a plausible scenario although it would undoubtedly strike the inexperienced man as being a sick one. It is in keeping though with the female desire for a challenge.

Either explanation is possible but I happen to know now that she did like me because she followed up the first gift with another fifth a month later. Again, I was cordial and grateful as I am unaccustomed to receiving presents, but it was irrelevant because I no longer had any interest in her. As an epilogue to the story I again ran into her in 2004. It was near my new condo which is far to the south of Dickville. She was standing in front of me in the checkout line of a supermarket. She turned around and called my name, but I had no idea who she was. She had dyed her hair dark brown, yet her body remained immaculate. We talked about nothing and I never saw her again. Her recollection of me on that occasion suggests though that one of the two scenarios indeed was correct. Oh well, I tried—at least I did in the beginning.

In the final analysis, her adopting a foolish strategy that either of her grandmothers would have been far too smart to attempt thwarted any possibility of romance between us. For her, like it does with so many other women, the refusal to express interest doomed our chances.

Please realize though that the purpose of this book is not for me to play consigliere to the modern women, but if I were asked to help them—I probably wouldn't—but if I had to I would identify the effort deficit as being the area most in need of amelioration. Women should act receptive to men whether they are interested or not. By being reflexively receptive, women allow themselves more opportunities in the long run. It enables them to continue to be the choosers as a man will rarely make sacrifices for a woman who ignores him. Showcasing affinity is the most effective way to land a man and keep him. Of course, no females will ever ask me for my advice. Why would they when they can always purchase a self-help book which will assure them that they never are to blame for the predicaments in which they find themselves.

10

Let's Not Make a Deal

Midway through Lauren Fox's first novel, the book's heroine, Emily, envisions herself as an exhibit at the local natural history museum: an unhappy mannequin lounging in an apartment-diorama titled "Twenty-First-Century Psychological Mess." The exhibition card would read: "This species of American female was known for muddling her love life beyond repair. Fortunately, she did not reproduce."
—Michiko Kakutani[311]

What bountiful days these are for women who exude loyalty, charm, kindness, and a plantation full of femininity because most of their peers have effectively abandoned the reproductive battlefield. For these types, finding a man has never been easier as the average modern woman is incapable of competing with them.

As for the modern woman, well, as General Chuikov said of the German lines in the last days of the Second World War: "Today is a great holiday for my country. How it is for you over there it is rather difficult to say."[312] It seems as if contemporary females are following a master [sic] plan which enables them to suppress their natural splendor while promoting the traits that most of their predecessors would have been ashamed to possess. By exhibiting dominance, self-absorption, corpulence, and rampant materialism they have forced themselves to find a man who will overlook what is unquestionably a bewildering multitude of flaws. In short, without realizing it, they have drawn up an order that can only be filled by a complete loser, a sucker or a closeted homosexual who is in need of a beard with which to mask his lifestyle. We can all agree that theirs is a position in which we would never want to be placed.

Were they not cursed with empowerment and a culture incapable of questioning them, they would realize that advanced age mightily decreases their attractiveness and that the time for being choosy went out with the big hair of the eighties. Their imitation self-esteem will not allow for the abandoning of the ideal and the act of reconciling themselves to what is possible. For many an older woman—although much of what I say below is not exclusive to them—it is wise to take what they can get. They must rise above their emotions and make a deal, but this is something that their egos will not allow them to do. What is the root of their paralysis and their concomitant refusal to adapt to new situations? In my view there are five basic reasons for their maladaptive response to changing conditions.

I. Unrealistic Expectations:

The first obstacle to the satisfaction of many women is their own inaccurate perception of self. An inflated sense of personal worth clearly sabotages any attempt to find happiness, and this will be true in a variety of circumstances even those outside of the reproductive context. The only way to know if what you want is obtainable is to recognize what your own personal strengths and weaknesses are. This is obvious, but most of the modern women that I know seem to have a quixotic opinion of their standing with the opposite sex.

Part of this is due [once again!] to a staunch refusal on the part of feminists, the media, and individual women to consider the dynamics of male sexuality. Do we fetishize body parts? Yes. Is body more important than face to most of us? Yes. Do we care about a woman's status or wealth? No, such issues are about as pertinent as the weather forecast for Borneo. Yet, a failure to contemplate the psychology of the opposite sex is a one way ticket to Waziristan, but that is exactly the kind of mindset that many older women have for themselves.

Retreat is impossible, the future is bleak, and the past is gone forever, and it is all a result of their finding objective self-appraisal too painful to initiate. After all, sterile evaluation is unromantic and emotional involvement in judgments is something of which women are today taught to be proud. Creating a ledger, either in print or in one's imagination, which tallies up strengths and weaknesses is not something that the average woman will ever consent to do. Yet their refusal costs them. I agree that comparing oneself to others, particularly those who are more talented than you, can be a painful business (assuming it is done properly), but it is the only way in which we can properly align our own standards to those of the world around us.

Women would be wise to follow a standard tactic that is often used in poker when you get dealt a decent, but not great, hand. You bet out to see where you are at, and then make your decisions from there based on what you know about the game conditions and the style of the other players. A feeler bet or two, or in this case several feeler attempts at self-examination, would do immeasurable good for the average woman; particularly as the stakes are far higher than they are for a rounder.

A coworker I once knew perfectly epitomized this intelligence failure. There was a major disconnection between what she took her to be her worth and what it actually was. She used to come into my office every morning and tell me woeful tales from her love life. I felt rather sorry for her because it seemed like she was living among a group of people whose language she could not understand. She would mention to me guys at work that she wanted to date and she seemed to be the only one who did not know that they would never have anything to do with her. I often had to suppress the desire to come out and say what I was thinking as she overweight to the point in which many of her facial features were no longer definable. Her waist sagged down into a large pooch which then sagged further down until it met her quadriceps.

Of course, she did have a very good personality. She possessed positive attributes such as intelligence, humor, reliability, and a good work ethic. These traits make for an excellent friend, but, when it comes to male sexual attraction, they never outweigh obesity. Finally the tragedy of her stories got to me so I asked her to tell me what qualities she was looking for in a man. She gladly consented and went on like an auctioneer for about ten minutes. She had all kinds of expectations.

When she was done I asked her, "Now what do you have to offer a man?" She turned pink and was silent for over a minute. She then mentioned her fine personality, good family, and that she was a truly good person. She was right on all counts, but what she said was only relatively material to the question I asked. The type of man who embodies all the attributes she listed is very rare. I know this because I certainly did not meet them. Therefore, in all likelihood, there was zero chance of this Prince Abdullah ever appearing in her life. Rich, handsome, youthful, and romantic men, even when found outside of their natural habitat which is between the covers of a Harlequin romance novel, generally avoid girls who could suit up for the New York Jets. Luckily, my friend eventually got married…to a total schlep. Maybe she was listening to me after all.

By pretending that their ideal man is someone who will fall in love with them due to factors that have nothing to do with lust, many women delude themselves and thereby diminish their chances of being happy. Why would the average man subject himself to a juridical charnel house by marrying a woman who makes him cringe every time she takes her clothes off? He would not. A woman's appearance can never be discounted due to factors that *they* think men should appreciate. The supposition that we will ignore the same stimuli which enraptured males since the beginning of time is preposterous. If this were true then more men would marry collies, yaks, or lamas as there would be no copulative expectations and it would have the added advantage of saving money during the dissolution process (not to mention the obvious loyalty dividend). That women neglect to examine themselves in light of male desire is disastrous and self-defeating.

II. *"He'll Love Me No Matter What."*

Will he? Of course not. Just as with women, men have certain requirements that are near universal and they will not be modifying them due to a person coming along with a kind heart—see the opinions of young Master Robin on this subject in Chapter 6. Reality aside, many women indulge themselves into thinking that there is a man out there who will love them for, or in spite of, their flaws. Once he accepts them he can then be relied on to put up with absolutely anything.

Countless times have I heard women utter the phrase, "If he loves you then he won't have a problem with _____". In the blank space all sorts of major deal breakers accumulate such as obesity, alcoholism, mental illness, wastrel spending, and even infidelity. This kind of magical thinking is fueled by a culture that has no respect for its male members. It is rather appalling, but let us take up the burden of rejoinder anyway and give the position the respect it is not due.

Why might a man love a woman who is a mess? Well, they could be one of the losers or suckers that I mentioned a few paragraphs ago or they could be a rescuer type. I have met quite a few of these fellows over the years. Their goal seems to be saving a basket case wherever they should find one. When they see an unmade bed they immediately go into maid mode and begin cleaning the sheets of stains and debris. Yes, this breed is in circulation but they are far from being representative of the average man. So, aside from these carnival act types, there does not appear to be many men who will sign up for a project to which there is no likely solution.

I recall the time in which I wrote a couple of pieces concerning marriage and the need for modern men to have a presumption against it.[313] The response from many women was vehement to say the least. Generally, these individuals were on a first name basis with delusion. One even labeled my stance as being "selfish" due to my recommendation that men should ask themselves, before committing, what they expect to gain from a modern union. I guess we are not supposed to be asking any questions at all. The fairer sex would prefer our happily signing on the dotted line and eschewing all examination of later effects. Man as Sacrifice has become the basis of an entire culture.

Again, what brings about man's love for woman is rooted in biological factors. Once that initial spark occurs he may then become attached and devoted to his mate for a variety of reasons but what is essential to remember is that this occurs *after* the initial chemical reaction made it possible. An unattractive woman cannot suddenly become viable based on personality alone. A minimal of physical criteria must be met first or she will never get her foot in the door. No amount of charm can override the ennui caused by a flat bottom and a concave chest. When a woman tells another, "The man who loves you won't care about your weight," she lies to both herself and her "friend." The truth is that the man she takes an interest in will invariably fail to reciprocate because human beings are not automatons. They do things which advance their needs, and that is a very good thing. If we followed any other mandates we never would have survived.

III. Chasing the Dragon: The Bigger, Better Deal.

Countless women have willingly estranged themselves from stable, loving, caring, productive, and competent men because the blokes lacked some idealized and/or ethereal quality. Perhaps for vague and fleeting reasons, they did not qualify as "soul mates." Girls envision a perfect man who comes along and embodies a wondrous mélange of masculine and feminine traits. These consummate characteristics will enable them to become immaculate companions, lovers, fathers, and providers. However, for many women once a man makes his mortal tendencies known he must be unceremoniously discarded. There begins an unvarying cycle which may continue until death as no man will ever meet the conditions of such unrealistic criteria. Women really believe that a man who is the "complete package" will come around eventually, and, unlike with Santa Claus, whether they have been naughty or nice will not matter. He will be above banal concerns like physical appearance and have everything in common with her including a love for network television shows, a love for shopping, and an appreciation of diverse sweets. He will cherish her and respect her in every sense while expecting nothing in return. Just being with her will be good enough for him because…because she is a woman.

As we all know, no such men exist. How paradoxical it is that the status of men in society has never been lower but women's expectations from them have never been higher. What women want from their suitors is beyond the scope of human possibility as it is an assignment which could only be completed by a Cyborg. Even if a woman finds a man devoid of interests and who exists for her alone, such an automaton will never really be human. He will be a Replicon straight out of the movie *Blade Runner*. The quest for "perfection" will result in the weeding out of equals, and our equals are the members of the opposite sex for whom all of us should pay the most attention. A preference for phantasmagoric apparitions is a mug's game.

Unbeknownst to the modern woman, even as they prowl around for upgrades their value declines steadily. Upon entering their thirties they will soon find that the men who once wanted to marry them are now long gone. Or, as Danielle Crittenden brilliantly put it: "But if a woman remains single until her age creeps up past thirty, she may find herself tapping at her watch and staring down the now mysteriously empty tunnel, wondering if there hasn't been a derailment or accident somewhere along the line. When a train finally does pull in, it is filled with misfits and crazy men…The sensible, decent, not-bad-looking men a woman rejected at twenty-four because she wasn't ready to settle down all seem to have gotten off at other stations."[314]

This will not occur to most women. Business will be too brisk and they might be having too much fun to contemplate the future. They look forward to the Bigger Better Deal: a dreamy man who will be a tremendous improvement over past boyfriends yet one made of flesh and blood. He will be a hero on a white horse who will be loyal, devout, exciting, handsome, wealthy, and romantic. With such a demigod on the way why should they settle for the mundane? Once again, they deserve the best because...they are women. Has the dysfunction of empowerment ever been more evident?

Well, it does not take much of an imagination to guess what the future will bring. Society supports women both in their hyper-choosiness and hyper-self-esteem which turn out to be a twin axis of personal destruction. Perfection, as I noted earlier, is but a chimera. All of us are flawed (although some to a greater extent than others). None are more disfigured than those who think they are worthy of the sublime. Given that these women are opposed to objective reflection concerning their own worth, their prognosis is quite bleak.

Soon they will discover that the window of time is more fleeting than they ever anticipated. They never will get married because they are incapable of making a deal. Suitable men are rejected continuously until a girl's stock has fallen to the level of Enron, and no analyst in the world will have anything to do them. The final outcome for these women is not a treaty or even an armistice, it is unconditional surrender. The battle will be lost and only smoke, corpses, and memories will remain. Like Napoleon, they will be relegated to a Saint Helena and be left with only domestic servants to dominate. With bitterness rich and palpable, most men will avoid their company at all costs.

The media will not write any exposes about these ladies, but they will play up the idea that the woman who gets married in her prime is a sell-out. This is a direct misrepresentation of the truth as the woman who "settles" early is actually the one who is very wise. She has made a deal from a position of strength, and recognized that finding a stable, affectionate, caring, loyal, and marriage-minded man in the current environment is a lucky windfall. Their sisters once had a chance to take such men but turned them down to await the arrival of their Zeus/Hera who, in the end, turned out to be just another figment of mythology.

IV. Cost-Benefit Analysis.

Romantic relationships are all about negotiation as opposed to romance. Fantasy is something that belongs between one's ears and should never form the basis of worldly expectation. The person we end up with is someone with whom we made the best deal possible. They provide us with the traits that we must have while exhibiting few of the attributes that we cannot tolerate. Your narrator has three basic needs in a woman: physical attractiveness, affability, and average intelligence. Even though these parameters for exclusion are rather lenient, it has been a serious challenge to find a woman who meets them. My current girlfriend is totally satisfactory but finding her was quite fortunate. I know that should she leave she will not be easy to replace.

For the modern woman, the fable of the soulmate is a major obstacle that must be overcome. What they do not seem to understand is that most soulmates happen to be members of your own sex. The person you have the most in common with is generally a coeval. This is particularly true with men as there are few women who passionately share male interests.

Automobiles are an example of this. Numerous men are infatuated with them but never in my 37 years have I come across a female car enthusiast (but I acknowledge that a few do exist). Another example can be found with sports. In the Introduction I alluded to a fanatical female hockey supporter I used to know but her kind are as rare as straight male fashion designers. With sports, when a team wins a lot they become popular and one of the signs of their newfound status is the sudden growth of their female fan base. This was the case with the Chicago Bulls in the nineties as it seemed like every girl I met was the "world's biggest Bulls fan," although women were the first to abandon them when they began to lose. They even used to refer to the players by their first names as if they were personal friends. How often I heard the phrase, "Michael and Scottie" but once Jordan left, female support evaporated quickly. Even with their recent success, I have not met any girls who claimed to be major Bulls fans since 1998.

I can say the same thing about the Bears as their 2007 Super Bowl appearance coincided with the sudden emergence of thousands of female devotees. Where they were when the team was merely good is not known. It is true that there are hundreds of women in my city who love the Cubs, but whenever one speaks to them they have little of substance to say about their play. The main focus of the female Cubs fan seems to be on drinking and having fun at Wrigley Field. Few know much about the players or the team's record.

Small group loyalty, an appreciation for detail, and a love for specifics and strategy are traits more ubiquitous to men than women. That most men have far more in common with their friends than they do their wives or girlfriends is a truth so self-evident that it deserves only passing comment. One's brothers not only have similar interests, but they also rarely judge or nag. Furthermore, they never invite their relatives to stay in your house, and will no longer remain your brother if they continually try to wheedle you out of money.

Male friendship is an end in itself and the boundaries between liking someone and lusting them are never crossed—apart from in the hills of Hollywood when they are putting together a film like the previously mentioned, *Chasing Amy*. I have established the fact that our reproductive engines may or may not be directed towards those with whom we feel personal affinity, but any such bond, if it occurs, is formed long after the initial jolt of electricity has been chemically transmitted.

For their part, many women do not take this into account and are completely mystified by the nature of male friendship as they find bewildering our need to spend time with our brothers. They wonder why the hours spent with our significant other are not fulfilling enough. Well, they are but only on television or in the other regions of mass produced fiction. Rather than castigate and condemn male friendship, most women would be better off trying to emulate it.

The successful and self-actualized woman understands that the male they find will not be a Me, Junior. She accepts that their relationship will be based on the concept of "there's you, there's me, there's us" rather than one formed between apocryphal soulmates. What we call "the one" should be the person who best fits our needs and desires. He or she will offer us the most benefits with the least amount of costs. Bliss and contentment are rooted more in logic and reason than in anything else. Certainly, my definition of a joyous pair-bond will not be enshrined on a Valentine's Day card but it is far more reflective of truth than the hocus-pocus which most women believe at the present time.

What then is the road to interpersonal happiness? It is the ability to conduct cost/benefit analysis in any given situation. Cost/benefit analysis focuses on one's needs in the context of how a real life person can meet them. It grants that "the other" is an independent human being who is appreciated for their own unique merits.

V. Accepting the Cards You Have Been Dealt.

Knowing ourselves and knowing others is the surest road to contentment. Ignorance, like cocaine, can only produce short-term highs and its after-effects are never worth the initial thrill we receive. Accepting who we are and identifying the type of person that we deserve is what results in enchantment and felicity. This can never come about in those whose inflated self-worth is a product of self-deception.

What is the best definition of happiness? It is the act of being pleased by what you can get. Should the reader doubt it then I advise him or her to take a look around at the people they know. We know many individuals who are pleased with their lives. Their appearance, mood, and actions tell us all that we need to know. Joy is the inevitable outcome of accepting the hand you have been dealt.

Wealth, legions of admirers, and endless free time are aspects of existence that most of us will never know, but reaping the harvest of what is available is the key to fulfillment. Holding onto our resentments is like drinking a glass of poison every day and expecting the other person to die.[315] A better practice is to survey what is around you and cherish all that you have been given.

When I was an intern at a mental hospital in 1995 I used to ask some of the patients a fairly simple question. What if you were to receive 25 million dollars in exchange for the removal of every person that you know from the planet? Would it be a worthwhile transaction? Not one of them, despite a plethora of problems that most of us can only imagine, said that they would accept such an arrangement. If mental patients have the ability to see the value of their social connections then what does that say about normal people who continue to hold out for the Bigger, Better Deal? Obsessing over the unobtainable is a mental state from which endless toxins emit. It is best to remember that none of us deserve anything, and that we are fortunate to have what we have. What more do we need?

Being appreciative gets easier the more you practice it. Your narrator was not raised to think in such a fashion, and was not born with an appreciative disposition. But upon accepting real life, instead of the hunt for utopia, I quickly became more healthy, generative, and insightful. I now see women for what they are: a wonderful enhancement to life. They should never be regarded as the main purpose for drawing one's breath. The change in mindset has been very liberating. In relationships, I am content to enjoy whatever time I spend with the fairer sex. I realize that I am not the only one who sets the course for my life. There are many events and outcomes that are completely beyond my control, and acknowledging this has been a relief. Provided that I make sound decisions in the present, I have no reason to fear for the future.

I have been seeing the same girl for over a year, and while I do love her, should she break up with me, I will not despair over lost time.

The months we have had together were not wasted as her presence has made my days more enjoyable. She, like most of the girlfriends I have had in the past, has added irreplaceable texture to my life and I thank her for it.

VI. A Formulaic Interlude.

For the visual learners among us, I will sum up the discussion with a formula. Let us graphically showcase the hell that women's high expectations make of their lives:

> Women today have far greater expectations in regards to prospective suitors than their predecessors had. When this is juxtaposed with the essential and unchanged nature of man it results in frustration becausethe romantic desires of individual women cannot, by definition, be met.

↑ Expectations + Unchanged Male Nature= Unmet Expectations.

> When their refusal to consider the male perspective, along with their aversion to dispassionate self-analysis and their endemic belief in their own superiority, meet the actual interests of men the inevitable result is their own disaffection.

↓ Knowledge about Men + ↓ Knowledge of Self + Assumed Supremacy = Disaffection.

> Age and bitterness then depreciates the value of the average women.

↑ Age + ↑ Bitterness = ↓ Female Value

> Despite the devoted efforts of every media outlet, older women soon discover their declining worth, and their reaction to this eventuality is non-adaptive. Rather than blame the social engineers who misled them in the first

place, they choose to blame men for being the way that males have always been. They become depressed and vengeful towards the direct sex.

↓ Value =↑ Rage Towards Men

Like a dictator thrust into exile, many women are left with decades on their hands in which to reflect upon what once was. Unlike your average man, they were societies' queen and darlings, and no rulers can ever accept diminished status with aplomb. They will not negotiate or adapt, as those actions are beneath them; instead, they will plummet into the abyss. For them it was always everything or nothing…which now means that they have nothing. Their attitudes will deteriorate along with their appearance. Disadvantage then feeds upon itself as their personalities become less and less palatable to the opposite sex. Their inappropriate expectations were the cause of the quagmire in which they now find themselves.

Inflexible Expectations + ↓ Morale + ↓ Receptivity = ↓ Male Interest

Their dreams have become inverted. Rather than possess a secure love that would be the envy of their peers, the barren older woman now becomes an object of pity. Her greatest goals—being esteemed by society, establishing a permanent sense of connectedness, and finding an everlasting love—can never be realized. Devoid of fertility (a pulsating representation of "the force that through the green fuse drives the flower,"[316]) along with the ability to settle, they are now finished. Their emotional fecundity has vanished as well. They will succumb to depression and eventually despair. The queen has been checkmated, and the Checkmate of the Queen is what we shall term this scenario. The phrase is an accurate reflection of the new rules that our society has crafted for the fairer sex.

↓ Male Interest + Zero Fertility + Despair = The Checkmate of the Queen.

They will refuse to acknowledge that their fate was of their own choosing. They were empowered, they were the ones who called the shots, and yet they were the ones who lost the battle. Had the decisions made in their Halcyon days been informed and generative, their end would have been radically different. Like Icarus, they flew too close to the sun, and, like Napoleon, their final days will be spent in painful obscurity.

11

Blockade Running: The Foreign Bride

Anywhere is Better than Here.
                    —The Replacements.[317]

These are not American women…They do not care about your age, looks, or money.
And you are not going to have to talk to them for half an hour and then have your
testicles handed back to you! Let me tell you: over here, you're the commodity; you're the
piece of meat. I've lived in St. Petersburg for two years, and I wouldn't date an
American woman right now if you paid me!
                    —Words of a Tour Guide in Russia.[318]

Who better to begin our discussion with than with my legendary friend, Johnny Q-Bacca. Mr. Q-Bob is not a subtle man. Two years ago, after four decades of living in Lady America, he was suddenly offered an opportunity to relocate to South Korea—ostensibly for the purposes of work. Upon arriving in Seoul, he spent several months steeped in joy, vitality, Soju, and his own swelling sense of gratefulness for the young Asian women he was able to devour. He flew back to O'Hare drained but inspired. Upon his return he quickly became disillusioned. In Korea his prospects with women were limitless, but now he is just another member of a domestic legion of "not good enoughs." He wears his dejection like a goat-tee. The other night, he mumbled mournfully into several Double Diamonds about obesity rates, yuppies, and materialism for over three hours. By the time we left the bar he vowed to take his action elsewhere, preferably to Central or South America.

Concerning dissatisfaction with the western lifestyle, it is hard to know just how representative someone like Johnny Boy is. Certainly, he is far from being alone in his dissatisfaction with American women. More and more westerners have gone overseas on a quest for female companionship of one kind or another. The desires these men have are not very complicated. They would like to procure a woman for the long-term who is both attractive and appreciative. Their overall perception of our own women is that most of them are looking to mold their husbands into house cats.

As a testament to this, the global internet dating scene is booming.[319] There are over 200 types of dating service companies[320] which pair American males with foreign females and have names like Cherry Blossoms, Mail Order Brides, A Foreign Affair, and T.L.C. Worldwide. The main areas from which they come are Southeast Asia, Russia, and Central America. Each year it is estimated that between 6,000 to 8,000 American men[321] marry foreign women; although, as many as 15,000[322] foreign born women meet our citizens via the aide of these brokers.

Undoubtedly, going to such strange lengths to find a woman will strike many people as being quite odd; however, it is a decidedly American practice whose tradition dates back to the early eighteenth century.[323] What is important about the subject is that its increasing popularity tells us much about the relations between men and women in this country because, unlike a few hundred years ago, there is technically no "shortage" of women in the United States. For men to look elsewhere illustrates the extent to which men are dissatisfied with the modern western woman.

Regardless of the ease with which one can travel to Guadalajara or Cartagena, flying to foreign lands and negotiating miles of red tape seems extreme to most people. Therefore, asking what comparative advantages foreign brides offer over indigenous women is certainly legitimate. From what I have read and been told, the upside is significant.

As I have already noted, in our country, female status has run amok due to our habit of treating women more like idols than human beings. A man's target constituency offers them little but asks for everything. In the next chapter we will see why today's marriages are unions in name only. *The Road to Serfdom* is more than just the title of a magnificent book, it aptly embodies a man's experiences upon the road to engagement and marriage. Servitude is integral to being a good husband. The beau must follow commands and reply to them with, "yes, Dear," "where's my honey-do list?" and "Thank you, mam, may I have another?"

The idea of equality, quid pro quo, and tit-for-tat is now culturally anathema. Like Jack Nicholson's character in *Batman*, today's husband turns over a card and finds that it is he who is the joker. His wife's emotional and financial reciprocity is an unknown and independent variable which is wholly dependent on her individual discretion. Giving back to him is optional and done on a case-by-case basis. To be a suitable husband one must provide economically, provide emotionally, provide physically, and follow these heroic acts up with the Houdini trick of fulfilling his wife's every fantasy. Such expectations are ridiculous and more in keeping with a group of deities who dwell upon Olympus rather than in Seattle.

A bond with an American man offers a foreign women a great deal. They can move to a land in which the drinking water is always clean, where the homes sparkle with constant electricity, and where practically every child and mother survives the birthing process.

Most western women are not grateful for any of these eventualities. They take them as givens. The decadent female is like a gigantic Pac-Man whose mission is to consume material items, food, and entitlements. The American woman is largely ignorant of the suffering of her non-western peers. They take for granted that their own lives will continue indefinitely, but view the right to abort the lives of their offspring as being a central tenet of good government.

By looking to a foreign country a man seeks to run the blockade. His goal is to find a woman who has not been debauched and denatured by our culture of female supremacy. He longs for a woman who is not contaminated by state mandated privilege, self-obsession, and ill-obtained self-esteem. In many countries, one's daily survival is something that is never guaranteed and their female citizens are more likely to be religious than our own. They would scoff at the notion that we have been placed upon this earth to be major players in a cosmic empowerment and enrichment scheme. Foreign women intuit that work is a prerequisite for both existence and happiness. As the clever Fred Reed pointed out in regards to Mexican women, "shopping does not give meaning to their lives."[324]

What the groom receives from the imported arrangement is considerable. They often procure women who are younger and more attractive than the ones they could obtain at home. The personality upgrade cannot be underestimated either. Acquiring a wife who is excited about being a mother is also a major improvement. Who needs a brooding Hamlet who laments the inevitable sacrifices and changes in lifestyle that children bring about? Happiness is contagious and finding an agreeable person to round out one's days with is an end in itself. In light of the American woman's current mindset, the odds seem quite favorable that one will find a higher quality mate elsewhere.

In return for this new and prosperous life, the husband of the foreign bride hopes that his love will be appreciative for what she now has. This is quite possible as she came from a society in which the word tradition was not synonymous with hate. What he provides to her with will be a major improvement over what she had previously. The husband as soulmate is probably not a role that ever occurred to her; the husband as guarantor of survival could well be enough. Men in the non-western world are still deemed the appropriate complement to the opposite sex as they are not expected to be therapists, wet nurses or maids. Masculinity is not seen as a viral condition or a problem in need of a radical cure. These girls desire security and a future, and that is usually what they receive upon saying "I do."

A great many testimonials illustrate that these marriages often end happily. One fellow noted: "Dating or being married to an American woman is like driving a beat-up

Ford Escort. If you are only used to driving a beat-up Ford Escort, then you have no idea what it feels like when you drive a Bentley or Ferrari. You need to at least test-drive a Ferrari, so you'll have a reference point on what a real car feels like."[325]

Most of us will have to take his word for it, but our own women are well aware of the possible advantages offered by the foreign bride. They are smart enough to be threatened by what they see coming over the horizon. The last thing they need is somebody arriving and destroying their market price. The best comparison of the two female entities stems from the 1970s with the foreign bride being a Toyota and the indigenous female being a Ford LTD. The Toyota was a new competitor who outclassed the Ford in every way yet also managed to be a cheaper product. Our own vehicles were so cumbersome, poorly engineered and defective that Detroit had to adapt or face extinction. The modern western woman, however, is not known for her adaptive capacity.

Therefore, the foreign born woman is Satan to American females. The usurper's refusal to subjugate her biological imperatives must greatly perplex our indigenes. These women are poorly educated in comparison to their western counterparts, but yet have the good sense to save money, avoid promiscuity, and to realize that obesity is a state of decline which should be avoided. Most imports are appallingly resistant to the allures of the mythic career, and do not wish to forsake children and family on an unholy crusade to work oneself to death. Of course, it really would be difficult to sell the idea of labor as glory to any other species of mammal on this earth. The American woman is undoubtedly astounded that anyone would want such a primitive, but, due to their belief in male inferiority, they will refrain from examining the subject. Why should they when they can explain it away with their preconceived notions of male insecurity and limited cognition?

Naturally feminists, who wish men to be miserable at all costs, condemn the practice of males attempting to limp around the sistahood's Maginot Line. As always is the case in regards to male prerogative, they explain the fascination with aliens as being a sign of pathology. Here is what one had to say about the phenomenon: "The Internet has created what bell hooks aptly titled a 'neocolonial cyber-space.' Mail order brides are bartered and traded women, attractive because of their submissive nature, their natural beauty, and their potential naiveté. An American man, perhaps disillusioned with American women, turns to the Internet to find a woman who will fit these requirements. Thus it seems that the problem might not rest squarely in the proliferation of mail order bride Web sites. Perhaps the source of the problem is the motivation of a man who seeks to buy a bride."[326] Yes, the man who wishes to find a kindly, trustworthy, and attractive bride is a person who we all must condemn.

We should not be surprised by such a stance as there has never been one inter-sexual conundrum in history for which feminists have failed to blame men. Objecting to any aspects of female behavior is a thoughtcrime in contemporary America. Another feminista observed, in regards to a law that I will soon discuss, "Obviously this is a very important law and we are glad it was passed. **But does anyone else see something really really wrong with men *buying* their wives online?** And don't even get me started on the hideously violent and disempowering relationship between the Western man and the *third world woman* subject/object and stuff (clearly I have no patience today.)"[327] Undoubtedly, she will have no patience today, no patience tomorrow and no patience forever. Sometimes I pity the feminist as the truth never seems to ever fit into their ideological template.

There are a great many things to say in response to the above two quotations. First, men who marry foreigners do not "buy" their wives. The women are not paid for, and the companies who profit from the arrangement promise their customers nothing. All they do is set up an opportunity whereby individuals can meet. That is it, no imperialism required. Second, women voluntarily explore these opportunities and are not coerced into them. They do so because it is in their best interest which is in keeping with the behaviors of all psychologically healthy individuals. Had this allegation been made in regards to a fictional Afghanistani or Sudanese dating service there would be some merit in it, but the majority of the women American men pursue are from Russia, Mexico, Columbia, and Peru. They are not coming from countries in which women are enslaved by the laws of Sharia. They are free individuals who make free choices, but the notion of people making choices for themselves is something that has always infuriated feminists.

For many women scratching out an existence on the equivalent of $30 a month, the idea of marrying an American man portends robust health and survival for herself and her children. Given the socioeconomic circumstances of those who live in poorer countries, moving to this land of bounty has always been a positive expectation play. One commentator noted that their interest in American men goes far beyond dollars and cents: "While there is little demand among foreign men for American wives, there is a huge demand for American husbands. Thousands of foreign women are seeking husbands in the international bride market. Most of these women seem to prefer an American man if they can find one. American men are highly sought after because, compared with (what these women know about) the men in most countries, American men simply make better husbands."[328] If feminists actually cared in the least about their sisters then they would rejoice in the improved quality of life that the foreign bride obtains. Their lack of empathy is entirely predictable as it is in keeping with their nature.

I have already torched the argument that men objectify women so there is no reason to bore readers with a restatement of it here. All I will say is that when extralocal females arrive on our shores, they are not treated as objects because the state grants them a myriad of rights. How could it be any other way? Both parties in the arrangement get something out of it, but anything desired by men is deemed suspect by feminists.

Further blurring this picture are people like my former physician. She was born and raised in India, but moved here in the mid-nineties. If I asked her out would I have objectified her or fostered the injustices of colonialism? I suppose her making about 100 grand more than I do would not have mitigated the damage caused by my query. The idea that I would be somehow exploiting her by dating her is risible, but feminists make no distinctions between thoughts, words, and acts so I am sure that they would attribute my doing so as a desire to misuse people of color. Perhaps the doctor's prolonged exposure to my amorous company would have resulted in the reformation of the British Raj or the Belgians re-invading the Congo.

No matter how fallacious the claim, when it comes to harridans in self-imposed distress the government always finds the time and budget to placate them. Research regarding extraterritorial nuptials was initiated by Robert J. Scholes and funded by the Immigration and Naturalization Service. Scholes arrived at various conclusions and some of them were positive—such as the rate of divorce for foreign bride marriages being less than that of the rest of the nation—but some were quite negative such as his statement: "The true character of the men is well expressed in Glodava and Onizuka (1994:26), who note, 'those who have used the mail-order bride route to find a mate have control in mind rather than a loving and enduring relationship.'"[329] I find this statement, as applied to men in general, to be totally absurd.

The act of partaking in marriage, especially in the United States, makes clear to any suitor that he is embarking on a serious undertaking, and one from which there will be no easy extrication. The attitude of the government ensures that this arrangement, one way or another, will be an *enduring* relationship. Nowadays, most men realize that marriage is a never an avenue to control. The man who gets married in America forwards to his wife and the Leviathan the future direction of his life. One cannot deny though that, as with any population sample, there will always be a few sadistic individuals in the mix. Yet there is no reason to think that there are more of these poisonous persons pursuing foreign brides than there are within any other cohort.

The word submissive is quite important because, as we have already seen, it is reflexively affixed to women who do not adhere to the feminist agenda. It is a universal way of describing those females who have traditional interests and goals. That the newcomers might be happy and satisfied by the arrangement they enter into only serves to feed the feminist position because women who eschew complaint and outrage are submissive by definition in their eyes. Activists would be wise to stop deriding extralocals and learn to imitate them instead. This would serve the modern woman well as there are many ways to get what you want in life, and the subtle approach is almost always best.

What is clear though is that foreign wives, or practically any other woman that the narrator has ever met, are not submissive at all. Most of what the modern woman labels as submission are situations in which equitable expectations are displayed. Equality in male/female relationships is not common here and the rejection of female privilege strikes many an indigene as being an act of self-hatred. Foreign wives are more likely to offer a husband a quid pro quo relationship in which their efforts are complementary but not the same. Their increased desires to raise a family and acknowledge that marriage is about fulfilling the needs of both parties indubitably seems backward to the American woman, but it is not remotely submissive.

Were a foreigner truly submissive then they probably would have never left their own country in the first place. Immigration is not a passive act; it requires bravery and will. Pursuing western men is proactive. Rather than complain, cry or litigate, they are actively seeking to improve their own lives. Being more accommodating, or at least passive aggressive instead of aggressive-aggressive, is a cultural difference that is a result of non-baby boomer parenting along with one's hailing from a less gynocentric culture. Obviously though, increased amiability never equates with submission. Congeniality is not a mark of defectiveness. Treading lightly on others is commendable and a proven way to forge love.

American women have two non-mutually exclusive options in their attempts to deal with the unexpected source of superior competition that is the foreign bride. First, they can try to change foreign women, and, second, they can incite our female-pandering legal system to enact some form of protectionism. By using mother's little helper—the government—they can pass laws to save their cartel, and, thereby, ensure that their exclusive proprietary relationship over the America male continues for the indefinite future. Variations of both strategies have been initiated and have proved fairly effective thus far.

Luckily for the modern woman, all that needs to be done in order to corrupt, alter, and spoil the foreign woman is for our culture to be exported to their homeland. Then, essentially, the work gets itself done by itself. The allure of the androgynized, unserious life is well-known as selfishness, self-absorption, and materialism are traits which more than aptly sell themselves. In fact, based on our experiences after the 1960s, they seem to be highly addictive. Preferring ease to effort may well be instinctual. Narcissism, the placing of one's needs and desires upon a holy altar, is far easier than integrating oneself with the outside world.

Should a country prove resilient to our siren song, then the next possibility for corruption occurs after the foreign wife's arrival. The fear of every prospective husband is that the woman he brings here may soon take on the qualities of the women he wished to avoid. Figuring out who the losers are at the starting gate is the aspiration of every husband-to-be, but doing this is a serious challenge due to the brevity of the romance period. The documentary film, "Cowboy del Amor,[330]" showcases such a situation. It treats viewers to the perspectives and practices of a sixtyish cowboy matchmaker. He is a folksy, cheesy, but insightful fellow who loves traditional women as much as the men for whom he gets paid to arrangement introductions. Despite his sunny disposition, there are moments of great seriousness onscreen. In one, he recounts his own tale of bringing a Mexican wife over and the disaster that ensued. Soon she was ordering him about and telling him how to run his home and life. He divorced her and lamented that she had turned into an American woman.

This situation is alluded to in the film *Monsoon Wedding* as well. The plot involves a successful Indian-American man who returns to his homeland for the purposes of an arranged marriage with a "virgin." It is not long before we discover that the man's bride-to-be happens to be quite experienced and is participating in an illicit affair with a married television producer right up until the night before her wedding. In this variation of adultery, and contrary to the notion of caveat emptor, the female protagonist decides to confess the scandalous situation to the groom. As one might expect, he is outraged. He barks at her [something to the effect of], "Well, you'll fit in just fine in America!" His comment was perfect even though I was the only one in the theatre who responded to it with applause. My glee was short-lived as modern movies seemingly are forbidden to end with a conclusion in keeping with the edicts of logic or evolutionary psychology. The young man—rich, good looking, undoubtedly prized by 500 million Indian women who would kill to line up for his passported persona—decides to go ahead and get married anyway. He thereby became the "perfect feminist groom"[331] as he readily accepted the cuckoldry which most men fear more than going broke or getting drafted. By pretending otherwise, the filmmaker "rewrote" males into an image of her own liking; which may well explain why the film was so popular in America. As we know from our chapter on deception, western women prefer male alteration fantasies to stories that concern the way men actually are.

Unlike with other issues, women are not content to limit their disdain to men. Foreign wives have reported hostility being directed towards them from native females. In the course of my research, I came across a particularly amusing posting[332] addressing this eventuality. Despite its coarseness,[333] I am sharing it with you in its real form as narrative summary would render it impotent. The young lady confides: "I am tired of getting nasty comments anytime I am with my American boyfriend, and someone overhears my accent. I am tired of women telling me that I am nothing but a little house slave for my boyfriend just because I cook for him everyday when he comes over to do his laundry." After making this admission, she compiles for readers a list of her experiences with indigenous women:

1. *The way they are nasty to foreign women and assume we marry American men to get a green card. I am LEAVING THIS COUNTRY once I graduate!!!!*

2. *The way they blame men for all of their problems.*

3. *The way they believe any woman who likes to cook and clean is a submissive slave.*

4. *The way they make fun of Christians and say they are close minded.*

5. *The way they are rude and snobby.*

6. *The way they feel threatened by foreign women. Sorry if we take YOUR men away from you! Maybe you should not nag him so much! Learn to bake or something!*

7. *The way they get pregnant by their boyfriend on purpose to trap him into marriage. That is evil and wrong!*

8. *The way they look at me when I tell them my boyfriend's job. What is wrong with working construction? He is a very responsible hard worker! They want a boyfriend who will work in business and make a $90,000 salary.*

9. *The way they tell me I should get my hair cut. It is down to my waist and I will NOT cut it off! I love it too much!*

10. *The ugly fat pimply whales who make fun of skinny women and talk about how being fat is beautiful. Big beautiful women?! I don't think so!*

What is eerie about this irritable young lady's confession is just how precisely it correlates with the impressions of the American male. Her criticisms about our women are remarkably similar to the ones that we ourselves make. It is doubtful that the average bachelor could have put together a more compelling critique.

Yet, as with all things relating to the modern woman, government intervention is their favored solution. Insulting native males and their imported wives may make them feel better, but it does little to deter the practices they abhor. It did not take long for the federocracy, our Conanesque liquidator of individual rights, to find a way to meet the needs of women. In 2005, they passed the International Marriage Broker Regulation Act (IMBRA)[334] whose unstated goal was to protect foreign nationals from our own citizens (which, is a bit of a departure from idealized state practice). Usually, a country's rulers are not so blatantly obvious in their attempts to oppress a major segment of their own population. Of course, the wording of the law does not single out men. The "petitioner" can be of either sex, but only men intentionally seek spouses from elsewhere— although, it is quite humorous to imagine how the average yuppie female would react to having a Russian husband. Pretending that this is somehow sex neutral is like saying that taxes levied upon tampons apply to men as well.

This omnibus law, which will inconvenience thousands of American citizens looking to better their quality of life, was adopted as a result of the murder of two women in Washington State.[335] The law stipulates that prospective husbands must provide extensive background information concerning themselves before they are allowed to make contact with foreign women.[336] Preceding correspondence of any variety, a personal history report—containing information far more extensive than a simple criminal background check—must be sent to "the foreign lady client in her native language."[337] She must then sign and give written consent concerning the man in particular before the communications can begin. Should this draconian procedure not be followed, it can result in a "$25,000 civil fine and up to 5 years in federal prison."[338] This is levied against any company that initiates the introduction.

It is in the specifics of the law where we find the lipstick traces of our discriminatory nanny state. Having to proclaim banal bits of information such as the locales in which one has lived, the amount of times that one has been married, and the number of children one has sired are not the stuff of major oppression, but the sharing of these tidbits in the United States is only mandatory for those who wish to break the cartel. These procedures apply to no other citizen. All the added bureaucratic hurdles have been very effective as this pernicious law has already held up 10,000[339] marriages in the time since it was enacted.

As is generally the case, this act of government has caused more harm than good. The biggest problem with the law is that it is a major violation of free speech. That one is barred from even talking to these women functions as a prior restraint on our First Amendment Rights.[340] It is also a major violation of our privacy rights.[341] Aside from creating a layer of bureaucracy that will bankrupt scores of corporations and frustrate countless men and women,[342] the law is completely redundant as domestic violence information is already provided to foreign citizens via the Visa Petition Process.[343] IMBRA makes every American male appear to be a potential abuser and codifies into law the notion of the ugly American.[344] Its covert goal is to add a veneer of disrepute to the simple desire to communicate with a foreigner. IMBRA implies that our citizens are international undesirables.[345]

Manipulating Congress into passing this totalitarian malarkey was not difficult. Those peacocks operate within the framework of chivalry justice and see it as their duty to protect, not all citizens, but women; which, as we know, equates with giving in to their every desire and demand. The socialism of feminist activist groups fits in well with the statism that is predominant among our legislators. The two groups see something they do not like and sputter out instinctively, "There ought to be a law!" A few emotional and irrational speeches later there is one, and we all become a little less free as a result. This is certainly what happened in the case of foreign bride legislation[346] which was spun as affecting "mail-order brides" and "marriage brokers" despite its purview extending far beyond unions and even into the region of saying hello to strangers.

All of this non-sense was enacted as a direct result of a couple of murders. That anybody is murdered is unfortunate, but we already have laws on the books that deal with psychopaths. There is no need for any more legislation on the matter. It is an issue for the police as opposed to one for the Senate. Despite the fantasies of leftist utopians, no Bill that could ever be passed will prevent a psychopath from acting psychopathically. Killing, exploiting, torturing, and terrorizing others is what those people do. The response should be to catch them, prove their guilt, and punish them, but there is little that can be done in terms of prevention in a free society. Rational people are completely ineffective in anticipating the behaviors of the irrational. The one thing in which we can take comfort is that there are but a few psychopaths among our nation's 300 million persons. Yet to make this point is futile as common sense has no dominion in 2007; our political discussions have been fueled solely by emotion for the past several decades.

Is the Personal Political?

Obviously, my spirited defense of men who opt for foreign brides may give readers the impression that this is my own viewpoint. That would be a reasonable assumption but it would also be an incorrect one. In this debate, as in practically every other, I stand firmly on the side of anti-statism. Whenever I hear the words "government solution," I reach for my keyboard. My disdain for socialism, as opposed to a desire to sire Vietnamese children, is what drives the positions I express. This is but another area in which we find that the personal is not political.

Spending the rest of my life with a woman would be ideal, but marrying a foreign bride would probably not work for me. My personality is too introverted and low stimulus seeking for such an endeavor. I suspect that my own solitary inclinations would greatly exhaust a young foreign national's patience. Naturally, she would originally come to these shores under the assumption that I would junket over her relatives from Kenya each month. She would also expect me to pay an annual tithe to her tribe back home, but would soon find that I would not be much help when it came to enriching her family. As for me, I would definitely resent her attempts to get me to go her homeland or to bring all of her relatives over here or to deposit a large portion of my paycheck into a foreign bank account. Further, the woman would arrive completely on her own and devoid of friends and relations. She would become as dependent on your narrator as an infant is on his mother. To an introverted person like me this would be a nightmare from which I could not awake. Phone calls would paralyze me at work, and my nights would be spent trying to entertain my newfound love. Weekends would become a blurred ordeal of leading tours in the hopes of managing boredom. This is definitely not the life that a low maintenance man like me wishes to lead. I have no desire to permanently become someone else's Master of Ceremonies. No time to hang with my friends, read, write, watch football or play poker would make your kindly narrator as angry as a radical feminist. No, the foreign bride is not for me.

Caution!

I will now proffer a few points with which to put the situation into the proper perspective. Numerous complications can arise from marrying a foreign bride; although, politically, I agree that it is a noble venture.

1. The amount of time preceding engagement and marriage is too small a window in which to really know someone. This is due to financial and geographic considerations, and lust is inevitably a factor which does not play out in a man's favor. One needs a certain number of months to ensure that the wondrous curves of a

Latina have not displaced one's ability to accurately assess their personality.

2. What a man finds endearing and precious about them may be environmentally dependent. Without their families and homeland, they may quickly *adapt* to their surroundings, and, hence, their pristine nature will become spoiled. Soon the wife may visit McDonalds as much as Martina Navratilova did back in the seventies.

3. Female Backlash: A man must not underestimate how irritated indigenous women will become once they find out that he has successfully outrun their blockade. These barbarous types will soon attempt to *befriend* his wife, and subtly work to instill her with their own anxieties, anger, insecurity, and materialism. With friends like that around, it will not be long before the Garden of Eden gets morphed into a strip mall in which the husband serves as parking lot valet.

4. At this time, our courts have no sympathy for male citizens. Regardless of being the indigenous party, a man could be pilloried during divorce proceedings just as he would at any other hearing. In all likelihood, judges will display even greater bias when it comes to foreigners than they do for indigenous women. The treatment the husband will receive will make him think that he has been cast in Ned Beatty's role for a local production of *Deliverance*. My friend Varnelli married a Columbian, and their divorce brought her citizenship along with a fifteen year stipend enabling her to never work again. Our courts do more for today's women than ten husbands ever could.

5. One terrifying possibility is that some foreign women could have seen and heard plenty about how hen-pecked American males are and wanted to come here to get in on the action. They could show up anticipating a dominatrix gig, and surmise that their husband will become the houseboy they could never afford in Peru. Yes, adopting our lifestyle and fleeing the men they grew up with could be the entire reason why they plotted to come here.

6. It could also be that the really happy foreign women are the ones who stay at home. After all, Horace's observation, "they can change their souls but not their skies," is absolutely true. The depressed seek happiness all over the earth...but remain depressed. It is a possibility that cannot always be ruled out.

7. Lastly, should one's wife divorce him and return to Fiji or Moscow, it may be the last time that a father ever sees his children again. What is even worse is that other countries—quite rightly—favor their own citizens in custody proceedings so the American husband can expect no mercy from any court on this earth.

Thus, on aggregate, marrying a foreign bride is certainly a risky endeavor, but the current situation is so deleterious for men that it might be worth braving the anarchic variables and giving it a go. For those with limited status and limited options in America, corralling a young, attractive woman might outweigh the inherent dangers that I outline above.

12

The Anchor, Marriage in its Totality

Men Don't Commit, they surrender.
—Chris Rock.[347]

A man is incomplete until he is married. Then he is finished.
—Zsa Zsa Gabor.[348]

If divorce has increased by one thousand percent, don't blame the women's movement. Blame the obsolete sex roles on which our marriages were based.
—Betty Friedan.[349]

Well, my reader, you and I have reached our endpoint. Only the issue of whether or not marriage remains a feasible institution is left to us. I guess *only* should be placed in italics as it is probably the most important question that we can address in regards to male/female relations. I will surprise no one by saying that, for most women, marriage remains an excellent proposition. It is full of benefits, entitlements, and power, while, for most men, it has devolved into an option of last resort. Indeed, given the nature of man's precarious position within society, the direct sex should now have an active presumption against it. Oh, that is not to say that marriage is akin to joining the Foreign Legion, wherein one has no future and has no past because that would be to mildly overstate the case. Again, it is important to remember that with this subject we are dealing with statistical means as the basis for our discussion. No doubt that marriage is a hell for some women just as it is a long reading of the beatitudes for some men.

Marriage came about for the best of reasons, and, in the past, it was a binding societal force; not only for this nation but for every nation. However, the last four decades have irreparably damaged the institution in the west. Those who criticize America for its inequalities but fail to mention the devastation wrought by the state's intrusion into our private romantic affairs are illegitimate. Indeed, the refusal of such partisans to address the government's bias against men showcases their being more interested in politics than they are justice. The Leviathan has entered our bedrooms and completely altered the rules by which we live. Feminists think their doing so is highly commendable—which should, by itself, make men wary of embracing the arrangement. Over the course of this chapter I will examine marriage from every possible perspective in the hopes of analyzing whether it continues to be a worthwhile endeavor in the present misandric environment.

A Girl's Best Friend.

No, I am not doing a commercial for the DeBeers Company by using the phrase "girl's best friend." What I am referring to are not diamonds but marriage itself. Matrimony, once an equitable arrangement, is now a contract that conveys to women more pleasure and privilege than they could have ever obtained elsewhere. One indicator of this being true is the positive attitude that the fairer sex continues to have towards it. The sharp divergence between male and female perceptions in regards to the ceremony is directly reflective of just how much the institution favors one sex over the other.

The simple fact is that far more women want to get married than do men. Were we to poll the population about this matter in the same way that we do politicians, in my opinion, we would find that marriage had an approval rating of about 70 to 80 percent among women but only 20 to 30 percent among men. This is due to the increasing recognition on the part of the citizenry that formal vows are more beneficial to one sex than the other. Could anyone deny that the most happy woman on this earth is the one who just recently got engaged?[350]

The rate of marriage in the United States has declined massively[351] in recent years; it is now 50 percent lower than it was in 1970.[352] As of 2005, US Census information indicates that there are over 89 million single and unmarried adults in America.[353] Evidence suggests that much of this decline is due to a change in male attitudes. Male reluctance and angst regarding matrimony were confirmed by the Rutgers 2002 *State of Our Unions Report*:

> *Overall, men are not optimistic about the future of marriage as a life-long commitment. They are acutely aware of the risks of divorce. Although they hold out the hope that their generation will work harder at marriage than baby boomers, they say that they are already seeing the first wave of divorces among their friends and this shakes their confidence in the future. Also, they believe that adults continue to change and "grow" and this makes it much harder to stay married to one person for a lifetime. One man said that he thought a contemporary marriage partnership of equals is more difficult to achieve than the traditional marriage with strict gender roles. As with the respondents in our earlier focus groups and surveys, these men do not believe that there is much that can be done to strengthen marriage on a society-wide basis.[354]*

Between 1960 and 2000, the percentage of married males within the important age bracket of 35 to 44 fell from 88 percent to 69 percent.[355] Many now view cohabitation as being a viable alternative: "In the U.S., about 10 million people are living with a partner of the opposite sex and most of these couples are 25-34 years old. Cohabitation is like 'marriage insurance,' a way to screen possible life partners and avoid divorce if it doesn't work out."[356] If cohabitation allows us to have the milk without buying the cow, why then do so many men persist in getting married?

I hold that their primary motivating factor for doing so is to please the women in their lives. Furthermore, as we all know, women can be very persuasive when it comes to obtaining the things they desire. And desire marriage they do. It almost seems as if a yearning to be married is hardwired into the brains of the fairer sex. Feminists and the mainstream media have promoted the idea of marriage being a "comfortable concentration camp,"[357] but the average woman knows better.

Many females respond to social pressure and the trendy disapproval of conjugal bonds by publicly denying that it is something that matters to them. Over the years I have met scores of females like this who tell me, soon after I meet them, that marriage is not something in which they are interested. But the vehemence of their disavowal is highly suspicious. In the words of Shakespeare, "The lady doth protest too much, methinks."[358]

One such protester is my friend Frankie's girlfriend, Hazel. They have been together for 13 years. When I first met her in 1999 she was very much a Womyn's Studies radical. Her state of mind was something that I was made aware of in advance so I never mentioned anything political in front of her. Hazel had no use for marriage whatsoever so Frankie thought he had it made. In his opinion, it would be the status quo forever.

Eventually though, the subject came up in 2002 as the three of us sipped free Scotch at a promotional night in a Lakeview pub. As the evening wore on we continued to drink and scrunch our faces, but around the fourth or fifth tumbler Hazel informed me that the two of them would soon be wed. I thought she was kidding and laughed out loud. I soon noticed that she was glaring at me. She was serious about what she said. My eyes widened (alcohol notably decreases my inscrutability) and I asked her why she suddenly had a change of heart about the institution. She did not answer but demanded to know why it was "a change of heart." I told her that Frankie mentioned a few years back that she thought there was no point in tying the knot as it was just a piece of paper. Hazel went ballistic and started yelling at the two of us. She then began to demonstrate menacingly around the tavern and demanded that I tell her all the other secrets that Frankie had shared with me. I never suspected, nor did Frankie, that her views on matrimony were a secret. Wouldn't he be expected to discuss major life decisions with his friends? No, as it turned out.

I looked into my glass and mumbled that Frankie had not ever said anything else to me of a personal nature the entire time that I knew him. For the sake of irony I should have also added, "I have not now, nor have I ever been, a member of the Chapin Intelligence Service." My disavowal of all agency activities pleased Frankie but not Hazel who did not seem as if she was ever going to cool down. She continued to berate the two of us so I decamped for home after about five minutes. I was grateful that she did not belt me. Despite her ungluing that night, it is now five years later and Frankie is no closer to getting hitched than he is to shacking up with a *Penthouse* pet.

I have found that this type of opinion reversal is fairly common with modern girls. They seem to forget that most of us take their rhetoric at face value and believe they mean what they say. After all, we do, but then again, we are the direct sex. If their utterances came with a Surgeon General's warning then we would all be better off. Hazel's attitude towards legal amalgamation is similar to that of other women as it arises not only from a desire to hoodwink men but also from a need to fool themselves.

Conformity works both ways with marriage. The culture strongarms women into loving the rat race, independence, and the acquisition of power, but the increased societal status that married women have is palpable. The media does its best to overpower them with the negative case for the institution and that it is better to be unmarried[359] but their efforts are largely ineffective. One source stated that 90 percent of married women feel that marriage "makes them happy all or most of the time..."[360] That is a powerful statistic as is the next one concerning British wives. One study found that two-thirds of those surveyed believed that the best sex of their lives occurred during marriage.[361] Redbook reported that 77 percent of women who experienced a series of one night stands were unable to attain orgasm during the course of events with a stranger.[362]

Marriage's perennial popularity among women can be directly attributed to the increased social esteem which arises from their entering into the institution. Women are known to have a greater desire for intimacy and this is apparent even during childhood.[363] Women fear being alone, along with its accompanying loss of social status, much more than do men. Modern women, just like their pre-feminist grandmothers, have a strong desire for attachment.[364] A study conducted at University of Virginia found that the happiest couples were those living within traditional frameworks which featured the husband as the family unit's main provider.[365] How surprised should we be by this in light of the fact that our modern customs violate 200,000 years of established practice?

Once the ring is slipped onto her finger, a woman has irrefutable proof of her popularity and importance. She also has proof of her social connectedness. Wives immediately become members of a club that has been around for several millennia (in one form or another). Marriage gives women something of tremendous value as they long for public and social recognition of their romantic relationships. The ceremony illustrates to the world the centrality and exclusivity of their bond.[366] With the addition of a formally enmeshed partner, a woman now has documentation of her belonging. Should he abandon her, the legal punishment is such that most husbands believe "it is cheaper to keep her." They could well be right.

The social power of wedlock cannot be underestimated. In 2003, I got engaged for the second time which had the predictable effect on my fiancée's mood. Shortly thereafter she made the mistake of sharing her bliss with her unmarried best friend. The result was the termination of their friendship. Her pal abruptly stopped speaking to her due to my ex-fiancée's emailing a picture of the diamond ring that I bought. The friend interpreted this as an attempt to demean her. She felt my ex was disrespecting her by putting the ring "in her face." Perhaps an aphorism of G. C. Lichtenberg reveals the rationale for her ire: "In the misfortunes of our best friends we always find something that does not displease us."[367]

Contrast the transcendent sentiments of women in terms of marital anticipation with those of men and the expanse between the sexes will never seem wider. How many fellows fantasize about their "Big Wedding Day" and buy magazines featuring extravagantly overpriced knick-knackanalia and other gilded accoutrements? I have not met one in over three decades of life on this planet.

Marriage can also mean the end of work for the lucky bride and this is something of which most of them are fully aware. Numerous women take advantage of this cultural labor schism and voluntarily become unemployed. Unfortunately, a great many husbands are taken aback by their wives' post-matrimonial indolence, but this is generally not the case for those wives who plan on becoming mothers. Over my 12 years in education, I have known about 15 women who went on maternity leave and never came back. Childbirth marked the end of their "careers" and it was a decision I often heard them boast of when they returned later for a visit. Options like these are not available to most men. Even if a man consciously attempts to find a woman who is rich he is generally reluctant to accept a tradeoff between financial security and physical attractiveness. Regardless of how much easier life could be for him, nothing is worth having to share a bed with Diane Feinstein.

The Advantages for Men.

You don't want to eat the same vegetable every day.
     —A Muria man from India.[368]

This is a somewhat more difficult position to illuminate. Modern marriages' benefits to men are not immediately apparent. We could never have said this a century ago, however. Sexual satisfaction used to be a serious motivating factor behind the decision to wed. Previously, matrimony was the only way in which a man could satiate his physical lust without having to pay for it. Luckily for us, the sexual revolution changed everything. A minority of women even think that they are the ones doing the using when they have sex. [The narrator recommends that everyone be supportive of such brainwashed persons and encourage them to continue with their male exploitation projects.] Even apart from the ranks of the deluded, a high percentage of modern women make themselves physically available to men at what is, historically speaking, a most early juncture in the courtship process. Thus, most of us know that our relationships will be consummated sooner rather than later so there is no cause to bother with promise rings, engagement rings, or the M Word at all. Ah, even during our initial encounters with the modern woman, the end zone is always in sight.

Erotic fulfillment is no longer the main motivator for "getting hitched," but, even back when it was, sex was always of short-term significance alone. This is due to something I call the **marriage paradox**. I have no doubt of the veracity of the survey above in regards to women believing that the best sex of their lives occurs during wedlock, but this finding could not be replicated with men. The main reason as to why concerns the male love for novelty. A girl with whom a man has not slept has considerably more value than one with whom he has. To put it more crassly, in the words of a fellow I used to work-out with, "For every hot chick out there, there is some guy who is sick of f*cking her." He is undoubtedly right.

The love for novelty is most acute in married men who, based on the ones that I have known, love pornography more than any other segment of the population. Since I turned 21, the only times in which I was ever asked to go to a strip club were by married men. Generally, single men will have nothing to do with those places. Most of us understand the futility of paying coke whores and societal free riders to pretend that they like us. I have been friends and/or associates with hundreds of men, and there is no question that the married ones are always the fellows most ravenous for meaningless, mechanical sex—which could well be due to their intimacy needs already being met in the confines of their conjugal relationships.

The fact is though that a decrease in physical attraction for one's wife is quite adaptive. We cease being obsessed with the women we have and this allows us to better notice the other women around us. Our roving eyes increase the likelihood of our finding more women for the purposes of copulation.[369] And this enables man to spread his seed to new individuals, and, thus, increase his reproductive yield. In the west, the frequency of sex with one's mate decreases steadily over the course of a relationship.[370] The man's disinterest is part of a greater plan that allows him to produce far more offspring than he could otherwise. For this reason, marriage never really did offer a long-term sexual solution for men.

Appealing to *Cosmopolitan* or the cult of misandry will not do a frustrated woman any good due regarding this matter. Men are far more influenced by their genes than they are the harridans of the media. In what is termed the *Coolidge Effect*[371] the dynamics of male sexuality are readily evident. The effect got its name after former President Calvin Coolidge. One afternoon, he and his wife Grace were out taking separate tours of a government farm when the guide told the missus that the rooster before them copulated dozens of times each day. She said for him to "please mention this fact to the president." After the message was relayed, President Coolidge asked the guide, "Always with the same hen?" The man told him that no, the rooster did it with all different hens. The President said, "Please tell *that* to Mrs. Coolidge."[372]

The Coolidge effect is pronounced and occurs across various mammalian populations.[373] To the annoyance of many a social constructionist, the effect is observed consistently in mammals such as rats, sheep, cattle, and rams. Just as with humans, male animals give hearty responses to the presence of novel females.[374] Group sex and wife swapping are behaviors that almost always originate with men.[375] A married man is no different from a bored sheep in this respect. Looking at the exact same centerfold each day, particularly one whose brushstrokes sag and decay with the passage of time, will never provide the type of reaction that our social engineers wish it did. In fact, men engage in extramarital affairs chiefly due to their being bored with wives who are long past their prime.[376]

Despite a bevy of evolutionary, and logical, evidence, our opinion makers continue to blame men for the fleeting of desire, but when a behavior manifests itself in a majority of a given population it cannot be considered "abnormal." A bit of President Coolidge is in all of us. As David Barash noted, "...the biological fact remains that inside the most faithful husband there is a fervent philanderer—and, at least in part, a hopeful harem master—just waiting to emerge."[377]

Should a magic wand be waved, ala Tony Robbins, and men awake the day after being wed to discover that they no longer have roving eyes it would be of little consequence in terms of their eventual sexual ennui. This is due to men generally not selecting salacious females to become their long-term mates. Women who are wild and love freaky zoo sex do not make for good wives. The person a man weds should have some functional value beyond the giving of pleasure. Marriage should bring two people together who possess shared goals and aspirations. The raising of children is a perfect example of the couple's symbiosis. Being fruitful and rearing offspring promises the pair eternal life.

As with all meaningful endeavors, inherent to matrimony is considerable labor, sorrow, and joy. Modern woman's obsession with her self and her own fulfillment is a millstone that drags down the couple's prospects. The banal and mundane aspects of matrimony are not likely to appeal to her. As I earlier noted, the modern woman is not used to hardship and will not revel in its diversity. Worries about bills and debts will not be welcomed by someone expecting a forty year parade of Macy's gift cards, designer outfits, and Vicodined emotions. Reality will prove profoundly disappointing to her even though she can make herself feel better by blaming her husband for what are the vagaries of life.

Should a man be marriage minded it is now more important than ever to find a wife who is not spoiled, and who understands that upturns and downturns are an inherent part of our existence. Thus, the most important criteria in wife selection—assuming, of course, that one finds a person who meets the minimal criteria for attractiveness and intelligence—is for a man to find someone who is loyal and supportive. These are not traits commonly found in pornofetish chicks, however.

Most of us are not holding out for a girl who is just like dear old mom, but we absolutely do not want one who has to be fumigated every time she returns home. I grant that the sex with such creatures can be enthralling, but marrying them is out of the question. A party girl is lots of fun…for 30 minutes, but the post-orgasm conversations are absolutely barbarous. One also has to be careful not to fall asleep due to concerns about what they could steal after you drift off. Freud was right, sometimes a skank is just a skank. All men would be wise to remember that women we think of only in a sexual light are not suitable choices for life partnership. Indeed, it is the very non-whorishness of an attractive woman which makes us consent to marrying them in the first place. The characteristics of loyalty, honesty, and trustworthiness do not make for good topless dancers, but they do make for excellent qualities in a wife.

That wives are so disappointed by the Marriage Paradox is understandable but also irrational because domestication is nothing if not the process of systematically eliminating a man's animal instincts. Decreasing their husband's freeform lust was a prevailing goal when they married him, but it proved to be one rife with unforeseen consequences. Wives do such a good job of defanging their husbands that they ultimately become dissatisfied with the eunuch sleeping alongside them. Low testosterone attitudes and behaviors in husbands are ideal...until they correlate with lowered testosterone levels and lowered animal interest in the bedroom. All the competitive edge that once fueled his prowling evaporates with the saying of "I do." Even if his body continued to release the same levels of hormones that it once did it would only make things worse for him psychologically. His lust for random women would either drive him mad or propel him into divorce court. Rather than express pride in their good little milquetoast, many wives instead express dissatisfaction. That hubby prefers a nap to the karma sutra should be entirely expected. As George Gilder observed: "Marriage means giving it all up. Give up love? That is how it seems to the single man, and that is why he fears it. He must give up his hunter's heart, forgo the getaway Honda growl, shear off his shaggy hair, restrict his random eye, hang up his handgun, bow down and enter the cage. At bottom, what he is is hunter. No way he will be hubby. And yet, he will."[378]

Cooling off sexually at that point is also quite adaptive. Despite what the talk shows would have us believe, there are good biological reasons for it just as there are good biological reasons for having a roving eye. If man's initial lust for a woman did not wane then we would never have survived as a species. We would have starved to death due to our eschewing hunting, the building of shelters, and the avoiding of predators in the hopes of getting more sex.

Furthermore, we have names other than lover for those who sleep in close proximity to us. For example, they are often called sister or mother. That desire is not present in our domestic interactions is the norm for most of our lives, and that is how it must be. It is unremarkable that a husband grows to regard his wife as being a close friend or a biological relation.

Lust is a very unstable element in our interpersonal relations, and it can become de-constituted rather quickly. For this reason, were my wife enceinte, I would refuse to be present during childbirth. If I did otherwise there is no question that my opinion of my beloved's nether regions would change irrevocably. There are some things that you just do not need to see. Curiosity might not kill a cat but it certainly kills an erection. I feel the same way about shutting the door when one uses the facilities.

Waste elimination is something that everybody does but sex is reserved for those with whom we feel special. Not everything in life has to be experienced together and individual boundaries must be maintained. When men come to regard women in the same way that they do the dude in the adjoining stall, then romance is officially over—forever.

So we can set sex to the side for the moment in terms of male marital motivation, but what about children? Well, I think that they remain an important influence on a man's decision-making. There is no question that kids from unmarried homes are at a serious disadvantage in life. It is the boy without a father who is the one most likely to end up in prison. Certainly, wedlock is best for offspring, and I truly believe that this is something on the minds of many men. Our yearning for sons and daughters is massively underrated by society. We make much of the maternal instincts that women possess, but often pretend that paternal instincts are non-existent. Of course, many of us have a sincere desire to raise the children we sire. We enjoy influencing the young and appreciate the affection with which they sometimes shower upon us. Men do not often verbalize the pleasures we obtain from our interactions and this clouds the issue further.

A child's utter spontaneity and enthusiasm is something lacking in our daily interactions with adults. The rewards of rearing them can be monumental. The joy produced by our efforts becomes perpetually reinforcing and the feeling that one matters to a child is quite satisfying. I can testify to this based on my own experiences outside of fatherhood. For this reason, many single men dote on their nieces and nephews along with the children of their friends. Assuredly, the need to have "legitimate" children is also something that many men think of when they walk down the aisle.

In the current era, our longing for progeny is far less conflicted than our desire to wed. The allure of being a father remains powerful. Its hold varies depending on the individual, but, in the narrator's case, it is the only factor that could spur him to get married again. If my prospective wife had no interest in children or was past reproductive age then my I would not consent to take part in the process. I can safely say that if I never enter to another contract with a woman and the Leviathan it will not matter to me, but I cannot say the same thing about never having children.

Another determinant for a man taking on a wife is the pleasure he derives from pleasing the women in his life. This is the most politically incorrect of assumptions and will never be formally acknowledged by the members of the Female Therapeutic Nation. The fact is though, when we love someone we want to make them happy and most of us are more than a little aware of how much propping down upon one knee can mean. This is why go along with the program against our better judgment and make an extravagant purchase at the jeweler as a means to necessitate it. Such a truth will never be expounded upon by the media as it humanizes men to a disagreeable extent.

Honor may be the final impetus to our signing a treaty with the state. Honor is a term that has fallen into disrepair and disrepute as of late. James Bowman wrote a book[379] by which to commemorate its lost societal function. The feeling arises in those of us who have had a woman on the line for a fairly lengthy amount of time. We reckon that she has stood by us unselfishly and now "deserves" to be married. Honor exists in a mental vacuum and demands justice for our woman. We figure that they have given us their best years so now we would like to balance the ledger. The legal arrangement is the ultimate form of a loyalty bonus. For the woman who has endured through an Iwo Jima of interpersonal calamities, marriage is sometimes awarded as if it were the Congressional Medal of Honor.

A friend of mine once had a fine woman issue him an ultimatum. He did not know what to do. I unexpectedly argued on her behalf. I said, "Well, she did stay with you for that year when you were unemployed. How many other girls would do that?" Perhaps it was reckless for me to say that, but her devotion to him was highly irregular and I had to accede it. Like my friend, sometimes a man gets married because he knows it is the honorable or right thing to do under the circumstances.

The Realities of our Simon Bar Sinister State.

In America, just as in England, Canada, Australia, and most of the west, the state now takes its role as overseer for our personal lives quite seriously. It has expanded its encroachments into our privacy more with each passing decade, and refuses to be an honest broker in our relationships. It takes sides and its presumption always lies with the fairer sex. Our courts and our legislators manifest an explicit bias against men in the decisions they issue and in the laws they craft. Much of this has been previously elucidated so here I will only address the unique specifics of the Leviathan's influence in the realm of matrimony.

a. _Divorce._

Mary was a friend I'd say 'til one summer day. She borrowed everything I owned and then simply ran away…
          —Phish.[380]

Regardless of what most people think, the clear-cut beneficiaries of divorce are lawyers. In absolute terms, the dissolution process substantially impoverishes both parties: "The study of about 9,000 people found that divorce reduces a person's wealth by about three-quarters (77 percent) compared to that of a single person, while being married almost doubles comparative wealth (93 percent). And people who get divorced see their wealth begin to drop long before the decree becomes final."[381]

Why then, with such extreme consequences for both parties, are there so many divorces? For the most part, only women can answer the question. Despite the cultural cliché about men leaving their wives or trading them in, the reality is radically different. About two-thirds of divorces in America are initiated by women and the figure is even higher in Canada.[382] Feminists habitually lie about the impact that divorce has upon women[383] in the hopes of convincing them to throw away what they already have. Even though overall wealth is slashed for the woman who has never worked or who earns far less than her husband (again, in the aggregate sense) there are economic gains to be had. After the attorneys are paid off, the couple's worth is diminished but what becomes the wife's is a nest egg that she no longer has to share with anyone and was likely never hers to begin with. She is now free to do what she pleases with what used to be _their_ money.

The profile of family operations that is put out by the media in our country is entirely fallacious. Husbands may earn a higher salary than their wives but they have less authority over financial decisions and family resources.[384] The poor oppressed wife who clings to her husband as a means for economic survival rarely exists. In America, women control 51.3 percent of the nation's wealth.[385] This provides an independent illustration of there being no patriarchy, and further, that there is no reason to slant judicial decisions in their favor.

That does not matter though as the husband always gets brutalized during divorce proceedings. A goal of feminism has always been to find a way for women to become totally independent of men, and separating a man from his wealth is the quickest means by which to do so.[386] The politicization of the universities and law schools has virtually guaranteed that those who fly the absurd tricolor of Gender, Class, and Race are the ones who come to dominate our jurisprudence. One female district attorney even made the mistake of publicly admitting this semi-secret. She said, in regards to a defendant's murder of her husband, that there was no need to take such drastic action. She chided, "For Heaven's sake, a man is cheating on you, you do what every wife in this country does: You take him to the cleaners. Get his house, car, kids -- make him wish he was dead."[387] We should be grateful that this legal functionary was honest about the dynamics of state influence as she provides much needed evidence of the current system's corruption. That she made this observation before a gender mixed jury illuminates the way in which people have grown accustomed to injustice in contemporary America.[388]

Far more extraordinary were the words of another functionary, former Canadian justice minister Martin Cauchon. He proclaimed: "Men have no rights, only responsibilities."[389] To regard men in such a fashion is to reduce them to the status of helots who can do nothing better than serve their female Spartan masters. I have found that sentiment like his is fairly prevalent. Since I turned 30, I have dated many a divorced woman. What has perplexed me most about this is that several of them have bragged to me [of all persons!] about how financially "set" they were as a result of the proceedings. Many of them laughed about the way they had made their husband's pay for what they did—either cheating on them, ignoring them, or supposedly drinking too much. They must have figured that my genitalia meant that I was too low functioning to ascertain that past behavior is a reliable indicator of future performance. I made a point of thanking them for the tidbits and encouraged them to tell me more; the Chapin Intelligence Service is a great appreciator of all types of information.

With women being about as fearful of court decisions as men are of invitations to the Playboy Mansion, why wouldn't they be the main catalysts for divorce?

Comedians and writers have had great fun with the saw, "if we get divorced then she gets half of my stuff," but this may be an underestimate in regards to the viciousness of the actual settlement. When two 30-year-olds wed they have, in effect, bequeathed the running of their future financial affairs to an East Germany politburo because our judges are quite fond of using coercion as a means to redistribute wealth. Many of our black-robed chancellors mistake for justice the act of granting a wife an inordinate amount of marital swag. Yet for what logical reason would a post-divorce woman be entitled to one cent more, inflation aside, than what she once earned before entering into the arrangement (assuming she quit her job)? There can be no reason. The state has no right to use the dissolution of a relationship as a means to grant women a pot of gold.

Forbes[390] compiled a list of the Top 10 most costly celebrity divorces in history. Guess how many of those settlements were paid out be women? If your guess was "none" you would be correct. The reporters had a ready excuse for the disparity. It seems it is "a reflection of the historic dominance men have played in the entertainment industry." No it is not, but their explanation is a fine example of media bias. The disparity is due to our courts refusing to treat women in the same manner they do men. At any rate, the top four entries feature some obscenely large digits. At the four spot, Harrison Ford paid out 85 million to his ex but the settlement also featured her getting a slice of all future earnings. The number three position went to Steven Spielberg who paid Amy Irving 100 million in exchange for four years of marriage. He even had her sign a pre-nuptial which was, of course, rendered null and void. Number two went to Neil Diamond who had 150 million dollars carved out of his hide in penance for his consenting to live with his wife for 25 years. Diamond, as brainwashed a male as I have ever encountered, said it was "worth every penny." Really! And how many of those pennies did she earn? Michael Jordan, Chicago's most beloved former citizen, came in at the top position on this list of shame. His Airness had to pay upwards of 150 million as no exact figure was cited in the article. Not addressed in the piece was Paul McCartney who had to pay his wife 80 million[391] for four years of service. Even for an ambitious gold digger, 20 million per annum is a handsome rate of return.

The whole judicial charade involving these persons is appallingly offensive, but our main objection to it is rooted in its unfairness. The courts punish men systematically because they believe that women are always the victims and that men are always the villains. With such a worldview, women derive all kinds of goodies once the relationship fails to work out. Yet marriage, to be practicable, has to be an arrangement between two equal parties. No side is entitled to reparations from the other. That such inequitable decisions occur is a travesty of justice. Almost any counter-plan would be better than the status quo. If judges were to average the woman's salary for the three years before she got married, proceed to double it, and then adjust the product for inflation it would be a far more ethical method than the present one—although it would remain unjust.

With the celebrity examples we can vividly see the tremendous bias of our courts at work. Husbands must pay out half of their total wealth as opposed to half of what they earned while they were with them. Why would these women ever be entitled to the dollars their man made before they met? Michael Jordan got married four years into his professional career but that salary was never subtracted from the funds he was ordered to transfer to his wife. This means that what most of us take to be the worst case scenario—that our exes will get half of what we made while we were with them—may, in fact, be the best case scenario.

In terms of the average man with an average income, it is easy to see how his life could be completely destroyed not long after he walks down the aisle. The narrator is no celebrity but he is not in the gutter either. Most of my savings are in retirement vehicles, but were I to get married today and divorced a decade from now my wife would abscond with more than half of my earnings. This would be due to her receiving half of the capital gains and dividends produced by my mutual funds over the period in which we were together. That the principal upon which these payments were based was earned long before I had ever met her will not matter.

Anti-male loopholes are apparent with illiquid assets like real estate as well. If a man buys a house before marriage and his wife moves into it, upon divorce, she will be entitled to half of its appreciation over the years in which they were together. The way that the courts will configure its pre-marital value will be a real horror show. The last thing they will do is attempt to index its worth based on the market's progress over the span of the relationship. What they will do instead is to credit the husband with what he paid for it originally and then dole out half of the rest.

A case in point concerned a poor schlep of a teacher I used to know. I went to his retirement party in 2003 at the end of the school year. When the staff returned in the fall I found him at the front table filling his mug full of coffee. I was shocked. I said, "Dougie, what the heck are you doing hear? What happened?" He looked forlorn and stammered for a bit. "Oh, ah, gee, my wife left me. She met some guy at the mental hospital."

"The mental hospital?"

"Yeah, the mental hospital. She was real depressed and had been for several years. Anyway, the two of them fell in love there and then she divorced me. She got the house and a third of my pension. It looks like there will be no retirement for me. I'll be here forever, man."

I patted him on the back and promised that I would tell others his story. The character of Worm in the movie *Rounders* summed up the situation quite admirably: "In the game of life, women are the rake." In terms of divorce, had he substituted marriage for life his statement would have been even more correct. The more we analyze matrimony the more we see that the courts' manipulations on the behalf of women are both erroneous and oppressive.

Prenuptial Agreements, as Spielberg found out, are not the solution they should be. They evolved as a means of allowing both parties to stipulate the way in which their assets would be partitioned in the case of their separation, divorce, or death.[392] Unfortunately, these agreements are often not upheld. A variety of factors are used to dismiss them such as the proximity of the contract to the actual wedding date, whether both sides had representation or even should one party claim that they did not understand what they were signing before they signed it.[393] Like Social Security, a prenuptial agreement is never a vehicle in which one should entrust their future.

b.   The Slaughterhouse: Custody Law.

As it stands today, when a woman and a man part ways the mother, barring bizarre circumstance, is the one granted custody of the children. This outcome is standard practice but there is no good reason for how it came about. Before the nineteenth century the situation was far different.[394] At this point, however, there appears to be no likelihood that the presumption in favor of the mother getting custody will ever be reversed. Here again the state has exerted a pernicious influence on the lives of its citizens as the court is slanted against fathers. Often their child support payments are increased for political reasons[395] due to the judiciary being unquestionably influenced by the agenda of radical feminists. Consider the words of feminist psychologist Peter Jaffe, an educator of family court judges, "[J]oint custody is an attempt of males to continue dominance over females." Who knew? I thought it was a way to maintain relations with one's children, but if urinating while standing up is an expression of patriarchal authority then we must not be perplexed by the desire to maintain relations with one's offspring also being an expression of it.

The case law is as depressing as it is infuriating. In one fantastic proceeding, a man had to pay 96 percent of his take-home pay to his wife, and his plea to have the amount lowered was soundly rejected.[396] Obviously, the victimization of that fellow will not be something that NBC, CBS or ABC will be profiling anytime soon. But they will happily rail against "deadbeat dads," and commit plenty of errors of omission. What they will not report to the public is that women, when they are the ones who pay child support, have a lower rate of compliance than do men.[397] Why comply when you are guaranteed favorable treatment? Injustice comes quickly to the man who is behind in payments as he soon finds himself thrown under the tracks of an M-1 tank. The government's zeal in prosecuting fathers exceeds that with which they prosecute cocaine dealers. The latter typically serve 20 days out of their 30-day jail sentences while a "deadbeat dad" in arrears serves out the entirety of his sentence.

There is, unlike with promiscuity, truly a double standard here. Men are being set up to fail by Uncle Sam. Columnist Cathy Young observed: "In the end, our society sends men quite a mixed message. If your partner gets pregnant and decides to keep the baby, you're liable for 18 years of child support, whether or not you want to be a father. If she doesn't want to be a mother, she can give your child to strangers and there isn't much you can do. Then we complain that men don't take parenthood seriously enough."[398]

The message really is not that mixed however. What men soon learn is that marriage is a sanctuary for women and a killing zone for men. Males are second class citizens in this country and it is nowhere more apparent than in custody dispute law. Regardless of his possible financial limitations, the husband will be bled ashen. Should his condition improve and his salary increase, his ex-wife can make sure he experiences no increase in living standards. She can petition the court to insist that he pay her more. Conversely, if he experiences an economic disaster, such as his savings being wiped out, he must still make the payments specified by his juridical masters.[399] For fathers, there is nothing just about this justice system. That fatherlessness correlates with criminality, lowers self-esteem in female children, and produces a host of other social pathologies is immaterial to the Leviathan. The government is neither moved by reality nor what the future will bring. As more and more men opt out of marriage due to their rational fears of bureaucratic vengeance, our ruling elites will continue to pour billions into social programs that only exacerbate root problems and would be largely unnecessary had men been empowered to remain in the home.

c. "Equitable Paternity."

Within the larger context of divorce and custody law, comes a decision from the summer of 2006 that made the few remaining hairs on my head change color. It is so reprehensible that it deserves an independent entry in this chapter. The legal doctrine of "equitable paternity" is so outlandish that it does not even seem to have been dreamed up by feminists. The concept, in a nutshell, is that if a man believes he is the father of a child and pays child support then he is legally liable for the maintenance of that child until he or she reaches adulthood—even if DNA evidence later proves that he is not really the biological father.

John Caher explained the idea in full: "He who acts like a father, is a father—if not biologically than at least legally—the Court of Appeals said Thursday in imposing 'equitable paternity' on a man who wrongly assumed he had fathered a girl and acted accordingly. The court in Matter of Shondel J. v. Mark D., 40, upheld the trial court and the Appellate Division, 2nd Department, in ordering a man to pay child support on behalf of a child he did not father. In doing so, it recognized the legislatively endorsed concept of 'equity paternity,' or paternity by estoppel (see Family Court Act §§18 [a] and 532 [a])."[400]

Parent by arbitrary fiat is a more truthful way to describe the process. Permeating this decision is the debilitating reek of the sensitivity state. The court crucified Mark D. because they felt it was best for the child even though the youngster was not even his. One cannot help but wonder how much a need to be self-righteous had to do with the outcome. The justices must have felt very superior as they pronounced the decision into their Dictaphones. They "saved" a child by pummeling a dupe. Ah, what a magnificent justice this turned out to be. What will be done with this precedent? Will I have to donate half of my check to strangers in public housing projects because that is what is best for them? Who knows? Anything is possible in our misandric United States.

Would the justices do the same thing to a wife who married, and later divorced, a man who came into the arrangement with children from another woman? Never. Here, as with affirmative action, the state has emphasized the rights of one group of citizens—children and mothers— over those of another (fathers). There is no moral justification possible for this, and it is particularly vile given the specifics of the case. Mark D. was intentionally hoodwinked by the baby's mother.

For the record, the dissenting opinion described the litigant as being "completely innocent"[401] so it is comforting to know that not all of our robed masters are vile and debased. I have discussed equitable paternity with many people, and even my ideologically enemies acknowledge that there is something foul about the practice. With this kind of juridical hocus-pocus in the ether, marriage will soon decline to the point of it becoming an alternative lifestyle for our lunatic fringe.

d. *Marital Rape.*

While not as offensive as equitable paternity, the issue of "marital rape" is a most unsavory concept that has mind-boggling implications. It "can be defined as any unwanted intercourse or penetration (vaginal, anal, or oral) obtained by force, threat of force, or when the wife is unable to consent."[402] It has not been around for long and was first officially recognized in 1976 when Nebraska did away with the Marital Rape Exemption.[403] Fast-forward 30 years and it is now the law in every state even though some states make the punishment for it more lenient than the one meted out for non-married rape.[404]

Now we have to be careful with this subject because rape is a very serious crime and there is no rationalization for a man raping anyone, but "marital rape" statutes are rife with the potential for abuse. First of all, it should be that every state, not merely a few of them, treats the offense in a different fashion than they do other kinds of rape. Obviously, sexual relations are intrinsic to the idea of matrimony. If a person does not want to have sex with their partner then they have no business walking down the aisle with them in the first place. Of course, this is no excuse for men to be physically violent but we should not pretend that their doing so is a common occurrence. Furthermore, it is never the same thing as forcing oneself upon a person to whom you are not married. The right thing for a woman stuck with a husband for whom they do not want conjugal relations is to leave him at once. Getting him jailed for life is the height of evil.

Second, marital rape grants women unprecedented power over the lives of men. Anytime they want rid of their husbands, or merely wish to ruin their lives, they can make an accusation and their guy is basically done for. She could just get up from her bed post-coitus, run down to the station house and say that the intercourse that just occurred between them was a product of coercion. A good amount of the evidence for her allegation would be right there swimming inside her. When the authorities examine the evidence, they may not find any bruises or scrapes, but his DNA would be at the point of entry so what would our courts do? Well, as they already have an anti-male bias, they would be most likely to believe the wife over the husband. I have no doubt that a sizable minority of our officials continue to believe that women are incapable of lying about rape. These justices will immediately take the wife at her word and put her husband in jail for 25 years.[405] Perhaps they will even take comfort in the fact that once he is there the husband will be raped for the remainder of his days.

Third, consider the vagueness of "unable to consent" which is something that should make all men tremble. Who among us has not once, while ensconced in the lascivious joys of a new relationship, made overtures to a partner who was sleeping or at least very tired? What was previously a major reason to get up early on the weekends has now become a shuttle bus to the penitentiary.

All of these factors amount to one thing: women are in charge of any relationship they enter into. Legal concepts like marital rape so alter the balance of power that a husband can be sent to prison on spousal whim. Laws such as these make a mockery of the man who thinks that marriage will improve his quality of life because years spent in Stateville, Marion or Pelican Bay are not life at all.

e.   *"No Thanks": The State's Impact.*

Like so many other disastrous government programs, marriage has become a tool of state oppression and another showpiece of bureaucratic incompetence. As noted above, fewer and fewer men are now getting married and the downward trend will continue as long as the courts forge malevolent legal doctrines like equitable paternity [which was born in 2006]. An ever-increasing plurality of men are slowly realizing that wedlock is more for Rosie O'Donnell than it is for them. The drama of dealing with the opposite sex for 40 years is daunting enough, but having to dodge the stamping of the federocracy's million ton feet is enough for most of us to have a presumption against marriage.

As Matthew Weeks argued in an article called *The Marriage Strike*, "By advocating government as a surrogate husband in the case of single motherhood, they [feminists] have eliminated the disincentive for women to file for divorce. And through decades of litigious activism, they have given rise to the bloated and intrusive family court system and stacked it so egregiously against the men of this country that it now appears they are subconsciously engaging in what could be called a 'marriage strike'; preferring to play the odds rather than assume a massively disproportionate amount of risk."[406]

A shortage of males who consent to signing on the dotted line is the unintended consequence of this government chicanery. The commentator's conclusion is entirely correct. In their attempt to benefit the fairer sex the state has so skewed the terms that even the least reflective of men will eventually begin to notice that marriage is a negative expectation play. And, as those with a background in probability can attest to, the Risk of Ruin for a negative expectation game is 100 percent.[407]

In the long term, fatherlessness and single parenthood will destabilize society and make women as disposable as Bic razors. Politicians care more about looking sensitive and feeling good about themselves than they do the calamities which arise from their warm and fuzzy policies. The allure of "caring" about people is more important to them than actually improving conditions for the citizenry. This veneer of caring is what has kept housing projects across the nation, like Chicago's Cabrini Green, open because our representatives felt the people's pain and were there for them...and what they did made matters infinitely worse. The government is a major reason why so many men now forgo wedlock.

Marriage and the Modern Woman.

Every woman should marry—and no man.
        —Benjamin Disraeli.[408]

Never has the old question from JFK conspiracy fame, "who benefited and why," been more crucial than in regards to marriage. We already know that it is more enticing to women than it is to men, but, apart from the punishments exacted by the state, does marriage still offer prospective husbands any of the advantages that it once did? The short answer is no and the reason is that the modern woman's character is far different from that of her predecessors. She has been empowered and licensed to steal...and steal she does. Let us examine some of the ways in which our conjugal relations have now changed.

   a.   *The Progressive Marriage.*

Call it modern, call it progressive, or even call it post-modernist, but whatever you call it, the dynamics of contemporary wedlock are most unique. What all of our new arrangements have in common is that they are engineered with the idea of empowering women and disempowering men. No doubt that the extent of the changes varies based on one's socio-economic level as the higher up you go the more likely one is to encounter a woman whose notion of a husband is that of a cheerleader with muscles. In the micro-world of the aggressive wife, an emasculated husband will forever play Tonto to his turtledove's Lone Ranger. In our new world, man has become loyal sidekick and money machine. For most men, this outcome is a fate worse than death. When they get hitched they invite an occupying army into their lives, and the ceremony in which they participate will be one to celebrate their own unconditional surrender.

No entity can better describe the conditions of the progressive marriage than *The New York Times*. Here are a couple of questions they regard as needing to be answered before one can safely tie the knot. Couples should reflect on the following: "Have we discussed whether or not to have children, and if the answer is yes, who is going to be the primary care giver?...Have we discussed our expectations for how the household will be maintained, and are we in agreement on who will manage the chores?"[409] What once was obvious must now be negotiated.

The whole idea that men are as likely to consent to staying home and raising infants, dancing with the vacuum cleaner, and nodding affirmatively to the edicts of Oprah is absurd but the Gray Lady [*the NYT*] thinks otherwise. Their editors dream of a day in which men will willingly make such sacrifices without flinching, and that day will come —as soon as God allows the mainstream media take a blue pencil to his plans. Of course, there have been numerous examples of perfectly normal men being stay-at-home-dads such as men's rights advocate Glenn Sacks, but the majority of us will never be satisfied by playing the role of wife.

The entire idea of a "progressive marriage" is counter-intuitive. Marriage is a conservative institution and was never meant for radicals. The early communists knew this and renounced it as being an instrument of oppression. Progressive marriage, in which the woman reigns transcendent, is far more oppressive than marriages of the past. Modern women have altered its constitution and it is now something other than marriage. If they need any suggestions on what to call it I am partial to "bondage" or "serfdom," but it is doubtful that any of their representatives will be querying me on the matter. Progressive marriage will remain desirable for women as long as they continue to believe in their own supremacy, and see men as having no choice but to submit to their will.

b.   *Last Name Shame.*

Marriage is the triumph of hope over experience.
          —Samuel Johnson.[410]

    It used to be that you got married and your wife took your last name. That was how it worked...but not any more. As with everything else, concessions must be negotiated on an individual case by case basis. Nothing can be taken for granted, and it is best to bring up the subject before submitting the forms to the registry clerk. It has always been an important goal of feminists to convince married women to keep their maiden names. Young radical Jessica Valenti cannot understand why her peers would ever change their names. She offers to them her counsel, "You want future kids to have the same last name as you and your hubby? Hyphenate, b*tch! Or do something, anything, but change your last name. It's the ultimate buy-in of sexist bullsh*t. It epitomizes the idea that you are not your own person."[411]

    There are a multitude of things wrong with her denouncement. First, is not marriage supposed to be a declaration that you are not your own person? I thought it was. What I have always wanted for myself in an arrangement can be embodied in the phrase, "there's you, there's me, and there's us." It never occurred to be that a deal could be brokered predicated upon the maxim, "there's just Bernard." To my own credit, even if I did meet someone amenable to such terms, the deal would not appeal for me. Of course, the surest way to retain your identity is not to get married at all. Ladies like Ms. Valenti have missed out on the notion of union entirely. They would be wise to consult a biography of Abraham Lincoln for some important tips on this subject. They might ascertain that union and secession are not synonymous terms.

    Second, the name change is one of the few remaining stipulations of marriage that benefits men. Without this advantage, there does not seem to be much that separates cohabitation from wedlock. Should Valenti's views become more widely accepted, fewer men will incur the risks inherent to legally enshrining their relationships which will cause the marriage rate to further plummet.

Third, an obvious response to my position arises from the arbitrariness of the woman being the one who has to make a change. Why not the man? No wholly satisfactory answer to this argument can be given. The practice is not found in all cultures. Were we to be born members of the Iroquois Nation then it would be a different story, but the woman accepting her husband's name is a fixture of western tradition. Regardless of how waywardly the custom came about, it remains our custom. The bottom line here is that marriage is an old-fashioned act and once the tradition is ripped out of it then there is no point in entering the institution.

It was not until I began dating after college that I first encountered the aromatic and ethereal state of political correctness. In those guileless days, it was not unusual for young people to speak of marriage when they interacted with one another, and I certainly was a part of this majority. My ignorance of contemporary attitudes caused me to regard wanting a wife to change her name as being a normal assumption. I was not informed until later that our elites now hold it to be a sin against virtue. About a month after I got home from Cleveland, I went out with a delectable girl whose mode of conversation consisted of telling people about the way the world worked and what they should be doing with their lives. Unlike today, I was not smart enough to feign interest in her fascism and pretend to take mental notes as she spoke. I just kept staring at her body which did not seem to hurt my cause, but my mouth soon scuttled any chance that I had with her. She told me of her plans to reject her future husband's last name, and, although she did not solicit an opinion from me, I immediately interjected, "Well, I'd never marry you." Her retort was entirely predictable, but unforeseen by the 21-year-old me: "Then I guess this is all a waste of time." I made no recovery and that was the last time I ever saw her. Only a dumb kid gets dragged into discussions like that with women but a dumb kid was precisely what I was. Luckily, the exchange had a positive effect on my future behavior.

I suppose my refusal to come around to accepting the practice has to do principally with my own sense of honor. That a woman, in light of the jeopardy her prospective husband subjects himself to by entering wedlock, would shun his last name strikes me as being uniquely disrespectful. When they continue to go by Smith, Constantinov or Al-Bin Shaffi she has effectively announced to the world, "This jerk married me but I'm still available. Whoo!" Her stance makes it seem as if she continues to await a better offer from another party. The act suggests that she is not serious about taking herself off the market and that she will make no sacrifices today and no sacrifices tomorrow. The changing of name has value because it signals commitment in a commitmentless age.

When a woman refuses to change her last name she effectively distorts the supply and demand relationship between man and woman. As we know, in terms of sex, women are always the supply and men will always be the (eternal) demand, but that is not true with connubiality. Men will merrily form a line to enter a woman but never form one to enter a chapel. The plot of a film like *Runaway Bride* becomes more preposterous with each passing day. In this land there are untold legions of men like my friend Frankie who will jovially pay women to stay with them, provide them with food, vacations, and comfort but will have nothing to do with making their relationship official. Therefore, adding yet another—and very public—humiliation to the list of Versailles-like terms placed upon men decreases the likelihood that a woman will find any husband at all.

For a hardened minority of men, this emblematic issue remains a true deal breaker. The wife who insists on keeping her last name is akin to a merchant asking his customers to pay more for his wares because...he is worth it. He is not and it will always be worth the time and energy to walk a bit farther down the road to discover a more congenial merchant. Inflating the price is not the sign of someone who wants to move their merchandise.

Of course, with what was once the counter-culture now being the establishment, more powerful indignities are always on the horizon. Progressive marriage offers an even more abominable outcome than the wife keeping her maiden name as she could require her husband to cast off his own. Should readers be skeptical of this point consider the words of one charmer who was quoted in the Smith College *Alumni Quarterly*: "In other wedding news, Christie Rowe married Sila Thielke . . . in July. She sends apologies to 'all my Smithie friends who I told that I didn't believe in the 'heteronormative subjugation.' She adds, 'Sadly I couldn't get Sila to take my name, unlike Sarah (Cliffy) Clifthorne '02 who just married Scott Bailey Clifthorne and gave birth to Emerson Clifthorne!' . . ."[412] I guess that we should be comforted that there are few girls in America who share this young lady's inclinations on the subject, but what can we say about Mr. Scott Bailey Clifthorne? I have no encouraging advice to offer him. Sometimes there is nothing you can do for people. He has freely chosen his own fate. But if young Emerson is ever in need of a tutor then I will make my services readily available.

c.   *Running up the Score.*

The good hawk hides its claws.
        —Confessions of a Yakuza.[413]

*With the Bears winning 72 to nothing in the middle of the fourth quarter, Grossman
stepped into the pocket and completed a 50 yard bomb to Berrian...Umm, I don't
think the Raiders are going to be happy about this...[414]*

Considering the amount to which our modern unions favor the
wife it is incomprehensible that so many women ask for more favorable
terms than the ones they already receive. Demanding that a potential
husband take your last name has the disgraceful feel of a 70 point blow
out in the National Football League. Wedlock now offers men less that it
ever has, but it seems as if the modern woman thinks that we are too
mentally deficient to ever notice this fact. There appears to be no shortage
of females who taunt their spouses and let them know just how foolish
they were to ever consent to the arrangement in the first place.

For some brides, the ceremony itself has become an opportunity
in which to poke fun at the jerk who will soon be taking over the paying
of their bills. One source mentioned that risqué pictures are now frequently being used as a means for the bride to satirize her own wedding.
[415] Yet, a party girl acting like a party girl during a public event should be
expected. Irony, however, can be found in the woman with a bedpost full
of notches having the nerve to wear white on her wedding day.

For the civilized person it is bad form to taunt someone after they
make a grievous error, yet this is exactly what wives do when they publicly
humiliate their husbands. One of the few rich and successful fellows I
know got married to a woman who keeps a personal blog. Before they got
married she had been a college student who never had a real job in her
life. A friend of mine emailed me an entry she posted in which she
bragged of her plans to give her children a distinct last name which would
be randomly selected from one of the couple's eight grandparents' last
names. The paragraphs were so extraordinary that I had to read them a
second time to make sure my mind had not embellished their meaning.
Her idea had to be one of the most imbecilic ones that I have ever
encountered. That she would publicly embarrass her husband in such a
fashion is a reflection of her total ungratefulness for the security and
future that he bequeathed upon her. She appears to be more desirous of

engaging in politics than she is of being a mother. Her decision would definitely have a negative impact on her children, but I suppose ideologues view themselves as being above such concerns.

The marriage ceremony has always been all about the bride as it is her chance to become "Queen for a Day."[416] A female journalist proudly put forth her tale of male emasculation in a column she penned for "the paper of record."[417] Rather than have the wisdom to keep silent about her scam, she gloated over her triumph before the nation: "Tradition hardly seemed enough reason for me to take his name, and I didn't want to have a different name from my future children. I imagined them asking why and realized the only possible answer was patriarchy. I didn't want my family founded on that principle."[418] You go girl! One cannot help but feel that any man dense enough to stay with such a person deserves exactly what he gets.

As far as children are concerned, the issue of bastardry, like everything else that was once tied into tradition, has receded in importance. With women keeping their last names, there are few societal markers left with which to discern whether a father is a husband or "my baby's daddy."

d. Infidelity Chic.

When I ask men in their 30s and 40s why they have not married, they do not answer that female promiscuity makes it unnecessary. They say that they are reluctant to propose to easy women. One man put it this way: "I would be uncomfortable in social gatherings where 15 percent of the people had been in bed with my wife."
—Paul Craig Roberts.[419]

It is well know that men have always despised promiscuity in a prospective mate,[420] but it is an issue of ever-increasing concern due to the hyper-sexualization of the American female. Unfortunately, our culture's tramp-o-mania now percolates through the ties that once bound. Supposedly there has been a wave of wives who confused infidelity with the expression of their own independence. They now think that it is their right to cheat on their husbands. Some have even said that we are entering the "era of the yummy mummy."[421] What is far worse, and clearly a running up of the score, is that many of these wives are known to revel in the act of infidelity.[422] I suffered through a book[423] that addressed this topic. It documented the perceptions of various women who were largely euphoric over the illicit coupling that they had done. The tone of the narration was largely positive. Indeed, the author dubbed the confessors "amazing women." She relayed to her readers a tale of her own temptation to cheat on her husband for which he [predictably?] forgave her.

Apparently, the earlier passage I quoted from *The Onion* has now become a direct reflection of real life. Woman really is empowered by everything a woman does. I came across a therapist who had a startling take on this smutty business. He spun infidelity as "…an opportunity – to redesign one's life and love relationships in ways that create honor, joy and true intimacy."[424] Herr Goebbels would have been proud of such deliberate distortion, but the therapist is very wrong. There are no silver linings to be found in infidelity. For a man, a cheating wife is a worthless wife; a risqué mate is an undue risk. There is no double standard here as we are comparing Porsches to condominiums.

The evolutionary principal, "mommy's baby, daddy's maybe," is illustrative of the reason why infidelity on the part of wives can never be tolerated. A woman is always confident that she is the mother of her child, but the same can never be said about a man. A husband who has been tricked into raising another man's child will live out his days within the framework of a tragedy. The profits of his labor will go to non-relations and his entire life will be rooted in a lie. The children he will express pride in will not be his own. They will be a chip off of another man's block. His genes will die out at the same time that he does, and preventing this eventuality is the rationale behind male sexual jealousy. By our watching women closely and making note of their attitudes, behaviors, and proclivities we are best able to handicap how suitable they will be for mating. Those who are hyper-sexualized are the ones who must be avoided at all costs. As I mentioned earlier in the chapter, what they have done in the past is the best predictor of what they will do in the future.

One should be no more inclined to accept an unfaithful woman for a wife than they would one afflicted by herpes or addicted to heroin. It is a painfully absolute business no matter how many publications pretend that it is otherwise. *Sex in the City* was a television show and the situations presented were more reflective of the relations between gay men than they were between man and women. If women are silly enough to believe that the direct sex can have their neural pathways rewired by HBO then the vista which they gaze upon is the inside of a howitzer's barrel. Adultery affects a man's psyche in the same way that Chernyobyl effected the environment. Dr. David Buss noted: "Men frequently divorce women caught having sex with other men…Even if they are not abandoned, women risk physical and psychological abuse at the hands of jealous partners. Women damage their social reputations as a result of sexual indiscretions. They risk impairing their mate value should they need to go back out onto the mating market. They endanger the success of their children, since cuckolded men might abandon their children or curtail investment in them. They risk contracting sexually transmitted diseases from affair partners."[425]

I guess it is not as glamorous a practice as *Newsweek* makes it out to be. Also, the sad fact is that adultery will never appeal to women in the same way it does to men. They just are not as interested in novel erotic entanglements. One study found that while 48 percent of American males desired extramarital sex, only five percent of the women surveyed did.[426] It could well be that men were the real winners of the sexual revolution— unless one is foolish enough to marry one of the five percenters or the unknown percent of wives who "experiment" due to a pathological need to conform.

e.   *Androgyny Mania.*

The evidence is overwhelming: androgyny—the negation of male and female—is a political creation, an act of war against human nature…Data indicate that the measurable psychological difference between the sexes has "not decreased over a whole generation of American life."
    —Dr. Allan Carlson and Paul Mero.[427]

Women are transcendent and are expected to be aggressive and assertive; whereas, men are expected to be happy about their newfound political and personal impotence. Men are encouraged to exhibit their apocryphal "feminine side." Males should express their emotions, shave off their body hair, manicure their nails, and take medications to reverse male-pattern baldness. Women, in turn, should be durable, reliable, and strong. They can do it! The fairer sex now looks more like the direct sex and vice versa. I hold that this eventuality has cataclysmically impacted the nuances of heterosexual attraction.

Another element of progressive marriage seems to be that after the ceremony many wives soon decide that they no longer need to look like women at all. I made a joke to my girlfriend about some of the bigguns that she works with. She was talking about someone named "Donna." I said, "which of the fortyish, short-haired, married, and overweight chicks is that?" She laughed but it turned out to be a legitimate question as they all have husbands and are all built like deteriorating eunuchs. The one thing of which I am absolutely certain is that they did not look that way when they originally took their vows. One can come across hundreds of these denatured females in our local businesses, government offices, malls, Wal-Marts, and roadways. They, unlike gay Americans, truly are everywhere.

Recently, I heard a woman give this phenomenon a favorable spin. She said of a friend of hers, "Her husband really loves her. She's gained a lot of weight but he doesn't care. They're at the point in their relationship where she can get *comfortable*." Hmm, how does she know that he doesn't care? My bet is that he is appalled by it but is cognizant of the fact that there is nothing he can do. Recently, during a break at a conference I re-met a person who embodies this decadent trend. As I walked towards the drinking fountain I was approached by a very large woman who spoke to me with great familiarity. The only thing was that I had no idea who she was. I did my best to place her face but could not. Luckily, she wore a nameplate and I soon realized that she had interviewed me for a position back in 2004, but, in the brief intervening years, she had managed to buffet herself into Andrea Dworkin. As if aware of the plight of her poor joints, she mentioned to me that she had just had a baby but she was easily twice the size that she was before. Blow-ups like hers are not a normal byproduct of pregnancy.

Clearly, the recently married woman who commits herself to a four-year-plan of exponential physiological growth is committing a very aggressive act, albeit a passive one, against her husband. There can be no other explanation for this brand of Tostitos madness. I will further cite the case of a sincere social worker I once knew. Both she and her husband were fine Christian people whom I admired very much. When I first met her she was in her late twenties and occupied the borderlands between being pleasantly plump and corpulent. A few months into our acquaintance, she showed me a photo from her wedding the year before. She looked like another person. Indeed, I was so startled that I almost said so. In the picture her appearance was impeccable. She looked young, fit, and with features that were radiant. She then, unbelievably, asked me if she looked any different now. By then though I had gotten into character, "A little," I said. "Your hair was blonde." She was pleased by my response and then confessed to having gained 65 pounds in the 14 month period that followed their wedding—all at the age of 26. Why she did this to herself is unknown but I knew her to be an overeater. Her heft was not a result of hormonal or metabolic changes, and I felt tremendous pity for her husband.

In fairness, obesity is a problem for both men and women, but what makes it so uniquely hazardous to women is that feminists have attached political significance to the decision to make a barge out of oneself. They have associated rotundity with freedom and independence. The goofy claim that "fat is a feminist issue" continues to be championed by activists in our universities. One recently noted, "For most scholars of fat, though, it is not an objective pursuit. Proponents of fat studies see it as the sister subject — and it is most often women promoting the study, many of whom are lesbian activists — to women's studies, queer studies, disability studies and ethnic studies. In many of its permutations, then, it is the study of a people its supporters believe are victims of prejudice, stereotypes and oppression by mainstream society."[428]

Actually, it has nothing to do with any of things. Fat is a cardio-vascular issue and its negative assault on health is not vagina specific. It is a function of taking in more calories than you burn. Really, it is a fairly non-esoteric subject. That feminists could encapsulate it with such dramatic and victimological terms is just another indication of how little they care about the people who take their dogma seriously. It also show-cases their complete disdain for truth. For them, self-massage and self-esteem are more important than survival. Excess fat kills, but you would never know that from reading any of their treatises. Somewhat humorous-ly, I am sure that these same women complain endlessly about the lack of men in their lives, but they could get a ton of action if they simply empo-wered themselves to stay away from McDonalds and Taco Bell.

No amount of porcine self-indulgence makes any sense. Picking up pounds is a malignant definition of "getting comfortable." It is never anything to be happy about, but far more repugnant is the deliberate avoidance of exercise. Mammals need to move and there is no reason why any human should confuse entropy with comfort.

Hair length, which is a secondary sexual characteristic, is yet another baleful example. Lengthy locks enhance a woman's attractiveness, yet there seems to be an explosion of post-menopausal females that chop off their hair. By doing so it is almost as if they are deliberately trying to make themselves unattractive. When I have made inquiries about this fad I have been told numerous times that "it is easier" to have short hair. The same could be said about lying in bed all day but luckily most of us choose not to do it. Demi Moore got a buzz cut in G.I. Jane and lost about 20 percent of her appeal in the process. Even with the stark plummet in value she remained attractive—on a scale from 1 to 10, she went from being a 9.5 to a 7.5. But how many other members of the fairer sex can afford such a drop? Very few, I am afraid.

That we have reached a point in which so many women sabotage their seductiveness by intentionally adding blubber to their frames or slashing ringlets off their necks is an indicator of our culture's decline. It also exemplifies our rigid belief in female supremacy. Many members of the chosen sex think that anything they do is perfectly okay—after all, they were the ones who were doing it. That they generally wait until their men swear allegiance to them at the altar suggests to me that they are fully conscious of how much the union slants in their direction. Marriage not only appears to be a license to steal but a license to stop looking like a woman as well.

What's to Be Done?

Bachelors know more about women than married men.
If they didn't they'd be married, too.
                    —H.L. Mencken.[429]

Roll over Lenin and tell Mao the news because the average American man must make a decision in regards to marriage and there is nothing he can do involving the barrel of a gun. My foremost recommendation for men in a quandary over whether they should enter wedlock is to suggest that they use logic for the basis of their decision-making. Emotional thinking in this regard will lead to ruin. The contract is a monumental undertaking for the husband-to-be so he must carefully examine all possible variables before requisitioning the services of a priest.

With wives no longer being goddesses of the hearth, with continued fidelity a wildcard, and with many of them viewing motherhood as being an inauthentic pursuit, **modern man should have a presumption against marriage.** This presumption can be negated quickly if one comes across a spectacular prospect, however. I do not know the exact tastes of every male reader, but I can proffer up a few prerequisites that he should look for in a mate. At minimum, the woman a man marries should be reliable, attractive, loyal, and possess average intelligence. After that, you are on your own son. Obviously, girls who are unattractive, slutty, spend prolifically, and are mentally sick or debilitated must be avoided. I will express the logical justification for possessing a negative presumption below:

A. Marriage is a Traditional Act.

B. The benefits of marriage for men almost entirely accrue from their being in traditional relationships.

C. Today most women are not traditional, and are horrified by thoughts of an "old-fashioned" union.

D. Coyness, a seemingly innate female defense mechanism, has been cast off in favor of narcissism and the constant discussion of feelings so modern women are ridiculously easy to discern. Their dominant personalities are readily evident even at the earliest stages of courtship.

E. Thus, as the modern woman offers man no conceivable advantages in a long-term pair bond, most of them are not worth marrying. The majority of western women have been contaminated by our new dispensation so a negative presumption in regards to wedlock is a logical outgrowth of their altered state. Such a perspective offers males the best chances for both sanity and survival.

I have three procedural recommendations as well:

1. Men should ask themselves what exactly their interests are. They should even write them down if they have to. The most essential question to answer is "what do I want from life?"

2. Next they should determine whether or not marriage will increase or decrease the likelihood of fulfilling their desires.

3. Once they find themselves in a relationship in which a decision must be made they have to ask themselves, "What is in it for me?" If they cannot think of anything then they would be wise not to let the government trounce its way into their bedroom. Without known identifiable benefits, marriage is a disastrous decision.

In conclusion, I will emphatically state that spending one's life with a person you love and who loves you is the best of all possible outcomes. Contrary to what you will find in a woman's self-help book, I am not going to pretend that staying single is superior to finding a person who cherishes you. If one of my readers is currently in a rapturous relationship then I extend to them my warmest congratulations. Love and its reciprocation are a slow and steady high like few others on this earth. I have absolutely nothing bad to say about love, but have much bad to say about adding the government as a third party for your ménage à trois. Personally, I have fallen in love about eight or ten times and have no doubt that I will in the future as well. Happy couples are not unknown to me and I have met more than a few handfuls of them. However, while their unions are exemplary, they are simply not an option for most of us in the current environment.

For this reason, I have coined the term "bachelor equity" which I use to describe why I think it is better to remain single than to get married in the majority of situations. Progressive marriage is quite progressive for the fair sex, but is totally regressive for the direct sex. In most contexts, the deal that men receive is never worth its accompanying risks. To use a baseball analogy, negative presumption mandates that the tie cannot go to the runner. For most single men, the potential downsides outweigh the potential upsides.

Most of the relationships that normal males have with modern women occur in conditions that are far from optimal. I acknowledge that, as I clarified in Chapter 10, holding out for the "perfect person" is inimical to finding contentment in life, and most of the judgments that average men make exist in what we call the gray area. On some days all is well but on others you wonder why prostitution is not legal. The bottom line here is that remaining single is not such a bad choice. Life is good but rarely great, yet that is not such a bad spot in which to find oneself. A man wakes up on Saturday and Sunday to discover that his days are unstructured and entirely his own. He will undoubtedly miss having a warm body at his side, along with a person who, presumably, cares about him greatly, but being single is a serious improvement over rounding out your days with a person that you can barely tolerate. I have heard some people tell me that they fear dying alone, but being with someone whom you do not trust is not a solution. It is better to die alone with God than in the presence a person who is an embarrassment to you.

Arrangements that are formed merely out of a desire to be married are occasionally described as relationships of convenience or relationships bound by fear. Regardless of how they are termed they are in no way preferable to maintaining one's liberty because with that you can always live to fight another day. Men must realize that, as with Mother Russia, time can be traded for space. Our biological clocks are Rolexes and generally keep ticking until damp earth is poured upon them.

I grant that I have painted a rather bleak picture of matrimony but it is one that I believe to be accurate. Many men born in this era are disadvantaged when it comes to bride selection, but that is not to say that there are not legitimate women out there to be found. Indeed, even your skeptical narrator has seen some, but they are generally married to other men. That is the way it must be. Talent negotiates its own price so we should not be surprised that these women were swept up quickly. Despite all the things I have stated in this book I would still get married if a fine situation presented itself. I am not immune to allure of a bargain, and my current girlfriend may or may not be the one that I take off the market. My own presumption got neutralized when I discovered that she made twice as much money as I do. One's fear of divorce rapidly diminishes upon realizing that the woman you are dating can buy and sell you three times over.

I guess the essential thing is for men to remember to be open-minded about the women they meet. Don't give up! You should always take your stop-watch out and get data on whatever prospective candidates stop by for a tryout. The biggest thing I have learned in 20 years of dating is that nothing is ever as good or as bad as you think it is. Age is not the depressant for men that it is for women. The best part about getting older is that with each passing year there is a notable increase in the number of women who are younger than you—and this is a cause of endless celebration. Indeed, not long ago I thought 30-year-olds were ancient, but now I think they are young, hot babes. Yes, our standards are not what they used to be, and that is a wonderful development.

All we can do with our research, scholarship, advocacy, analysis, and study is to clarify small parts of the world. There are infinite situations that arise with women and it is impossible to be effective in every instance. I know quite a bit about the fairer sex but I am confident that they will continue to mystify me until the day that I die. I will never know all that there is to know about them, but the triumph of political correctness makes books like mine far more enlightening than they should be. Talking frankly should be normal behavior, but intellectual freedom is something frowned upon in America today. Being a man was much easier at other points in history, but as Gandalf put it to Frodo, "All we have to decide is what to do with the time that has been given to us."[430]

Please now indulge the narrator by allowing him to close on an optimistic note. To be a man in a world where the needs of women are paramount is no stay in Shangri-la. I grant that it is a formidable assignment, but we have immeasurable advantages and gifts for which to be grateful. This is evident when we reflect on the lives of our ancestors. We, and by "we" I mean practically everyone in the west, do not have to face lethal epidemics and the likelihood of an early death. Thanks to modern medicine we have age-spans that rival tortoises and unprecedented levels of health in every decade we reach. Our comforts are so great that they are a challenge to merely recall. With full stomachs and minds sharpened by sleep, we are in a better position to solve problems than were any of those who came before us. Things could be far worse than they actually are.

The corruption of the modern woman is most dispiriting for hete-rosexual males, but conceding the battle is unnecessary and totally coun-ter-productive. That males have been discounted and dismissed by society-at-large just makes our skills and assets all the more potent when they are used. Radicals have a gigantic lead in the culture war, but we only need three male virtues with which to reverse the tide. Logic, courage, and organization are enough to bring the nation around to equality for all persons—which is all we really need or desire.

Female supremacy is a lie. Justice Brandeis was right: "Publicity is justly commended as a remedy for social and industrial diseases. Sunlight is said to be the best of disinfectants; electric light the most efficient policeman."[431] Shedding light on the pathology of misandry is exactly what I have done in these pages. Men have built practically everything in this world. We were the founders and protectors of civilization, and we must point this out to people from here to eternity. Men should stand up for themselves with verbal zeal and contradict those who seek to demean us. We must counter-attack whenever possible and counteract the labeling of innocents as oppressors.

I, along with practically every one of my readers, has never op-pressed or tormented anyone. We must stand and fight with words that do not always come easy, but fight we must do. Our odds of success are better than we think. No house built by radicals can stand before a strong wind. We must breathe deeply and blow their works back into the earth. There can be no surrender. We are men so we must die as men. Only then, once we have been true to ourselves and our brothers and sisters, will we be fit to face God. We must act, not tomorrow, but today.

August 2, 2007
Bernard Chapin
Chicago, USA
veritaseducation@gmail.com

References

Arendt, Hannah. *Eichmann in Jerusalem.* (New York: Penguin (1963) 1994).

Barash, David P. and Barash, Nanelle, R. *Madame Bovary's Ovaries: A Darwinian Look at Literature.* (New York: Delacorte, 2005).

Black, Jim Nelson. *Freefall of the American University: How Our Colleges Are Corrupting the Minds and Morals of the Next Generation.* (Nashville: WND Books, 2004).

Bork, Robert H. *Slouching Towards Gomorrah: Modern Liberalism and American Decline.* (New York: ReganBooks, 1996).

Bowman, James. *Honor: A History.* (New York: Encounter, 2006).

Buchanan, Bay. *The Extreme Makeover of Hillary (Rodham) Clinton.* (Washington D.C.: Regnery Publishing, Inc., 2007).

Buss, David. *The Dangerous Passion: Why Jealousy is as Necessary as Love or Sex.* (London: Bloomsbury, 2000).

Buss, David. *The Evolution of Desire: Strategies of Human Mating.* (New York, Basic, (1994) 2003).

Burana, Lily. *Strip City: A Stripper's Farewell Journey Across America.* (New York: Hyperion, 2001).

Carlson, Allan C. and Mero, Paul T. *The Natural Family: A Manifesto.* (Dallas: Spence, 2007).

Celine, Louis-Ferdinand. *Death on the Installment Plan.* (New York: New Directions, (1936) 1966).

Chapin, Bernard. *Escape from Gangsta Island: A School's Progress Decline.* (Nebraska: iUniverse, 2006).

Chen, Bill and Ankenmann, Jerrod. *The Mathematics of Poker*. (Pittsburg: Congelco, 2006).

Chesler, Phyllis. *The Death of Feminism*. (New York: Palgrave Macmillan, 2005).

Chesler, Phyllis. *Woman's Inhumanity to Woman*. (New York: Thunder's Mouth Press: 2001).

Coulter, Ann. *Slander: Liberal Lies About the American Right*. (New York: Crown, 2002).

Crittenden, Danielle. *What Our Mothers Never Told Us: Why Happiness Eludes the Modern Woman*. (New York: Touchstone, 1999).

Cutler, Jessica. *The Washingtonienne*. (New York, Hyperion, 2005).

Diamond, Jared. *Why is Sex Fun? The Evolution of Human Sexuality*. (New York: Basic, 1997).

Etcoff, Nancy. *Survival of the Prettiest: The Science of Beauty*. (New York: Anchor Books, 1999).

Farrell, Warren. *The Myth of Male Power: Why Men are the Disposable Sex*. (New York: Berkley, 1993).

Fein, Ellen and Schneider, Sherrie. *The Rules: Time Tested Secretes for Capturing the Heart of Mr. Right*. (New York: Warner: 1995).

Fisher, Dr. Helen. *Why We Love: The Nature and Chemistry of Romantic Love*. (New York: Henry Holt and Company, 2004).

Fitzgerald, Matthew. *Sexploytation: How Women Use Their Bodies to Extort Money from Men*. (Willowbrook, Illinois: April House Publishing, 1999).

Forster, E.M. *A Room with a View*. (USA: Vintage, (1923)1986).

Fromm, Erich. *The Art of Loving*. (New York: Harper & Row, 1956).

Furchtgott-Roth, Diana and Stolba, Christine. *The Feminist Dilemma: When Success is not Enough*. (Washington, D.C.: AEI Press, 2001).

Gilder, George. *Men and Marriage*. (Gretna, Lousiana: Pelican, 1992).

Gilman, Susan Jane. *Kiss My Tiara: How to Rule the World as a Smart Mouth Goddess*. (New York: Warner Books, 2001).

Henry, William A. *In Defense of Elitism.* (New York: Anchor, 1994).

Hewitt, Sylvia Ann. *Creating a Life.* (New York: Hyperion, 2002).

Hilts, Elizabeth. *Getting in Touch with Your Inner Bitch.* (Bridgeport, CT: Hysteria, 1994).

Hollander, Paul. *Discontents: Postmodern & Postcommunist.* (New Brunswick: Transaction, 2002).

Horowitz, David. *Left Illusions: An Intellectual Odyssey.* (Dallas: Spence, 2003).

Indante, Dan and Marks, Karl. *The Complete A**hole's Guide to Handling Chicks.* (New York: St. Martin's Press, 2003).

Kernberg, Otto F. *Love Relations: Normality and Pathology.* (New York: Yale, 1995).

Kipnis, Laura. *The Female Thing: Dirt, Sex, Envy, Vulnerability.* (New York: Pantheon, 2006).

Klein, Stephanie. *Straight Up and Dirty.* (New York: HarperCollins, 2006).

Lasch, Christopher. *The Culture of Narcissism: American Life in an Age of Diminishing Expectations.* (New York: Norton, 1979).

Lasch, Christopher. *Women and the Common Life.* (USA: Norton, 1997).

Levy, Ariel. *Feminist Chauvinist Pigs: Women and the Rise of the Raunch Culture.* (New York: Free Press, 2005).

Lott, John. *Freedomnomics: Why the Free Market Works and Other Half-Baked Theories Don't.* (Washington, D.C.: Regnery, 2007).

Lukas, Carrie L. *Women, Sex, and Feminism.* (Washington D.C.: Regnery, 2006).

Marin, Rick. *CAD: Confessions of a Toxic Bachelor.* (New York: Hyperion, 2003).

McDermott, J.P. *Why Women and Power Don't Mix: The Perils of Feminism.* (USA: Patriarchic, 1996).

Mencken, H.L. *In Defense of Women.* (Chicago: Time-Life, 1963).

Miller, Geoffrey. *The Mating Mind: How Sexual Choice Shaped the Evolution of Human Nature*. (First Anchor: New York, 2001).

Minogue, Kenneth. "Democracy & Naiveté." *The New Criterion*. March 2006.

Morris, Desmond. *Intimate Behaviour: A Zoologist's Classic Study of Human Intimacy*. (New York: Kodansha America, 1997).

Mustain, Gene and Capeci, Jerry. *Murder Machine*. (New York: Onyx, 1993).

Nathanson, Paul and Young, Katherine K. *Spreading Misandry: The Teaching of Contempt for Men in Popular Culture*. (Montreal, McGill-Queen's University Press, 2001).

Nathanson, Paul and Young, Katherine K. *Legalizing Misandry: From Public Shame to Systemic Discrimination Against Men*. (Montreal, McGill-Queen's University Press, 2006).

O' Beirne, Kate. *Women Who Make the World Worse: And How their Radical Feminist Assault is Ruining Our Families, Military, Schools, and Sports*. (New York: Sentinel, 2006).

Parlamis, Franklin. *The Passive Man's Guide to Seduction*. (New Jersey: Symphony Press, 1996).

Patai, Daphne. *Heterophobia: Sexual Harassment and the Future of Feminism*. (Lanham, Maryland: Rowman & Littlefield, 1998).

Patai, Daphne and Koertge, Noretta. *Professing Feminism: Cautionary Tales from the Strange World of Women's Studies*. (New York: New Republic/Basic Books, 1994).

Person, Ethel. *Dreams of Love and Fateful Encounters: The Power of Romantic Passion*. (USA: Penguin, 1988).

Proust, Marcel. *Remembrance of Things Past: Swann's Way*. (USA: Vintage, 1989 (1913)).

Ridley, Matt. *The Red Queen: Sex and the Evolution of Human Nature*. (New York: Penguin, 1994).

Rhoads, Steven E. *Taking Sex Differences Seriously*. (San Francisco: Encounter, 2004).

Sajer, Guy. *The Forgotten Soldier.* (Washington, D.C.: Bracey's (US) Classic, 1971).

Saga, Junichi. *Confessions of a Yakuza: A Life in Japan's Underworld.* (Tokyo: Kodansha International, 1989).

Sammon, Bill. *Strategery: How George W. Bush is Defeating Terrorists, Outwitting Democrats, and Confounding the Mainstream Media.* (Washington D.C.: Regnery, 2006).

Schwartz, Howard S. *The Revolt of the Primitive: An Inquiry into the Roots of Political Correctness.* (Westport, Connecticut: Praeger, 2001).

Scruton, Roger. "Modern Manhood." Found in *Modern Sex: Liberation and its Discontents.* Edited by Myron Magnet. (New York: Manhattan Institute, 2001).

Shenk, David. *The Immortal Game: A History of Chess.* (New York: Doubleday, 2006).

Sklansky, David. *The Theory of Poker.* (Las Vegas: Two Plus Two Publishing, 1999).

Smith, J.D. *Life Sentence: The Guy's Survival Guide to Getting Engaged & Married.* (New York: Warner Books, 1999).

Sommers, Christina Hoff. *Who Stole Feminism? How Women Have Betrayed Women.* (New York: Touchstone, 1995).

Stains, Laurence Roy and Bechtel, Stefan. *What Women Want: What Every Man Needs to Know About Sex, Romance, Passion, and Pleasure.* (United States of America: Rodale Press, 2000).

Steyn, Mark. *America Alone: The End of the World as We Know It.* (Washington, D.C.: Regnery, 2006).

Strauss, Neil. *The Game: Penetrating the Secret Society of Pickup Artists.* (New York: ReganBooks, 2005).

Thornhill, Randy and Palmer, Craig T. *A Natural History of Rape: Biological Bases of Sexual Coercion.* (USA: MIT Press, 2000).

Tooley, James. *The Miseducation of Women.* (London: Continuum, 2002).

Townsend, John Marshall. *What Women Want—What Men Want: Why the Sexes Still See Love & Commitment so Differently.* (Oxford: Oxford University Press, 1998).

Tuttle, Cameron. *The Bad Girl's Guide to Getting What You Want.* (San Francisco: Chronicle, 2000).

Valenti, Jessica. *Full Frontal Feminism: A Young Woman's Guide to Why Feminism Matters.* (Emeryville, CA: Seal Press, 2007).

Valentine, Roy. *The System.* (USA: Eye Contact Media, 2003).

Vilar, Esther. *The Manipulated Man.* (London, Caledonian: 1998 (1971)).

Whitehead, Barbara Dafoe. "How We Mate." Found in *Modern Sex: Liberation and its Discontents.* Edited by Myron Magnet. (New York: Manhattan Institute, 2001).

Wright, Richard. *The Moral Animal: Why We Are the Way We Are; The New Science of Evolutionary Psychology.* (New York: Vintage, 1994).

End Notes

¹ Immanuel Kant as quoted at *Oomlist.com*. Here is the link:
http://oomlist.com/writers/immanuel-kant.html

² As quoted in David Shenk's *The Imortal Game: A History of Chess*. (New York: Doubleday, 2006). p. 18.

³ A ling taken from Lady Galadriel's monologue at the beginning of Peter Jackson's 2001 film, *The Fellowship of the Ring*.

⁴ Townser, Henry. "A History of the Review." *The Stanford Review*. Frosh Issue 2000. Here is the link:
http://www.stanfordreview.org/Archive/Volume_XXV/Frosh_Issue/News/news2.shtml

⁵ Lukianoff, Greg. "Larry Summers Announces His Resignation from Harvard." *Fire.org*. February 21, 2006. Link found at:
http://www.thefire.org/index.php/article/6806.html

⁶ McElroy, Wendy. "Judge's Book Fans Flames of Culture War." *FOXNews.com*. January 03, 2007. Here is the link:
http://www.foxnews.com/story/0,2933,240839,00.html

⁷ This is a phrase long associated with *National Review*. When Jonah Goldberg was the online editor they used to sell t-shirts with this slogan on it but they no longer appear to do so. William F. Buckley mentions the motto in the preface to this article:
http://www.nationalreview.com/flashback/flashback200501030730.asp

⁸ Chapin, Bernard. "Indoctrination U: An Interview with David Horowitz." *Frontpagemag.com*. March 5, 2007. Here is the link:
http://www.frontpagemag.com/Articles/ReadArticle.asp?ID=27231

⁹ By definition, both sexes are mediocre. All individuals within all populations revert to the mean.

[10] "Famous Quotes about Women." *Nomarriage.com*. Here is the link: http://www.nomarriage.com/famous.html

[11] Wiki quotes for Aristotle. Here is the link: http://en.wikiquote.org/wiki/Aristotle

[12] Bombardieri, Marcella. "Summers Remarks on Women Draw Fire." *The Boston Globe*. January 17, 2005. Here is the link: http://www.boston.com/news/local/articles/2005/01/17/summers_remark s_on_women_draw_fire/

[13] I realize there is very little censorship today, but here, and throughout the book, I make a point of asterisking out every swear word within the narrative itself but not on the references list.

[14] Marcotte, Amanda. "Movie review-cum-I swear I'm a manly man man article at MND." *Pandragon.net.* June 17, 2005. Here is the link:

 http://pandagon.net/2005/06/17/movie-review-cum-i-swear-im-a-manly-man-man-article-at-mnd/

[15] Yes, I'm using "man's man" here as opposed to "the woman's real man" which I profile in Chapter 5.

[16] Email exchange with Dr. Steven Rhoads on June 26, 2007.

[17] Pinker, Steven. *The Blank Slate: The Modern Denial of Human Nature*. (New York: Viking, 2002). p. 344.

[18] Definition of feminism from Dictionary.com. Here is the link: http://dictionary.reference.com/browse/feminism

[19] Sommers, Christina Hoff. *Who Stole Feminism? How Women Have Betrayed Women*. (New York: Touchstone, 1995). P. 22.

[20] Ibid, 21

[21] Ibid, 19

[22] "Poll: Women Strive to Find Balance." *CBSNews.com*. May 14, 2006. Here is the link: http://www.cbsnews.com/stories/2006/05/14/opinion/polls/main1616577 _page2.shtml

[23] Lott, John. *Freedomnomics: Why the Free Market Works and Other Half-Baked Theories Don't*. (Washington, D.C.: Regnery, 2007). Pps. 5-6.

[24] Gilder, George. Men and Marriage. (Gretna, Lousiana: Pelican, 1992). p.viii-ix.

[25] Sommers, 222.

[26] Tuttle, 9

[27] Hoff-Sommers, Christina. "Ms. Information." *American Enterprise Research for Public Policy Research*. February 23, 2003. Found at *Aei.org*. Here is the link: http://www.aei.org/publications/pubID.16709,filter.all/pub_detail.asp

[28] Nathanson and Young, 2001, 5

[29] Nathanson and Young, 2001, 215

[30] Lithwick, Dahlia. "Girl Fight: The Marginalized Debate Over Female Opinion Writers." *Slate.com*. March 16, 2005. Here is the link: http://www.slate.com/id/2114926/

[31] MacDonald, Heather. "Diversity Mongers Target the Web." *National Review.com*. March 30, 2005. Here is the link: http://www.nationalreview.com/comment/mac_donald200503300758.asp

[32] No author listed. "Buerk Attacks Women Broadcasteres." [See any bias in that title?] *BBC News*. August 16, 2005. Here is the link: http://news.bbc.co.uk/1/hi/entertainment/tv_and_radio/4155228.stm

[33] "Life Expectancy at Birth for the U.S. Population in 2004." Table 1. Found at the *Center for Disease Control and Prevention* website in their National Center for Health Statistics section. Here is the link: http://www.cdc.gov/nchs/products/pubs/pubd/hestats/finaldeaths04/final deaths04_tables.pdf#1

[34] Conant, Eve. "Cancer: A Fresh Diagnosis." *Newsweek*, taken from the *Msnbc.com* website. January 17, 2007. Here is the link: http://www.msnbc.msn.com/id/16677528/site/newsweek/

[35] Recall President Bush's appearance on the program. Transcript found here: http://transcripts.cnn.com/TRANSCRIPTS/0009/19/ip.00.html

[36] Schlafly, Phyllis. "Time to Defund Feminist Pork." *Eagleforum.org*. July 20, 2005. Here is the link: http://www.eagleforum.org/column/2005/july05/05-07-20.html

[37] Rosenthal, Mark B. "What About Battered Men?" *Lewrockwell.com*. August 18, 2005. Here is the link: http://www.lewrockwell.com/orig6/rosenthal2.html

[38] Furchtgott-Roth, Diana, and Stolba, Christine note in *The Feminist Dilemma: When Success is not Enough.* (Washington, D.C.: AEI Press: 2001), p. 14.

[39] Sommers, 78

[40] National Organization of Women. "Executrix" is a joke. I realize there is no such position.

[41] Hollander, Paul. *Discontents: Postmodern & Postcommunist.* (New Brunswick: Transaction, 2002). p.59.

[42] Henry, William A. *In Defense of Elitism.* (New York: Anchor, 1994). p.103.

[43] From Steven Pinker's article, "The Science of Difference." In *The New Republic Online* (tnr.com), February 7, 2005. Here is the link: http://www.tnr.com/doc.mhtml?pt=IZMZoxUzwPMhvmZIyM6y9R%3D%3D

[44] Minogue, Kenneth. "Democracy & Naiveté." *The New Criterion.com.* March 2006, p. 6.

[45] Gilder, George. Men and Marriage. (Gretna, Lousiana: Pelican, 1992). p. 141-142.

[46] Gilder, 141-142

[47] Gilder, 141-142

[48] Lowry, Richard. "The Great Feminist Pander." *National Review.com.* May 4, 2007. Here is the link: http://article.nationalreview.com/?q=ZDY1ZTE0NGNiNjU2OGIwZmQ0YzZiOTI1ZTUwMjEyMTE=

[49] Quotes from Kate Zernike's *New York Times.com* coverage of the speech called, "A Shift in Power, Starting with 'Madame Speaker.'" January 24, 2007. Here is the link: http://www.nytimes.com/2007/01/24/washington/24scene.html?n=Top%2fReference%2fTimes%20Topics%2fPeople%2fP%2fPelosi%2c%20Nancy&_r=1&adxnnl=1&oref=slogin&adxnnlx=1169855553-H6zJPWgdf6L6kovEqX3Tww

[50] Shriffren, Lisa. "Pelosi's Party: It Wasn't Much Fun." *National Review.com.* January 9, 2007. Here is the link: http://article.nationalreview.com/?q=YjUwMDllZWM0OWI3ZGFiNmQ5NDljYzdkY2Y4YWU3MmE=

[51] McLaughlin, Elliot C. "Pelosi Ready for House Helm; Battle Over Issues." *CNN.com*. November 9, 2006. Here is the link: http://www.cnn.com/2006/POLITICS/11/08/pelosi.speaker/index.html

[52] Buchanan, Bay. *The Extreme Makeover of Hillary (Rodham) Clinton*. (Washington D.C., Regnery Publishing, Inc., 2007). p.193

[53] Fletcher, Michael A. "Views Mixed On Nominee to High Court Being Female." July 14, 2005. *Washington Post.com* Here is the link: http://www.washingtonpost.com/wp-dyn/content/article/2005/07/13/AR2005071302392.html

[54] Sacks, Glenn. "VAWA Renewal Provides Opportunity to Stop Destruction of Innocent Cops' Careers." *Lewrockwell.com*. July 20, 2005. Here is the link: http://www.lewrockwell.com/orig6/sacks2.html

[55] Ibid.

[56] From the song, "Summertime Blues," by Eddie Cochran. Lyrics found at Azlyrics.com. Here is the link: http://www.azlyrics.com/lyrics/rush/summertimeblues.html

[57] Horowitz, David. *Left Illusions: An Intellectual Odyssey*. (Dallas: Spence, 2003). p.345.

[58] Lukas, Carrie L. *Women, Sex, and Feminism*. (Washington D.C.: Regnery, 2006). p.172.

[59] This book was supposed to contain a chapter on chivalry. That topic will have to wait for a bit, and I apologize for that.

[60] Dowbrowski, Jenny. "There's Still Plenty Left for Women to Fight For." *Baltimore Sun*. December 28, 2006. Here is the link at where the article was reprinted: http://www.commondreams.org/views06/1228-20.htm

[61] Email sent to me on January 26, 2007 by Mike Cross-Barnet, Op-Ed Page Editor, *Baltimore Sun*. No need to put his email address on here as he was nice enough to forward it to the Letters to the Editor department so I can't complain about the guy.

[62] How about 70 to 80 percent of television? One wants to say that sports are for men, but, with Prince, Justin Timberlake, and Janet Jackson all appearing as halftime entertainment at recent Super Bowls, I am no longer certain of it.

[63] This term is defined and expounded upon in the final chapter concerning marriage.

[64] Young, Cathy. "Six Years of Culture Wars." *Reason*. January 23, 2007. Here is the link: http://www.reason.com/news/show/118168.html

[65] Ibid.

[66] Schwarzschild, Maimon. "Liberty and Autonomy for All." *The New York Times.com*. June 15, 1986. Here is the link: http://query.nytimes.com/gst/fullpage.html?res=9A0DEFD71638F936A25 755C0A960948260

[67] Kaye, Walter H. et al. "Comorbidity of Anxiety Disorders with Anorexia and Bulimia Nervosa." *The American Journal of Psychiatry*. December 2004.

Here is the link: http://ajp.psychiatryonline.org/cgi/content/abstract/161/12/2215

[68] Really a "giving out speeding tickets at the Indianapolis 500" situation if there ever was one.

[69] Hoff-Sommers, Christina. "Ms. Information." *American Enterprise Research for Public Policy Research*. February 23, 2003. Found at *Aei.org*. Here is the link: http://www.aei.org/publications/pubID.16709,filter.all/pub_detail.asp

[70] Patai, Daphne. *Heterophobia: Sexual Harassment and the Future of Feminism*. (Lanham, Maryland: Rowman & Littlefield, 1998. p.108.

[71] Ibid.

[72] O' Beirne, Kate. *Women Who Make the World Worse: And How their Radical Feminist Assault is Ruining Our Families, Military, Schools, and Sports*. (New York: Sentinel, 2006). p.54.

[73] Ibid, 54

[74] Lukas, Carrie. "Money Isn't Everything." *National Review.com*. April 19, 2005. http://www.nationalreview.com/comment/lukas200504190751.asp

[75] Ibid.

[76] The phrase repeated in a myriad of places with Title VII of the Civil Rights Act of 1964. Document found at *The U.S. Equal Employment Opportunity Commission's* website. Here is the link: http://www.eeoc.gov/policy/vii.html

[77] Minogue, Kenneth. "The Goddess the Failed." *National Review*, November 18, 1991. p.46.

[78] Vilar, Esther. *The Manipulated Man*. (London, Caledonian: 1998 (1971)). pp.9-10.

79 "The Silent Epidemic." *That Loving Feeling.com*. Here is the link: http://www.thatlovinfeeling.com/silentepidemic.htm

80 As quoted from her book, *Reader's Companion to U.S. Women's History*, in Daphe Patai's *Heterophobia: Sexual Harassment and the Future of Feminism*. (Lanham, Maryland: Rowman & Littlefield, 1998). p.134.

81 Bork, Robert H. *Slouching Towards Gomorrah: Modern Liberalism and American Decline*. (New York: ReganBooks, 1996). p.193.

82 Schwartz, Howard S. *The Revolt of the Primitive: An Inquiry into the Roots of Political Correctness*. (Westport, Connecticut: Praeger, 2001). p.xiv.

83 Nathanson and Young, 2001, 13

84 Schwartz, 54

85 Nathanson and Young, 2001, 33.

86 Ibid, 30

87 Sommers, Christina Hoff. *Who Stole Feminism? How Women Have Betrayed Women*. (New York: Touchstone, 1995). p.18.

88 Sommers,199

89 Chesler, Phyllis. *Woman's Inhumanity to Woman*. (New York: Thunder's Mouth Press: 2001), p.2.

90 Ibid, 2.

91 Ibid, 4.

92 Chesler, 2001, referring to the opinion of educational psychologist, Norma D. Feshbach, p. 88.

93 Ibid, 117.

94 Ibid, 3.

95 "The Case of Andrea Yates." *CNN.com*. Here is the link: http://www.cnn.com/SPECIALS/2001/yates/

96 Lopez, Kathryn Jean. "NOW Makes it Official." *National Review.com*. August 28, 2001. Here is the link: http://www.nationalreview.com/nr_comment/nr_comment082801a.shtml

97 Lind, Bill. "The Origins of Political Correctness." An Accuracy in Academia Address. Here is the link: http://www.academia.org/lectures/lind1.html

[98] Schartz, 123

[99] Lind, ibid.

[100] Bork, 209

[101] Ibid.

[102] Nathanson and Young, 222.

[103] "Silencing the Opposition." *Forces.org*. Here is the link: http://www.forces.org/fparch/102000.htm

[104] Chesler, 16.

[105] Really, Feminitizi is more accurate as they don't possess a drop of natio-nalism; they are International Socialists as opposed to National Socialists.

[106] Nathanson and Young, 2001, 229.

[107] From a quotation of Marilyn French's found at The National Association of Free Men, DC Chapter donation webpage. Here is the link: http://ncfm-dc.org/donate.html

[108] Ibid.

[109] Henry, 104

[110] Schwartz, xv.

[111] Bork, 203

[112] Nathanson and Young, 2001, 63.

[113] Ibid, 64

[114] Ibid, 5.

[115] Ibid.

[116] Ibid, 11.

[117] Ibid, 26.

[118] Ibid, 246.

[119] Ibid, 26

[120] Ibid, 43.

[121] Ibid, 21.

[122] "Feminist Jokes." *Not Boring.com.* Here is the link:
http://www.notboring.com/jokes/gender/12.htm

[123] "Feminist Jokes." WMST-L in October 2003. Here is the link:
http://research.umbc.edu/~korenman/wmst/jokes.html

[124] Nathanson, Paul and Young, Katherine K. *Legalizing Misandry: From Public Shame to Systemic Discrimination Against Men.* (Montreal, McGill-Queen's University Press, 2006). p.100.

[125] Nathanson and Young, 2006, 354-355

[126] Black, Jim Nelson. *Freefall of the American University: How Our Colleges Are Corrupting the Minds and Morals of the Next Generation.* (Nashville: WND Books, 2004), p. 58.

[127] Nathanson and Young, 2006, 208

[128] Ibid, 368-369

[129] Ibid, 366

[130] Bork, 201

[131] Ibid, 201

[132] Henry, 106

[133] Nathanson and Young, 2001, 231

[134] Ibid, 8

[135] Ibid, 60

[136] Ibid, 26

[137] Mansfield, Harvey. *Manliness.* (New Haven: Yale Press, 2006). p.1.

[138] Patai, 4

[139] Nathanson and Young, 237

[140] Patai, 11

[141] Campbell, Matthew. "Feminists Trip Up on Man Tax." *The Times Online.com.* October 25, 2005. Here is the link:
http://www.timesonline.co.uk/article/0,,2089-1838453,00.html

[142] Connolly, Kate. "German men told they can no longer stand and deliver." August 17, 2004. *Telegraph.co.uk.* Here is the link:

http://www.telegraph.co.uk/news/main.jhtml?xml=/news/2004/08/18/wp inkl18.xml

[143] "Gender Bias in the Study of Politics." International Women in IWISE Science and Engineering.

Here is the link:
http://www.iastate.edu/~iwise/iwise/lectures/08Nov2001.htm

[144] Mills, Elizabeth. "What Gender Studies Teaches." *Davidson.edu.*

Here is the link:
http://www.davidson.edu/academic/gender/gendies_album.html

[145] Camille Paglia quote found at *Brainyquotes.com.* Here is the link:
http://www.brainyquote.com/quotes/quotes/c/camillepag159814.html

[146] hooks, bell. "Understanding Patriarchy by bell hooks." July 25, 2004. Here is the link:

http://arizona.indymedia.org/news/2004/07/20613.php

[147] "Associated Press, Joe Klein, and More." *The Weekly Standard.com.* March 28, 2005. Here is the link:
http://www.weeklystandard.com/Content/Public/Articles/000/000/005/37 3erfbt.asp?pg=2

[148] "Social Capital and Gender." *World Bank.org.* Here is the link:
http://www1.worldbank.org/prem/poverty/scapital/sources/gender1.htm

[149] "Global Issues: What is Gender Justice." World Alliance of YMCAs.

Here is the link: http://www.ymca.int/index.php?id=782

[150] Search conducted on November 25, 2006.

[151] Sommers, 204

[152] Ibid, 251

[153] Ibid, 235

[154] Ibid, 235

[155] Ibid, 235

[156] Ibid, 257

[157] Glabe, Scott L. "Mansfield, Manliness, and Masculinity." *The Dartmouth Review*. October 21, 2005.

Here is the link:
http://www.dartreview.com/archives/2005/10/21/mansfield_manliness_an d_masculinity.php

[158] Thornhill, Randy and Palmer, Craig T. *A Natural History of Rape: Biological Bases of Sexual Coercion*. (USA: MIT Press, 2000). p. 67.

[159] Ibid, 71

[160] Valenti, Jessica. *Full Frontal Feminism: A Young Woman's Guide to Why Feminism Matters*. (Emeryville, CA: Seal Press, 2007). p.65.

[161] Zepezauer, Frank S. "Believe Her! The Woman Never Lies Myth." *Institute for Psychological Therapies Journal*. Volume 6. 1994. Here is the link:
http://www.ipt-forensics.com/journal/volume6/j6_2_4.htm

[162] Ibid

[163] Tzu, Sun. *The Art of War*. "Chapter Three: The Principles of Warfare." Available online for free at *Sonshi.com*. Here is the link:
http://www.sonshi.com/sun3.html

[164] Skinner, David. "Oprah vs. Faulkner: Paradox Of This Summer's Book Club Pick." Originally at *The Weekly Standard.com* but reproduced at *CBSNews.com*. June 18, 2005. Here is the link:

http://www.cbsnews.com/stories/2005/06/17/opinion/main702770_page2 .shtml

[165] Klein, Stephanie. *Straight Up and Dirty*. (New York: HarperCollins, 2006). p.39.

[166] Oldenburg, Ann. "The divine Miss Winfrey?" *USAToday.com.* May 11, 2006. Here is the link:

http://www.usatoday.com/life/people/2006-05-10-oprah_x.htm

[167] Ibid

[168] Ibid

[169] A four part series that appeared at a few places. Here's a link to the first one which I wrote for *Mensnewsdaily.com*:
http://mensnewsdaily.com/2006/03/14/watching-oprah-my-venture-to-hell-part-i/

[170] *Depressionhurts.com.* Eli Lilly and Company. Here is the link:
http://www.depressionhurts.com/index.jsp

[171] The episode from *The View* was shown in Chicago at 10 am on December 28, 2006. The person who said the line was not immediately recognizable to me. Later, I went to their website and discovered that the face I saw was that of Joy Behar—biography link:
http://abc.go.com/daytime/theview/bios/joy_behar.html

[172] Author unknown. "Gender and Society: A Matter of Nature or Nurture." *Trinity.edu.* Here is the link:

http://www.trinity.edu/~mkearl/gender.html

[173] "Challenging Behavior in Individuals with Autism Spectrum Disorders: Advances in Understanding and Treatment." Delivered by Dr. Michael Powers of the New England Educational Institute on November 17th 2006 in a suburb of Chicago.

[174] Kipnis, Laura. *The Female Thing: Dirt, Sex, Envy, Vulnerability.* (New York: Pantheon, 2006). p.21.

[175] Ibid, 35

[176] Ibid, 24

[177] Goodnow, Cecilia. "What's wrong with being a nice guy? Plenty, according to a local therapist." *Seattle Post-Intelligencer.com (Seattlepi.com).* May 3, 2002. Here is the link:

http://seattlepi.nwsource.com/lifestyle/68913_niceguy03.shtml

[178] Ali, Lorraine and Miller, Lisa. "The Secret Lives of Wives." *Newsweek.com.* July 12, 2004. Here is the link:
http://www.msnbc.msn.com/id/5359395/site/newsweek

[179] Salholz, Eloise. "Too Late for Prince Charming?" *Newsweek.com.* June 2, 1986. Here is the link:
http://www.msnbc.msn.com/id/12940202/site/newsweek/

[180] McGinn, Daniel. "Marriage by the Numbers." *Newsweek.com.* June 5, 2006. Here is the link:

http://www.msnbc.msn.com/id/13007828/site/newsweek/

[181] Jackson, Kate M. "0 is the New 8." *The Boston Globe.com (Boston.com).* May 5, 2006. Here is the link:

http://www.boston.com/news/nation/articles/2006/05/05/0_is_the_new_
8/?p1=email_to_a_friend

[182] Quote from Mark Twain found at *QuoteDB.com*. Here is the link:
http://www.quotedb.com/quotes/2342

[183] Blake, Tom. "Dad's Dating Younger Women, His Daughter Thinks He's
Lost His Mind." *Yahoo Personals.com*. No date could be found. Here is the link:

http://personals.yahoo.com/us/static/dating-advice_younger-women

[184] Dowd, Maureen. "Men Just Want Mommy." *The New York Times.com*.
January 13, 2005. Here is the link:
http://www.nytimes.com/2005/01/13/opinion/13dowd.html?ex=1265518800&en
= 7e963a2552d179c1&ei=5088&partner=rssnyt

[185] Schwyzer, Hugo. "Closing the doors: men, aging, younger women, and
ego." October 26, 2006. This is Mr. Schwyzer's personal blog. Here is the
link:

http://hugoboy.typepad.com/hugo_schwyzer/2006/10/i_posted_last_t.htm
l

[186] Townsend, John Marshall. *What Women Want–What Men Want: Why the
Sexes Still See Love & Commitment so Differently*. (Oxford: Oxford University
Press, 1998). p. 96.

[187] Tooley, James. *The Miseducation of Women*. (London: Continuum, 2002).
p.168.

[188] Ridley, Matt. *The Red Queen: Sex and the Evolution of Human Nature*. (New
York: Penguin, 1994). p.267.

[189] Ibid, pp.20-21.

[190] Rhoads, Steven E. *Taking Sex Differences Seriously*. (San Francisco: Encounter, 2004). p.58.

[191] Buss, David. *The Dangerous Passion: Why Jealousy is as Necessary as Love or Sex*.
(London: Bloomsbury, 2000). p.11

[192] Fisher, Dr. Helen. *Why We Love: The Nature and Chemistry of Romantic Love*.
(New York: Henry Holt and Company, 2004). P.110.

[193] Ibid

[194] Barash, David P. Barash and Nanelle, R. *Madame Bovary's Ovaries: A Darwinian Look at Literature*. New York: Delacorte, 2005. pp. 78-79.

[195] Ibid

[196] Etcoff, Nancy. *Survival of the Prettiest: The Science of Beauty.* New York: Anchor Books, 1999. p.64.

[197] Ibid

[198] Ibid

[199] Tooley, 168.

[200] Wright, Richard. *The Moral Animal: Why We Are the Way We Are; The New Science of Evolutionary Psychology.* (New York: Vintage, 1994). p.65.

[201] Derbyshire, John. "November Diary." *National Review.com.* November 30, 2005. Here is the link:
http://www.nationalreview.com/derbyshire/derbyshire200511300810.asp

[202] Day, Vox. "Women! Someday is Today." *Worldnetdaily.com.* October 10, 2005. Here is the link:
http://www.worldnetdaily.com/news/article.asp?ARTICLE_ID=46746

[203] Ibid

[204] No author named. Article adapted from a news release issued by *Cell Press.* "Male Chimpanzees Prefer Mating With Old Females." *Science Daily.com.* November 21, 2006. Here is the link:

http://www.sciencedaily.com/releases/2006/11/061120130545.htm

[205] "Chimpanzee" entry at The Oregon Zoo website. Here is the link:
http://www.oregonzoo.org/Cards/Primates/chimpanzee.htm

[206] From *Science Daily* cited in endnote 205.

[207] Ibid

[208] Transcript from "Showbiz Tonight." Found at *CNN.com.* April 27, 2006.

Here is the link:
http://transcripts.cnn.com/TRANSCRIPTS/0604/27/sbt.01.html

[209] No author cited. "Are More Older Women With Younger Men?" From *ABCNews.go.com.* May 5, 2005. Here is the link:
http://abcnews.go.com/Primetime/Health/story?id=731599&page=1

[210] Ibid

[211] Same citation as from endnote 208 found at *CNN.com.*

[212] I predict that not long after this book is published, a great writer of our age will address this topic in an extended essay entitled "Women and Conformity"—don't ask me how I know.

[213] "Maternal Obesity and Pregnancy: Weight Matters." *March of Dimes.com.* April 6, 2005. Here is the link: http://www.marchofdimes.com/files/MP_MaternalObesity040605.pdf

[214] Ibid

[215] From W.L George's "Notes on the Intelligence of Women" (December 1915). Cited in "Flashbacks: Notes on the Intelligence of Women" in *The Atlantic.com.* May 18, 2005. Here is the link: http://www.theatlantic.com/doc/prem/200505u/fb2005-05-18

[216] "7 Deadly Sins." Found at *Deadly Sins.com.* Here is the link: http://www.deadlysins.com/sins/pride.html

[217] Chesterton, G.K. "Pride, the Sin of Lucifer." Christian Living and Literature website. Found here: http://www.abcog.org/pride.htm

[218] Definitions of empowered and empower from Princeton's Wordnet site, which is found at, http://wordnet.princeton.edu/perl/webwn?s=empowered

[219] "Women Now Empowered By Everything A Woman Does." *The Onion.com.* February 19, 2003. Here is the link: http://www.theonion.com/content/node/38558

[220] Henry, 108

[221] Nathanson and Young, 2006, 371

[222] Nathanson and Young, 2001, 215.

[223] Tuttle, Cameron. *The Bad Girl's Guide to Getting What You Want.* (San Francisco: Chronicle, 2000). p. 26.

[224] Markland, David. "Keeping Abreast with USC." *Metroblogging Los Angeles.* May 09, 2006. Here is the link: http://blogging.la/archives/2006/05/keeping_abreast_with_usc.phtml

[225] Lyrics to Christina Aguilera's song "Beautiful" found at *Thelyricarchive.com.* Here is the link: http://www.thelyricarchive.com/lyrics/beautiful.shtml

[226] Sajer, Guy. *The Forgotten Soldier.* (Washington, D.C.: Bracey's (U.S.) Classic, 1971). p.170

227 Schwartz, 114.

228 Cardinal Fitness: West Loop and Beverly locations.

229 "Cancer Facts and Figures, 2006." U.S. Institutes of Health, National Cancer Institute. Here is the link: http://www.cancer.org/downloads/STT/CAFF2006PWSecured.pdf

230 Granted, a few sources said that cancer was now the number one cause of death but I could not verify this from a government source. My statement comes from page 4 of the Center for Disease Control's *National Vital Statistics Reports*, Vol. 54, No. 19, June 28, 2006. Here is the link: http://www.cdc.gov/nchs/data/nvsr/nvsr54/nvsr54_19.pdf

231 *Purple Ribbon Project.com*. Here is the link: http://www.purpleribbonproject.com/index.html

232 "Recommended Reading" at *Purple Ribbon Project.com*. Here is the link: http://www.purpleribbonproject.com/reading.html

233 Carlson, Allan C. and Mero, Paul T. *The Natural Family: A Manifesto*. (Dallas: Spence, 2007). pp.157-158.

234 Stains, Laurence Roy., and Bechtel, Stefan. *What Women Want: What Every Man Needs to Know About Sex, Romance, Passion, and Pleasure*. (United States of America: Rodale Press, 2000). p.49.

235 Ibid, 15

236 Leo, John, "Another Harasser Brought to Justice." *Townhall.com*. August 18, 2000. http://www.townhall.com/columnists/JohnLeo/2000/08/17/another_harasser_brought_to_justice

237 Mansfield's is not an euphoric embrace of masculinity. He makes clear that these traits are only a virtue when they are not taken to extremes. I agree with him entirely.

238 Mansfield, 22

239 Ibid, 16

240 Ibid, 20

241 Ibid, 17

242 Ibid, 18

243 Ibid, 70

[244] Again, this is the ideal of what you should be. I am certain few men meet such criteria.

[245] Lyrics from the Bee Gees' song, "Stayin' Alive." Found at Lyricsfreak.com. Here is this link: http://www.lyricsfreak.com/b/bee+gees/stayin+alive_20015578.html

[246] Ms. Silverstein is quoted on page 17 of Roy Stains and Stefan Bechtel's *What Women Want: What Every Man Needs to Know About Sex, Romance, Passion, and Pleasure.* (United States of America: Rodale Press, 2000).

[247] Person, Ethel. *Dreams of Love and Fateful Encounters: The Power of Romantic Passion.* (USA: Penguin, 1988). p.285.

[248] Rhoads, 73

[249] I recognize he's deceased.

[250] I honestly believe that masochists are but a small percentage of this number.

[251] Blow, Joe. "What Women Want: Who Cares." *Mensnewsdaily.com.* September 30, 2002. Here is the link: http://www.mensnewsdaily.com/archive/a-b/blow/02/blow093002.htm

[252] Dhaliwal, Nirpal. "How Feminism Destroyed Real Men." *The Daily Mail.co.uk.* August 4, 2006.

Here is the link:
http://www.dailymail.co.uk/pages/live/femail/article.html?in_article_id=398998&in _page_id=1879&in_page_id=1879&expand=true

[253] I wrote an article about this guy and the poor choice he made by marrying a radical feminist. This quote comes from his mother's response to me. Yes, here we find that the real man is the one who has his mommy defend him. Here's the link: http://www.lolspeaks.com/2007/01/17/people-who-dont-know-what-they-are-talking-about-should-keep-still.html

[254] Pardon the *Pulp Fiction* reference.

[255] "National Organization of Women." *DiscovertheNetworks.org.* Here is the link: http://www.discoverthenetworks.org/groupProfile.asp?grpid=6186

[256] Line from Bob Dylan's "Ballad of Frankie Lee and Judas Priest." Here is the link: http://www.bobdylan.com/songs/frankielee.html

[257] Email received from Thomas Varnelli on February 6, 2007.

[258] Email received from Steve Wills on February 6, 2007.

[259] Lyrics from Bob Dylan's "Buckets of Rain" from *Blood on the Tracks* found at *Lyricsfreak.com*. Here is the link: http://www.lyricsfreak.com/b/bob+dylan/buckets+of+rain_20021192.html

[260] Lyrics from Billy Bragg's "Walk Away Renee" found at *Rare-lyrics.com*. Here is the link: http://lyrics.rare-lyrics.com/B/Billy-Bragg/Walk-Away-Renee.html

[261] Please note, I frequently make use of "respect my diversity" as a phrase because I have found that I am far more tolerant a person than the politically correct persons who originally coined the term. I boomerang the choice phrase back in their direction whenever possible and derive great satisfaction from doing so.

[262] Diamond, Jared. *The Third Chimpanzee: The Evolution and Future of the Human Animal.* (New York: HarperCollins, 1992). p.103.

[263] And yes, obviously someone could write of its complementary phenomena, The Fundamental Theory of Men, but I am not the person to do so nor would my readers be interested if I did.

[264] Della Cava, Marco R. "Disney Let's Girl into Whinnie's World." *USA Today.* December 6, 2005. Found at their website, here is the link: http://www.usatoday.com/life/television/news/2005-12-06-winnie-the-pooh_x.htm

[265] Wikipedia entry for "My Friends Tigger & Pooh." Here is the link: http://en.wikipedia.org/wiki/My_Friends_Tigger_&_Pooh

[266] This is a quote from Mark Steyn that he said to me in a phone interview. "Is Demography Destiny?" *Spectator.org.* May 31, 2007. Here is the link: http://www.spectator.org/dsp_article.asp?art_id=11513

[267] Lyrics from Orbit's song "Rockets" from their 1997 CD *Libido Speedway*.

[268] Zinczenko, David. "Are Women too Aggressive?" *Yahoo! Health* via yahoo.com. March 8, 2007. Here is the link: http://health.yahoo.com/experts/menlovesex/22610/are-women-too-aggressive

[269] Coulter, Ann. *Slander: Liberal Lies About the American Right.* (New York: Crown, 2002). p.2.

[270] Ellis, Bruce J. "The Evolution of Sexual Attraction: Evaluative Mechanisms in Women." Appearing on pages 267-288 in Jerome H. Barkow, Leda

Cosmides, and John Tooby's *The Adapted Mind: Evolutionary Psychology and the Generation of Culture.* (New York: Oxford University Press, 1992). Specific citation from page 274.

[271] Ibid, 274

[272] Ibid, 275

[273] Ibid, 275

[274] Ibid, 275

[275] Ibid, 275

[276] Ibid, 276

[277] Ibid, 275

[278] Ibid, 275

[279] Ibid, 277.

[280] Ibid, 276.

[281] Ibid, 277.

[282] Ibid, 278

[283] Henry, 107

[284] Nathanson and Young, 70-71.

[285] Rhoads, 152

[286] Rhoads, 153

[287] Klein, 37.

[288] Although, what if they are but a subtle variation of all women? That not so happy thought has occurred to me.

[289] "Dr. Phil's Advice to Controlling Women." *Oprah.com.* No date given. Here is the link: http://www.oprah.com/tows/pastshows/tows_2000/tows_past_20001114_c.jhtml

[290] Hey man, I have an excuse. I was conducting research. The book is more important than my being hip.

[291] Henry, Lawrence. "Yes, Dear." *The American Spectator.* June 30, 2006. Here is the link: http://www.spectator.org/dsp_article.asp?art_id=10031

[292] Schwartz, 45

[293] Rhoads, 107

[294] *Gene Expression (gnxp.com)*. July 16, 2006. Here is the link:
http://www.gnxp.com/blog/2006/07/women-in-science-part-
3595726061058.php

[295] Rhoads, 121

[296] De Coster, Karen. "Women and the Freedom Philosophy:
Is There Hope?" *Lew Rockwell.com.*

August 11, 2006. Here is the link:
http://www.lewrockwell.com/decoster/decoster117.html

[297] Brown, Allison. "Female Libertarians." *Lew Rockwell.com.* October 25,
2003. Here is the link:

 http://www.lewrockwell.com/orig4/brown6.html

[298] Day, Vox. "Spiting Their Pretty Faces." Worldnetdaily.com. February 3,
2003. Here is the link:
http://www.worldnetdaily.com/news/article.asp?ARTICLE_ID=30830

[299] Gilman, Susan Jane. *Kiss My Tiara: How to Rule the World as a Smart Mouth Goddess.* (New York: Warner Books, 2001). pp.74-75.

[300] Buss, David. *The Evolution of Desire: Strategies of Human Mating.* (New York, Basic, (1994) 2003).

p. 44

[301] Ibid., 44

[302] Ibid., 44

[303] A perfect example of this was an article in *The New York Times* entitled
"What Shamu Taught Me about a Happy Marriage" (June 25, 2006). Writer
Amy Sutherland talks about "improving" her husband in an article explicitly
featuring an animal training motif. Here is the link:
http://www.nytimes.com/2006/06/25/fashion/25love.html?ex=130888800
0&en=f3a9c33e07612db0&ei=5090

[304] Gilman, 15-16

[305] Rhoads, 129

[306] Ibid, 118

307 True story from when I lived in Ottawa, Illinois and got a visit one night after one of my ex-wife's frequent crying spells.

308 *Wiki Quotes* for Aristotle. Here is the link: http://en.wikiquote.org/wiki/Aristotle

309 I say this but, quite honestly, *The Rules* is one of the least objectionable books of this genre. Overall, it is closer to the truth than most of them are.

310 "The Science of Flirting." *BBC.co.uk*. November 18, 2004. Here is the link:

http://www.bbc.co.uk/science/hottopics/love/flirting.shtml

311 Kakutani, Michiko. "Unhappy Wife Untangles Herself in a Sad-Funny Mess." *The New York Times.com*. February 16, 2007.

312 I have read hundreds of war books since I was a child and I do not remember exactly from where I heard this phrasing of Chuikov's words.

313 Chapin, Bernard. The Presumption Against Marriage." *Strike the Root.com*. June 10, 2004. Here is the link: http://www.strike-the-root.com/4/chapin/chapin3.html

314 Crittenden, 65-66

315 I heard this line from Thomas Varnelli who heard it in an AA meeting he attended. I have no idea who said it first.

316 A line from Dylan Thomas's masterful "The force that through the green fuse drives the flower." A poem that I found online at *Undermilkwood.net*. Here is the link: http://www.undermilkwood.net/poetry_theforce.html

317 Line from The Replacements song, "Anywhere is Better than Here." Found at *Lyricsdepot.com*. Here is the link: http://www.lyricsdepot.com/the-replacements/anywheres-better-than-here.html

318 Quote from Kristoffer A. Garin's "On the Great Ukrainian Bride Hunt," *Harper's Magazine*. Found at *Harpers.org*. Posted online July 6, 2006, but appeared in their June of 2006 issue. Here is the link: http://www.harpers.org/AForeignAffair.html

319 Bootle, Olly. "'Cyber-brides' Vulnerable to Abuse?" *BBC.com*. May 18, 2004. Here is the link: http://news.bbc.co.uk/1/3700409.stm

320 The 200 includes those both online and off. Scholes, Robert J. "'The Mail Order Bride' Industry and its Impact on US Immigration." *The U.S. Citizenship and Immigration Services website*. Here is the link: http://www.uscis.gov/graphics/aboutus/repsstudies/Mobappa.htm

[321] McElroy, Wendy. "'Mail-Order Bride' Law Brands All American Men Abusers." *Foxnews.com.* January 10, 2006. Here is the link: http://www.foxnews.com/story/0,2933,180487,00.html

[322] Jordan, Lara Lakes. "Marital Bliss on Hold for Red Tape." *The Chicago Tribune.com.* June 14, 2006. Here is the link: http://www.chicagotribune.com/news/nationworld/chi-0606140148jun14,1,2047673.story?coll=chi-newsnationworld-hed&ctrack=1&cset=true

[323] From Garin's *Harper's* article.

[324] Reed, Fred. "Fimmel Wimming Persons In Messico." *Fredoneverything.net.* April 17, 2005. http://www.fredoneverything.net/FOE_Frame_Column.htm

[325] From the site, *Nomarriage.com* on his "Only Marry Foreign Women" page. Here is the link: http://www.nomarriage.com/why_foreign_women_are_better.html

[326] Barton, Julie Hill. "World Wide Wedlock: Russian Mail Order Brides on the Internet." *Women in Mind: A Feminist Journal Dedicated to all Voices.* Here is the link: http://www.southernct.edu/departments/womenscenter/wim/articles/mob.htm

[327] "International Bride Brokers Regulated." Feministing.org. March 5, 2006. Here is the link: http://feministing.com/archives/003064.html

[328] Scholes, Robert J. "How Many Mail Order Brides?" *Immigration Review # 28.* Spring of 1997. Here is the link: http://www.cis.org/articles/1997/IR28/mail-orderbrides.html

[329] Scholes, Robert J. "The 'Mail-Order Bride Industry' and its Impact on U.S. Immigration." Pdf file report found at this location: http://www.uscis.gov/files/article/MobRept_AppendixA.pdf

[330] You can find the DVD concerning Ivan at Netflix, but here's the film's internet address: http://www.cowboydelamor.com/

[331] Kurtz, Stanley. "Monsoons & Marvels." *National Review.com.* March 27, 2002. Here is the link: http://www.nationalreview.com/kurtz/kurtz032702.asp

[332] Discussion board post by Polygirl entitled, "I hate all American woman (from a foreign woman who lives here)," at soc.men of google. Here is the link:

http://groups.google.com/group/soc.men/browse_thread/thread/e6848594
6e701e2e/675c91d832b2a4c0

³³³ I corrected the more egregious spelling errors.

³³⁴ Great site on the law: http://www.imbra.org/. A bunch of goodfellas
have taken over the address to campaign against the travesty. It proclaims
that "IMBRA Traps American Men in American Marriages."

³³⁵ Bala, Gary G. "Press Release on International Marriage Broker Law."
Article found at *USA Immigration Attorney.com*. Here is the link:
http://usaimmigrationattorney.com/PressReleaseIMBRA.html

³³⁶ Ibid.

³³⁷ Ibid.

³³⁸ Ibid.

³³⁹ Found in Jordan's *The Chicago Tribune* article.

³⁴⁰ Bala's press release.

³⁴¹ Bala again.

³⁴² Tristan Laurent, proprietor of the website *Online-dating-rigths.com* told me
that he has spoken to several foreign women who are appalled by this law.

³⁴³ Bala again.

³⁴⁴ McElroy again, "'Mail-Order Bride' Law Brands All American Men Abusers." Cited above.

³⁴⁵ An argument I first heard from Tristan Laurent.

³⁴⁶ No author listed. "Mail-Order Bride Bill In Works." *CBSnews.com*. July 5,
2003.

Here is the link:
http://www.cbsnews.com/stories/2003/07/05/politics/main561828.shtml

³⁴⁷ From Chris Rock's *Bring the Pain* 1996 DVD.

³⁴⁸ Smith, J.D. *Life Sentence: The Guy's Survival Guide to Getting Engaged & Married.* (New York: Warner Books, 1999). p.41.

³⁴⁹ Quotation from Betty Friedan at *The Quotations Page.com*. Here is the link:
http://www.quotationspage.com/quotes/Betty_Friedan/

³⁵⁰ Rhoads, 120

[351] Doyle, Roger. "By the Numbers: The Decline of Marriage." *Scientific American*. December 1999. Here is the link:
http://www.scientificamericandigital.com/index.cfm?fa=Products.ViewIssue
Preview&ARTICLEID_CHAR=173A9E9E-3926-40EA-869F-
622D8C8CE8E

[352] Jayson, Sharon. "Divorce Declining but so is Marriage." *USA Today.com*. July 18, 2005. Here is the link:
http://www.usatoday.com/news/nation/2005-07-18-cohabit-divorce_x.htm

[353] "Facts for Features: Unmarried and Single Americans Week Sept. 17-23, 2006." U.S. Census Bureau site: *Census.gov*. August 10, 2006. Here is the link:
http://www.census.gov/Press-Release/www/releases/archives/
facts_for_features_special_editions/007285.html

[354] Whitehead, Barbara Dafoe, and Popenoe. "The State of Our Unions: The Social Health of Marriage in America 2002 Why Men Won't Commit Exploring Young Men's Attitudes About Sex, Dating and Marriage." *The National Marriage Project 2002*. Here is the link:
http://marriage.rutgers.edu/Publications/SOOU/TEXTSOOU2002.htm

[355] Ibid

[356] Sellars, Stephanie. "Cohabitation in the City." *New York Press.com*. 2007 (no month noted). Here is the link:
http://www.nypress.com/19/28/news&columns/lustlife.cfm

[357] Quote attributed to Betty Friedan from an article in *Reason* called "Betty Friedan's Unexpected Legacy" by Cathy Young. February 8, 2006. Here is the link: http://www.reason.com/news/show/32061.html

[358] Shakespeare, William. Quote from *Hamlet* found at *Enotes.com*. Here is the link: http://www.enotes.com/shakespeare-quotes/lady-doth-protest-too-much-methinks

[359] Yanek, Dawn. "Are You Better Off Single?" Dating and Personals at *MSN.com*. Here is the link:
http://msn.match.com/msn/article.aspx?articleid=6320&TrackingID=5163
11&BannerID=562427&menuid=6&GT1=8333

[360] Rhoads, 122

[361] Rhoads, 112

[362] Buss, 2003, 230

[363] Chesler, 2001, 109.

[364] Neave, Dr. Nick. "Sorry, but Women are Dependent on Men." *Daily Mail.co.uk.* December 4, 2006. Here is the link:

http://www.dailymail.co.uk/pages/live/femail/article.html?in_article_id=42 0513&in_page_id=1879

[365] Ibid.

[366] Liebau, Carol Platt. "Postmodern Bride." *The American Spectator.* June 14, 2006. Here is the link:
http://www.spectator.org/dsp_article.asp?art_id=9955

[367] Kimball, Roger. "G. C. Lichtenberg: A 'Spy on Humanity.'" *The New Criterion.com.* May 2002. Here is the link:
http://newcriterion.com:81/archive/20/may02/lichtenberg.htm

[368] Buss, 2003, 81

[369] Ibid, 80. He is quoting Donald Symons here.

[370] Ibid

[371] Ibid, 79-80

[372] Entire exchange from Buss on page. 80.

[373] Ibid

[374] Ibid

[375] Ibid, 193

[376] Ibid, 81

[377] Barash, David P. Barash and Nanelle, R. *Madame Bovary's Ovaries: A Darwinian Look at Literature.* (New York: Delacorte, 2005). p.18.

[378] Gilder, George. *Men and Marriage.* (Gretna, Lousiana: Pelican, 1992). p.187.

[379] Bowman, James. *Honor: A History.* (New York: Encounter, 2006).

[380] Lyrics from Phish's "Heavy Things" from the album "Farmhouse." From *Azlyrics.com.* Here is the link:
http://www.azlyrics.com/lyrics/phish/heavythings.html

[381] Zagorsky, Jay. "Divorce Drops a Person's Wealth by 77 Percent, Study Finds." *Ohio State Research News.* January 17, 2006. Here is the link:
http://researchnews.osu.edu/archive/divwlth.htm

[382] Nathanson and Young, 2006, 132.

[383] Ibid, 133-134

[384] No name given. From a television show I gather called, "To the Contrary: A Discussion of Issues from Diverse Perspectives." *PBS.org*. No date on transcript. Here is the link: http://www.pbs.org/ttc/society/philanthropy.html

[385] Ibid.

[386] Kay, Barbara. "Ideology Trumps Equality." *National Post*. June 21, 2006. Here is the link: http://www.canada.com/nationalpost/news/editorialsletters/story.html?id= 935bec7d-269b-404d-802b-c2b7dc98d729

[387] Ibid.

[388] Ibid.

[389] Ibid.

[390] "The 10 Most Expensive Celebrity Divorces." *Forbes.com*. April 12, 2007. Here is the link: http://www.forbes.com/2007/04/12/most-expensive-divorces-biz-cz_lg_0412celebdivorce.html

[391] "McCartney's $80m Divorce Deal." *SMH.com.au*. January 22, 2007. Here is the link: http://www.smh.com.au/news/people/fouryear failure-worth-80m-fortune/2007/01/22/1169330797836.html

[392] Kesselman, Elayne B. "Frequently Asked Questions: The Prenuptial Agreement." *Divorce Central.com*.

http://www.divorcecentral.com/legal/legal_answers_5.html

[393] Ibid.

[394] Nathanson and Young, 2006, 126

[395] Ibid, 137

[396] Ibid, 125

[397] Ibid, 136

[398] Young, Cathy. "Stigmatizing Fathers." January 24, 2005. *Boston.com* (*The Boston Globe*). Here is the link: http://www.boston.com/news/globe/editorial_opinion/oped/articles/2005 /01/24/stigmatizing_fathers/

[399] Perrine, Stephen. "Keeping Divorced Dads at a Distance." *The New York Times.com.* June 18, 2006. Here is the link:

http://www.nytimes.com/2006/06/18/opinion/18perrine.html?_r=2&oref =slogin&oref=slogin

[400] Caher, John. "N.Y. High Court Says Mistaken Avowal of Fatherhood Imposes an 'Equitable Paternity.'" *New York Law Journal.* Reproduced at *Law.com.* Here is the link:
http://www.law.com/jsp/article.jsp?id=1152534921526

[401] Ibid.

[402] Bergen, Raquel Kennedy. "Marital Rape." *Vawnet.org.* March 1999. Here is the link:

http://www.vawnet.org/DomesticViolence/Research/VAWnetDocs/AR_m rape.pdf

[403] McElroy, Wendy. "Spousal Rape Case Sparks Old Debate." *Ifeminists.net.* February 16, 2005. Here is the link:
http://www.ifeminists.net/introduction/editorials/2005/0216.html

[404] Ibid.

[405] Ibid.

[406] Weeks, Matthew. "The Marriage Strike." *Matthew Weeks.com.* Here is the link: http://www.mattweeks.com/strike.htm

[407] Chen, Bill and Ankenmann, Jerrod. *The Mathematics of Poker.* (Pittsburg: Congelco, 2006). p.294.

[408] J.D. Smith, 11.

[409] No author listed. "Questions Couples Should Ask (Or Wish They Had) Before Marrying." *The New York Times.* December 17, 2006. Here is the link: http://www.nytimes.com/2006/12/17/fashion/weddings/17FIELDBOX.h tml?em&ex=1167541200&en=7d2657da2b02af0f&ei=5087%0A

[410] Samuel Johnson Quote found at *Wisdom Quotes.com.* Here is the link: http://www.wisdomquotes.com/001344.html

[411] Valenti, 146-147

[412] As quoted in *The Weekly Standard's* "The Scrapbook." From the January 1, 2007 issue. Here is the link:

http://www.weeklystandard.com/Content/Public/Articles/000/000/013/11
8vvsrf.asp

[413] Saga, Junichi. *Confessions of a Yakuza: A Life in Japan's Underworld.* (Tokyo: Kodansha International, 1989), p.81.

[414] A completely hypothetical situation with a made up quote. I could have just as easily inserted "Detroit Lions" in there as they are every bit as bad as the Raiders...but it would have pained me too greatly.

[415] Liebau, Carol Platt. "Postmodern Bride." *The American Spectator.* June 14, 2006. Here is the link:
http://www.spectator.org/dsp_article.asp?art_id=9955

[416] Ibid.

[417] Rudoren, Jodi. "Meet Our New Name." *The New York Times.com.* February 5, 2006.
http://www.nytimes.com/2006/02/05/fashion/sundaystyles/05NAME.htm
l?ex=1296795600&en=2ac29eb92ad10a2d&ei=5088&partner=rssnyt&emc=
rss

[418] Ibid.

[419] Roberts, Paul Craig. "Men are the Greater Casualties." September 3, 2001. I first read this column at *Townhall.com.* His archive has been deleted, however, so I have no link to it. I emailed him and Mr. Roberts pasted it into an email for me on December 24, 2006. It is the property of Creators Syndicate.

[420] Buss, 2003, 79

[421] Skurnick, Lizzie. "Chick Lit, the Sequel: Yummy Mummy." *The New York Times.* December 17, 2006. Here is the link:
http://select.nytimes.com/gst/abstract.html?res=FA0710F639550C748DD
DAB0994DE404482

[422] Ali, Lorraine and Miller, Lisa, cited endnote 178.

[423] Shader-Smith, Diane. *Undressing Infidelity: Why More Wives are Unfaithful.* (Avon, MA: Adam Media Corp: 2005).

[424] Huizenga, Dr. Robert. "Extramarital Affairs: What Everyone Needs to Know and What You Can Do to Help." *Ezine Articles.com.* Here is the link:
http://ezinearticles.com/?Extramarital-Affairs:-What-Everyone-Needs-to-
Know-and-What-You-Can-Do-to-Help&id=2067

[425] Buss, 2003, 235

[426] Ibid, 192

[427] Carlson and Mero, 127-128

[428] Ellin, Abby. "Big People on Campus." *The New York Times.com*. November 26, 2006. Here is the link: http://www.nytimes.com/2006/11/26/fashion/26fat.html?ex=1186200000 &en=cfd5ee3f56f9c3f3&ei=5070

[429] J.D. Smith, 1

[430] *The Fellowship of the Ring*. Part One of The Lord of the Rings Trilogy. New Line Procductions, 2001. Special Extended DVD Edition.

[431] Brandeis, Louis. *Other People's Money, and How the Bankers Use It*, 1933. I found the quote at the website for Brandeis, *Brandeis.edu* in the Investigative Journalism homepage. Here is the link: http://www.brandeis.edu/investigate/sunlight/

Printed in the United States
90163LV00003B/7-21/A